Maritime Britain in the 21st Century

Maritime Britain in the 21ˢᵗ Century

BRITANNIA
PUBLISHING

This edition first published in the United Kingdom in 2024 by Britannia Publishing as an imprint of Britannia Museum Trust Press, Britannia Royal Naval College, Dartmouth, TQ6 0HJ, United Kingdom, in partnership with The Devonshire Press.

PB ISBN 978-1-917152-01-3
HB ISBN 978-1-917152-00-6
EB ISBN 978-1-917152-02-0

A CIP catalogue record of this book is available from the British Library.

Publisher: PWN Honeywill
Series Editors: Kate Jamieson, Kevin Rowlands and Andrew Young

Cover image: *Seascape, Mawddach Estuary* Nigel Waters

Typeset in Adobe Garamond Pro 11/14pt. Printed by Short Run Press, Exeter and by Print on Demand.

BRITANNIA
PUBLISHING

Contents

Industry and Prosperity

Security and Defence

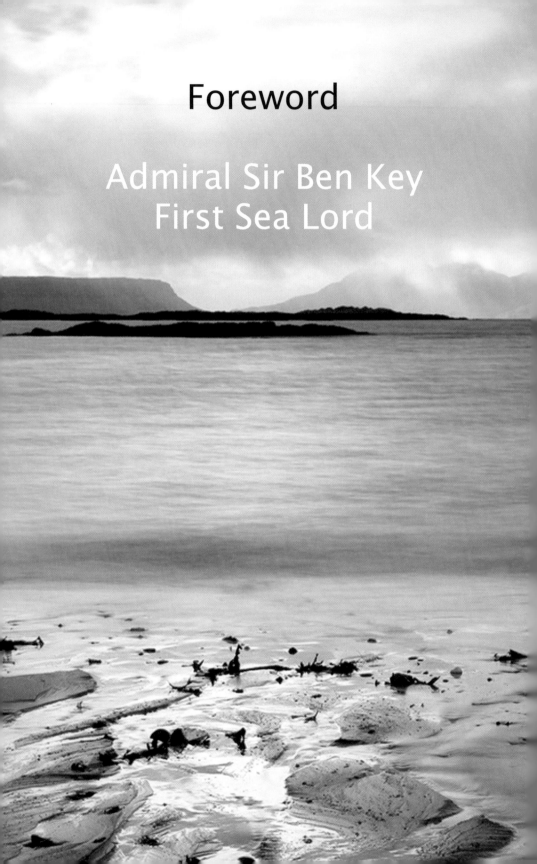

Foreword

Admiral Sir Ben Key
First Sea Lord

Re-Charting the Course: Reconnecting our Maritime Nation

Islands by geography, islanders by history, the United Kingdom has long woven its destiny with the sea. Yet in the decades following the end of the Cold War and with the onrush of Globalisation there has been a lull in our national maritime consciousness. It threatens to obscure the profound ways in which the oceans shape all of our lives. *Maritime Britain in the 21st Century* is not just a book, it is a clarion call to re-engage with the very element that sustains us.

This book has sought to bring together a range of diverse voices, exploring the power of cognitive diversity. It is not a singular narrative, but a symphony of perspectives. From the halls of academia to the engine rooms of industry, from the corridors of policy to the decks of ships, a range of contributors offer their expertise, weaving a tapestry that reveals the intricate relationship between Britain and the sea.

This isn't simply a story of trade routes and naval prowess, though these remain vital threads. It's about the communities that rise and fall with the tides, the cultural heritage shaped by winds and waves, and the very fabric of our nation that depends on a healthy maritime ecosystem.

Maritime Britain in the 21st Century asks us to confront our maritime dependency, a reality often taken for granted. It compels us to explore how our society and culture are intrinsically linked to the ocean and urges us to celebrate our rich maritime heritage.

By fostering a 'whole-of-nation' approach, the book extends its reach beyond borders. It includes a perspective from like-minded international partners, developing a shared consciousness, a global understanding of the profound impact the seas have on all our lives.

So I encourage you to dive into the perspectives, challenge and opportunities the book offers. It does not have all the answers, but hopefully it will help catalyse a renewed national conversation about Britain and the sea – a conversation long overdue, and one with the power to chart a more sustainable and prosperous future.

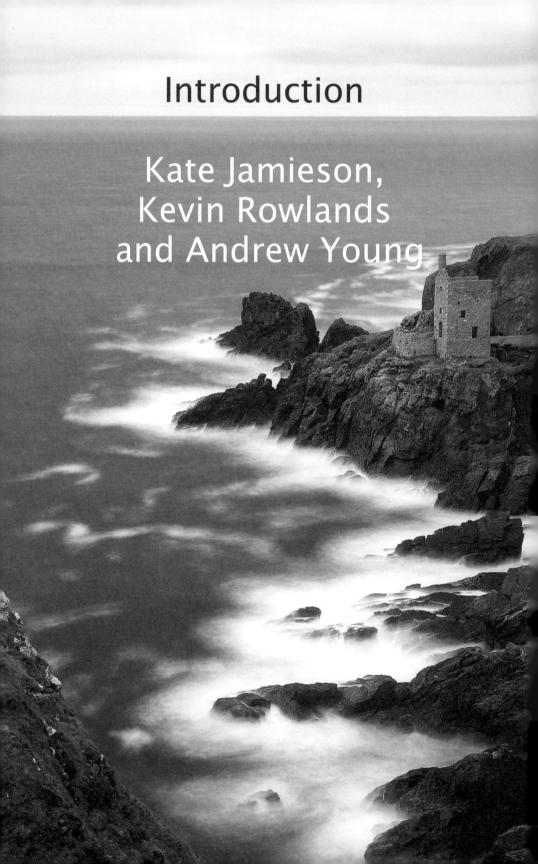

Introduction

Kate Jamieson,
Kevin Rowlands
and Andrew Young

What do we mean by Maritime Britain? How should we think about, conceptualise, and discuss Britain's relationship with the sea? And how can we mobilise resources to generate the instruments and capabilities demanded in an era of competition? These were some of the questions posed at the May 2023 Seapower Conference, held at Lancaster House, and proved the genesis of this edited volume. It is, by nature, an eclectic collection of chapters spanning the spectrum of history and culture, technology and industry, society and strategy, reflecting the diversity of contributors from academia, industry and the Royal Navy. All are joined by their passion for the maritime; our relationship to the sea is not limited only to those who transit or ply their trade on its waters, but every one of us. This book seeks to expose that truth.

In the opening section, authors explore and examine the relationship between the sea and strategy. Dr Rob Johnson focuses on the Grand Strategy of the United Kingdom; how this has adapted both in response to significant events and in cooperation with other state actors. He outlines the challenges and opportunities facing the United Kingdom today and a requirement to remember how dependent we are on our maritime sector. Putting these challenges and opportunities in historical context, Dr Matthew Heaslip asks what we can learn from the past. He asserts that 'maritime Britain is not synonymous with global Britain', and questions how riverine, coastal and 'blue water' policies have shaped discourse. His chapter explores how best to improve ocean literacy within Britain and, in doing so, develop and secure its maritime future.

The often-used aphorism 'culture eats strategy for breakfast' could set the tone for the next section. In his chapter on the 'Art of Admiralty' and the maintenance of naval power, Professor Andrew Lambert looks to address the question of how best to ensure a holistic approach to maritime engagement on a national scale. Through addressing how Britain has both succeeded and failed at this 'art' over centuries, he discusses the challenges facing the United Kingdom today, and how a renewed emphasis on how the sea – intangibly linked with our economy, industry, culture and identity – should shape our ongoing maritime strategy. As an island nation, our ties to the sea require an ongoing recognition on a wider scale; Lambert reminds us of the importance the sea has and will continue to hold for Britain. He is followed by Sub Lieutenant Joseph Reindler, combining being a practising maritime artist and serving Marine Engineer. With an eye to the intersection between British maritime heritage and the arts, his chapter looks at how and why warships have captivated so many, how maritime art can act as a first-hand communicative account, as a way of passing on a sequence of events, and how it can be utilised in the 21st century as a method of reconciliation between nations. Finally, Daisy Turnbull uses her chapter to investigate the heritage, culture and coast of maritime Britain today. Through the use of case studies, she highlights the existence of a maritime vacuum in our national consciousness, the need to grow ocean literacy, and the possibilities to repair the relationship between land and sea.

If culture and strategy tend to the abstract, they are grounded through the human experience, something that exercises our next contributors. Addressing the challenges of maintaining a fit and healthy workforce in an inhospitable environment, Dr Joanne Fallowfield and Cdr Mat Court suggest that civilian industry can learn a lot from the Royal Navy's experience. Taking a whole-of-systems approach prioritises retention of skilled personnel and maintaining well-being as individuals progress through their careers, even as they transition to shore-side roles rather than more active, sea-based ones. With an eye to the shore, Dr Melanie Holihead explores the absence of women from naval and maritime history despite the pivotal role they played at sea, ashore, and in the communities of maritime Britain. She asks what we can learn from the past and ponders how, and if, the voices of women today will be heard in a hundred years' time. It is a call taken up by Monica Kohli, who discusses the female experience of life at sea and in maritime industry. Charting a journey from her own childhood to today's realities, Kohli draws attention to the challenges facing women wanting to break into seagoing roles and staying there. Positively, she highlights the attractiveness of the sea cadets and youthful engagement in maritime training. Supporting and retaining that interest through-life will tap into hitherto ignored talent. That talent and opportunity is the subject of the next chapter. Dr Sophie Quintin, Dr Tegan Evans and Professor Pierre Failler propose a transformative blue governance agenda, to focus on both economic development and the responsible use of marine resources. The maritime security sphere has transformed in recent years, and Quintin discusses how interconnected seapower, safety, human security and the economy have become. They conclude by mentioning a requirement for a holistic approach with cross discipline collaboration between organisations.

We often visualise maritime power through what is seen. However, what goes on beneath the waves has assumed greater importance today, a view that our next trio of chapters discuss. Dr Carl Hunter expounds Britain's global economic opportunities and place as a leading sub-sea maritime power. This leadership is not uncontested, however; there are threats from global competitors that need to be addressed in partnership with our allies. These are predicated on the UK realising its research and development potential, becoming a 'science super-power'; a 'whole-of-nation' project across science, Defence and industry sectors. Matthew Bowden, Glenn Lipsham and Devon Johnson take us through a précis of the past, present and future of submarine cable infrastructure. The complexity of the system they describe, its inherent strengths and weaknesses, is both a source of confidence and concern; resilience and redundancy goes hand-in-glove with opaque ownership structures and practices. Exploiting and mitigating these requires greater Public sector scrutiny, understanding, and engagement. Offering one perspective and drawing on his professional experience, Gordon Meadow advocates new approaches to human-centred technology integration. He discusses the expanded role of behavioural assessments and continuous learning and adaptation, rather than relying on assumptions of a tech-centred nirvana, and concludes on a positive note for a secure, efficient and sustainable maritime future.

Going beyond the shores of our own island nation, Admiral Linda Fagan gives an alternative perspective on the importance of the sea. Despite the differences and America's two-ocean coastline (three, if Alaska and the Arctic Ocean are included), there are huge similarities to be drawn. She points out how America's place and power in the world today is anchored in the seas, just as the Britain's was and still is. That the idea of 'Maritime Britain' is obvious to an American seafarer should make us think and wonder why it is not always quite so obvious to us. We can also learn from closer to home. Commander Alex Westley's research, and the basis of his chapter, focuses on maritime security in proximate seas and he argues that the UK is at a crossroads, challenged by emerging threats and the necessity for strategic reform. Drawing insights from the French Maritime Prefecture system, he outlines a vision for the UK to transition towards a centralised maritime security model that promises enhanced cohesion, strategic clarity, and operational agility.

However we view and discuss the sea, what is clear from the contributors is that our relationship is very much human and reflects the realities of being land-dwelling societies. Calls for 'ocean literacy', 'whole-of-nation/society' approaches, and the regeneration of maritime culture exist across the full breadth of academia, policy and industry, and are necessary precisely because of maritime's centrality to our economy and way of life. Reliant as we are on the sea's bounty, its fruits, and the labour of those who work at, on or under the waves, we ignore this fundamental truth at our peril.

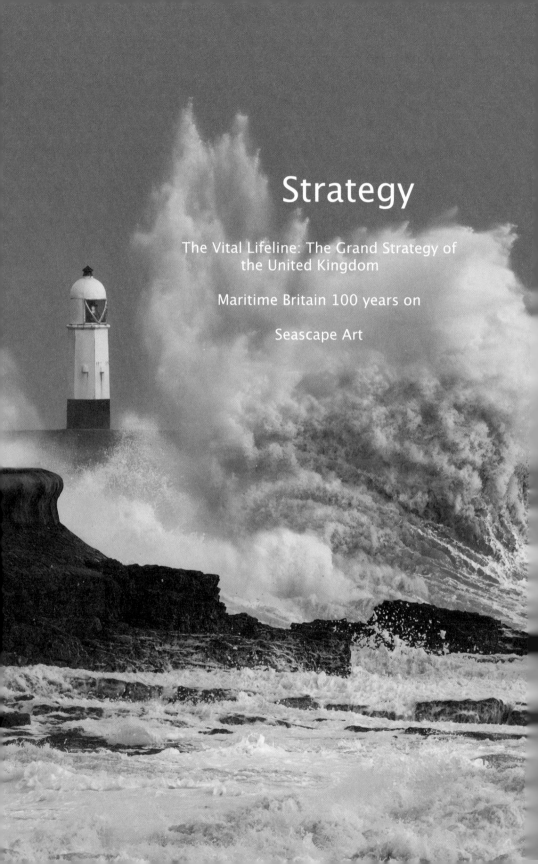

Strategy

The Vital Lifeline: The Grand Strategy of the United Kingdom

Maritime Britain 100 years on

Seascape Art

The Vital Lifeline: The Grand Strategy of the United Kingdom

Dr Rob Johnson

According to the Office for National Statistics (ONS), the total value of goods imported by the UK in 2022 was £155.5 billion, and the overwhelming majority of this came by sea.[1] This represents a steady increase over the last 5 years. In the financial year 2022 to 2023 the total value of trade was £1,749.6 billion.[2] In the first quarter of 2023, the total freight moved by rail was 4.07 billion net tonne-kilometres. Yet, ships can carry much greater volume than rail: A single vessel can carry 28,000 tons, which is the equivalent of two trains of 100 freight trucks each. In terms of liquid volume, the disparity is even greater. A single ship can transport 23 million gallons, but by rail the same volume would require seven trains each with 100 freight containers. Put another way, a single ship can move the equivalent of over 1,000 articulated lorries or road-borne tankers.[3]

The UK is dependent on the circulation of trade for its prosperity and its security. The UK's energy imports, to sustain its annual consumption of 300k GWhr p.a., are dependent on the sea, from both tankers and seabed pipelines in the North Sea and the Channel. This applies not only to the import of essential foodstuffs and goods in its regional waters, but also its electronic architecture, 97 per cent of which still relies on subsurface cables. The UK's financial sector, for example, is completely dependent on the fibreoptic cables across the world's ocean beds.

These raw statistics demonstrate the rationale behind the UK's strategic priorities, as set out in the recent *Integrated Foreign Policy, Defence and Security Reviews* (2021 and 2023), and the centrality of its maritime-air posture within the context of its regional alliance, the North Atlantic Treaty Organisation. In terms of its economy, the UK is a major global actor. It generates the equivalent of $2.8 trillion, or 3.2 per cent of the global share as a single nation. Its productivity per capita is $54 per hour. To put that in context, it is twice the size of Russia and five times higher than the productivity of China. With a population much smaller than China, at 67.5 million, its growth rate is 0.4%, whereas both the Russian and Chinese populations are declining. With a workforce of some 34.6 million, the GNI it generates is \$39,830bn, four times that of Russia and China. The UK is an efficient economy, and it has set out how to sustain its advantage through the embrace of science and technology, where it is ranked fourth in the world.

Grand Strategy is an explanation of enduring geographical setting, interests, and practices. The United Kingdom's geographical island setting has offered both opportunities and corresponding constraints, such as the need to focus on maritime security and an expeditionary military posture. Successive British governments have been clear about their enduring interests, namely the protection of sovereign territory and the people, their political economy, culture and way of life, and their economic prosperity. British practices of fulfilling their Grand Strategy made compensated for its relatively small size, compared with other continental powers, by fostering multilateral coalitions, and, where it did not curtail freedom of action, more lasting alliance partnerships.[4] In major conflicts, the United Kingdom served as a financier and supplier for its coalition partners, and used its maritime strength to continue the circulation of global trade. Periodically, and exceptionally, it has faced more existential threats, which required it to convert a portion of national wealth into defence resources, but, on the whole, the United Kingdom has preferred to exercise leverage through diplomacy and commerce. Britain made use of its wealth, influence, and patronage, usually under the encompassing heading of 'influence', to exercise a form of 'soft power'. The imperative has always been to encourage the global free flow of trade on which its logistical lifeline depends, and the desire to avoid either isolation or major war. Yet, in terms of ways, Britain has been prepared to exercise its 'hard power', through air, sea, and land operations and its continuous, at sea, nuclear deterrent.

What is clear is that the British have adapted their Grand Strategy to match their changing relative power position and in response to a series of significant events, both domestic and foreign.

The United Kingdom's Grand Strategy has been subject to the contestation of domestic politics, and perceptions of its world role: where some have favoured a proactive international posture, this has been tempered by a strong moral agenda. In the past, some political leaders have questioned more assertive foreign policies, but there was considerable ideological unity over the defence of democracy and liberties that carried Britain through the two world wars. In the Cold War, there were deep divisions about the moral responsibility to project power, and to protect the public and Britain's allies, but there was agreement to counter nuclear proliferation in foreign affairs and ringfence spending on a 'welfare state' at home. British self-perception has long been expressed in historical metaphors, but, in more recent decades, a new generation has favoured diversity, multiculturalism, and technological innovation, with a preference for international co-operation.[5] Yet, these remain peacetime interpretations, since challenges to British interests, including global terrorism or state threats, have generated a more traditional willingness to defy, deter, and deploy a range of instruments of national power.

There are elements of Britain's national interests which exist, but which are rarely expressed. The less often stated, but self-evident priority concerning foreign affairs and defence, is to remain close to the United States. Together, the United Kingdom's trade with the United States and the value of American inward investment dwarfs that of the European Union, both before Brexit and after. Crucially, the scale of America's forces, and its nuclear umbrella, compensate for Britain's diminished defence capabilities.

Another unstated but characteristic element of Britain's national interests is a pragmatic recognition of the need to adapt to changing geopolitical and economic circumstances. This sort of gradualism has been the long-term hallmark of the British in domestic affairs too, but that does not mean they are not prepared to act on principle. Indeed, the third element of their national strategy is their desire to uphold the international rules-based order, since history indicates to policymakers that the alternatives are far more detrimental to the UK's interests.[6]

Historically, the British government has utilised four grand strategic instruments.[7] The first was to use diplomacy to negotiate on any dispute with its antagonists to avoid war. The second was to seek new alliance partnerships to share defence burdens. Third, they could increase defence spending as a form of conventional 'deterrence'. Fourth, they could reconfigure their defence policy to meet new challenges.

The first, diplomacy, was successful to a point, but had its limits. International institutions can only function if there is sufficient will by the leading powers to compromise on their immediate national interests. It is precisely at times of crisis, however, that these powers will assert their own national interests and priorities. Britain's solution was to continue to work on pragmatic, bilateral agreements and focus only on areas of common concern. In recent decades, the apparent weakening of international institutions has once again raised the importance of bilateralism in British Grand Strategy. The UK is a leading power in NATO. It possesses a large air force, the third strongest in Europe, and Europe's most powerful navy.[8]

The second option, joining alliances, was not a favoured option for British governments until the Cold War, because of concerns about a loss of freedom of action. Today, Britain is part of an alliance network, not just in the North Atlantic region, but globally. The third and fourth options, defence spending, and changes to defence policies, have been interdependent. As a share of British GDP, defence spending has fallen steadily since the 1940s and more starkly since the Cold War, reaching its current level of 2.2 per cent. The cost of small-scale arms and equipment programmes is nevertheless higher, and the UK defence industry has only been able to offset these higher costs with increased overseas sales.

There are two aspects to the UK's Grand Strategy that explain the importance of the maritime setting. One, the domestic political debates that show how that although the UK changed over time, its enduring setting, interests, and practice remained; two, how UK Grand Strategy manages the opportunities and challenges of a shifting geo-strategic environment.

Managing Change: The UK's Enduring Grand Strategy

Britain possessed several objective strategic advantages because of its geography. As an island, it was relatively well protected from continental invasions, which, in turn meant it could afford to maintain a small army. It had a strong industrial base. It possessed large financial reserves, which could be converted into military and naval means if required. It dominated global communications and held numerous world bases. Diplomatically, Britain's maritime and commercial power gave it significant influence around the world, and Royal Navy provided a reassuring or intimidatory 'presence'.

There was always a risk that a breakdown in diplomacy would mean some form of commitment to defend Britain's national interests, but ordinarily this lay in the navy and avoidance of too large a continental land commitment. Britain's Grand Strategy could be summed up as a diplomatic effort to accommodate other states as long as its vital interests were not directly threatened.

Britain fought a successful war between 1914-1918 as part of an alliance and restored a European power equilibrium in 1919. Had it not been for the unexpected fall of France in 1940, the British desire for a balance in Europe would have been maintained in the Second World

War. In the first and the second world wars, the minimization of Britain's global commitments was sustained. The most vulnerable strategic locations for Britain in the wars, after the European theatre, were the Middle East, which was successfully defended, and South-East Asia (including routes to Australia), which was entirely lost. The Atlantic and Mediterranean were severely contested but were recovered. Nevertheless, the number of commitments in Africa and the Middle East increased, which catalysed decolonisation after the war.[9]

While Britain emerged as one of the victorious Allies in 1945, there was some concern that the United States might abandon Europe and the continent would fall to communism. Despite considerable diplomatic efforts, and membership of NATO, there was a decisive eclipse of Britain as a preeminent world power. Britain had been bankrupted by the war, its relative power was permanently damaged, and its share of global commerce had been diminished. By 1949, the international situation for the UK was grave. While British institutions and values had survived the war, with an even stronger commitment to social welfare and parliamentary democracy, the country was in a dire economic situation, Europe was in ruins, and the Soviet threat was existential. The overriding approach, later expressed by Lord Ismay as Secretary General of NATO, was to: 'keep the Germans down, the Americans in and the Russians out'.

The Grand Strategic priority of the United Kingdom from 1945 was to remain closely linked to the United States. The bond between Britain and the United States grew closer as Soviet assertiveness increased. Enshrined in NATO and intelligence sharing, the bond has remained strong, as a 'Special Relationship', ever since.

Economically, Britain's industrial base was too small to compete with that of the United States and the Soviets, once these powers had begun to industrialise at scale, unless it could retain a lead in technological innovation and productivity rates. The relative decline of the British economy reduced its strategic options. In the 1930s, Britain's international credit was less secure, it held less gold and dollars, domestic manufacturing was relatively weak, Britain was still emerging from the financial crash, and there was a shortage of skilled workers. In the Second World War, as in the first, there was intensive planning, but short-term war measures were unable to arrest the overall decline of Britain's global position. The idea of a Sterling Bloc, preserving its currency with fixed exchange rates in the regions where it had enjoyed considerable influence, was eroded by the dominance of the dollar and was effectively abandoned by the Bank of England in 1972. The 1973 'oil shock' exposed the UK economy to its dependence on foreign energy supplies profoundly. Nevertheless, the development of North Sea oil and gas, and the continued success of Britain's financial services, offset the decline in manufacturing and heavy industry, and its commercial strength was sustained by improving trade with Western Europe from the 1950s onwards. Domestically, in economic terms, Britain may have lost ground to other powers, but it was far more self-assured than its critics would claim.

British defence co-operation with Western Europe, its independent atomic arsenal from 1952, and its close relationship with the United States seemed to have placed Britain in a stronger strategic situation. Although there was some discussion of economic co-operation with Europe, and eventually membership of a European Economic Community, British politicians viewed European integration with suspicion. Instead, Britain developed global connections through SEATO (The Southeast Asia Treaty Organisation) and CENTO (Central Treaty Organisation), the latter with Turkey, Iraq, Iran, and Pakistan. The 1952 *Global Strategy Paper* reclaimed Britain's historic world-wide role, and this was enhanced by the development of a nuclear arsenal. In the 1960s, the Royal Navy acquired the responsibility for the UK's independent deterrent, and this sustained its global influence. There was also a focus on global bases, including important stations in Cyprus and Aden, although it was the controversy over the control of the Suez Canal Zone that caused the greatest rupture in Britain's Grand Strategy.

The prime minister, Anthony Eden, foundered on a departure in foreign policy of questionable legality or ethics. In Grand Strategic terms, Eden believed his seizure of the Suez Canal zone aligned with Britain's interests: he believed he faced an imminent and unprecedented threat, and that acting within a coalition would be sufficient justification to exonerate his actions. The instruments of Grand Strategy were limited – military tools with diplomatic preparation – but there would be no question of the full deployment of national resources. The crucial point was that the Americans had not been consulted, not treated as partners, and they punished the UK financially as a consequence.

The result was continued cuts in UK defence spending and capability with a greater emphasis on nuclear or alliance strength. In the 1957 *Defence Review*, the government announced reductions, and a steady fall in the share of defence spending as a share of GDP. Further attempts to reduce the size and deployments of the British armed forces followed, sometimes accelerated by financial crises, such as Wilson's devaluation of

Sterling in 1967. The imperative to pay for a burgeoning health service bill added further pressure to cancel defence procurement programmes (such as the F111 fighter) or to withdraw from the Gulf, Malaya, and Singapore. By the 1970s, both leading political parties began embracing the idea that Britain could redefine itself as a European power, integrated into a cheaper collective defence and an economic system. This seemed appropriate when the emphasis was on the dual Cold War conventional and nuclear defence posture, and Europe was the main theatre of operations.[10] However, once the Soviet Union collapsed as a major threat in the 1990s, and the predominant modality of war shifted to combatting international terrorism or multi-theatre insurgency by non-state actors, then the UK could consider once again a global strategy.

The enduring importance of Britain's relationship with America, rather than Europe, the need to retain a global naval expeditionary role, and the value of a military counter-terrorism specialism while holding on to a 'balanced force' for collective, conventional defence, were all justified in 1982 during the Falklands Conflict. Britain demonstrated that it possessed the capability and will to conduct a limited war of liberation of its own people against the Argentine Junta which had seized territory in contravention of the UN Charter. It also provided an opportunity to shape Britain's external situation. Despite its orientation towards European defence, the British government quickly assembled a naval task force. Its close relationship with the United States ensured the neutrality of other South American powers. Its amphibious operation, despite losses in ships and personnel, proved rapidly successful and the Falkland Islands were recovered before the arrival of winter. Critics, not least the Argentines, portrayed the British as unreconstructed imperialists, reckless in their pursuit of an outdated colonial prestige. London, however, adroitly avoided any such association, arguing clearly for the self-determination of peoples (for the Falklands islanders) and the upholding of international law (through an unambiguous UN Security Council Resolution).

In subsequent Defence Review documents, the British emphasised their adherence to international law and norms. In 1980, it had captured international attention by refusing to accept the takeover of the Iranian embassy in London, and its dramatic storming by 22 SAS, its elite Special Forces, marked the United Kingdom out as a state unlikely to allow its policies to be determined by terrorism. In fact, it endured three decades of terrorism in Northern Ireland and on the mainland, against Irish Republicans, using its military and policing instruments to contain and counter violence while searching for a political resolution. Against a background of improving economic conditions, the British government successfully brokered a final peace settlement a decade later, the so-called Good Friday Agreement, which involved diplomatic engagement with Eire. It continued this theme of upholding the international order in its participation in the Gulf War against Saddam in 1990-91 to liberate Kuwait, and then in its deployment of peacekeeping forces into Bosnia. Britain demonstrated its preparedness to accept international agreements that might not necessarily be in its own national interests by the peaceful transfer of power of Hong Kong in 1997, and diplomatically protested the Chinese repression of pro-democracy demonstrators at Tiannamen Square in 1989, and against Burmese military actions during that decade.

A consistent theme for the United Kingdom was also its 'prosperity agenda' and generosity in providing international aid. Successive British governments have seen the rising GDP of the country as a key policy imperative, but equally there has been an altruistic pride in the UK's willingness to support both Commonwealth and poorer countries. There are evident benefits for Britain in its aid packages, in terms of influence and access, but the drivers are altruistic not Machiavellian.

The divisions in Britain's Grand Strategy were most evident in its approach to Europe. On the one hand, its membership of NATO made it an integrated power and few questioned the benefits of free trade after joining the European Common Market in 1973. The problem instead lay in the European Commission's desire for an 'ever-closer political union'. Pro-Europeanists argued that the Special Relationship with the US was not one of parity and that American interests diverged from Europe, a charge made more emotive by Britain's participation in the Iraq and Afghanistan wars. They claimed that Britain could no longer think of itself as an independent global power. There had instead been the promise of an industrial boom, an increase in British invisible earnings, and the benefits of cheaper consumer products caused by an economy of scale in Europe.

In fact, none of these materialised. European co-operation in defence procurement projects proved more expensive than its American commercial links. Cheaper consumer products were available from East Asia and, less significantly, from Europe. The industrial boom failed to materialise, and instead British heavy industry declined, with all its associated social and political unrest. The service sector also thrived less on European markets, than on global ones. In purely defence terms,

NATO allies in Europe spent a lot less on their armed forces or equipment, with the consequence that military interoperability declined. Worse, European powers asserted 'national caveats' and restrictions on operations outside of Europe. Furthermore, with the recovery of Russia in the early 2000s, newly joined Eastern European members argued that they needed to focus on the conventional threat posed by Moscow, not global interventionism under the so-called 'Responsibility to Protect'. It is striking that Britain is regarded as one of the leading defenders of Eastern Europe with its enhanced forward presence deterrent deployments in Poland and the Baltic States. Additionally, NATO allies only inconsistently committed to operations in Afghanistan. The British, with the largest European contingent, took on the troublesome province of Helmand, and fought there in brigade strength alongside the Americans. Other European countries, however, made only token deployments. If, as some critics claimed, Britain was only a European power, it was at the very least the most dedicated one from a defence perspective.

The 9/11 terrorist attacks in the United States in 2001, and subsequent Jihadist terrorism in Britain and Europe; an increasing number of cyberattacks emanating from Russia, China and their proxies; the violent aftermath of the Middle Eastern uprisings known as the Arab Spring, which produced Daesh (the so-called Islamic State movement) and its wave of barbarous attacks, all seemed to indicate a period of instability. Indeed, the UK's 2010 *National Security Strategy* described it as 'an age of uncertainty.'[11] Given these events, it was logical to expect some enhancement to Britain's defences and the articulation of a Grand Strategy. There was certainly a strong expression of values and aspirations in the report, with references to global reach, a continuous sea-based nuclear deterrence, new aircraft carriers to project power, an expeditionary army of two divisions and an air arm possessing the latest strike, surveillance, and lift capabilities. Its armed forces work continuously in a joint posture, and the Combined Joint Expeditionary Force deployed to Eastern Europe consists of an all-arms British force within a NATO structure.

In support, Britain established a national cyber security centre to augment the work of GCHQ, a government communications centre, and continued to develop its whole-of-government approach to a range of non-conventional threats. The government adheres to three principles: budgetary investment in new technologies; strategic capabilities for 2040, including the new Dreadnaught class of nuclear submarine, new

F35 fighters and cyber projection; and stronger international partnerships and coalitions, under the umbrella phrase of 'international by design'.[12] Committed to learning from the Iraq Enquiry and the conflict in Afghanistan, the government also placed its decision-making processes under review, and set itself the objective of regularly updating its strategy.

The Iraq War of 2003-09 had an undeniably negative impact on British policy-making. The Iraq Enquiry, the 2.6 million-word report published in 2017, revealed, amongst its many findings, an absence of understanding of grand strategy amongst the UK's decision-makers. One former Defence Minister admitted that there was too much optimism, and mistakes were made, some wilfully, by members of the government of the day.[13] Cross government co-operation had been lacking and civil-military relations had been marred by misunderstandings. The report focused on the lack of preparedness for the reconstruction phase of the conflict. But the most egregious error was the premature withdrawal from the campaign in 2006, at the precise moment when the Americans were calling for a surge of forces. The British contribution had been to support the United States, so the decision to pull out appeared to be particularly inconsistent.

The seed of these problems had emerged earlier. The end of the Cold War, the multinational efforts to liberate Kuwait (1991) and those to resolve the Balkans conflicts (1994, 1999) produced over-optimism in successive governments. But the defence cuts they orchestrated as part of the post-Cold War 'peace dividend' meant they could not fulfil the expectations they set out for themselves in their defence reviews. In the early 2000s, the Labour government of Tony Blair emphasised its desire to align Britain's foreign policy, and thus its strategic influence, with the 'millennium goals' of eradicating poverty in the Global South, but, despite its generous aid budget, the scale of the problem and international trade restrictions made this unlikely. The Foreign Secretary, Robin Cook, had claimed that Britain would pursue an 'ethical foreign policy' and immediately ran into a diplomatic storm with Israel when he argued in favour of a Palestinian state and border revisions.[14] Britain's aspiration to sustain the international-rules based system to preserve the status quo seemed increasingly unlikely, given Russia and China's efforts to assert themselves as global powers with revisionist intent. Above all, the decision in 2003 to invade Iraq in order to eradicate a Weapons of Mass Destruction (WMD) programme and democratise the Middle East turned out to be ill-considered. The WMD programme was practically non-existent, the intelligence was deliberately manipulated to justify intervention, and the invasion created chaotic destabilisation. Curiously, when democratising movements emerged in 2011, during the so-called 'Arab Spring', Britain only reluctantly intervened in Libya as part of a coalition. The subsequent empowerment of local militias and the collapse of authority led to protracted violence there and a flood of refugees into Europe.

In a multipolar world, there are evident limits to the techniques of Grand Strategy that have worked historically. Like their predecessors in 1914 and 1938-9, government officials find that diplomacy has its limits. In the 2010s, North Korea, Iran, China, and Russia have been unwilling to adhere to the injunctions of the Western powers. Critics stated that the cost of the conventional maritime forces of the carrier groups was prohibitive and appeared at odds with the investment in new technologies and counter-terrorism, which seemed more pressing. Yet, there were also doubts about the entire resilience of the United Kingdom to address combined forms of attack, from a DDOS (Deliberate Denial of Service) cyber offensive on critical financial infrastructure to the conventional destruction of forward-deployed forces and the ability of the public to stomach resulting heavy casualties. There was further confusion in 2017 when British Prime Minister Theresa May tried to reassure the British public that there would be no further expeditionary operations comparable to Iraq or Libya, while the armed forces were still postured for land intervention missions.

In 2016, the majority of the British public voted for Brexit, the departure from the European Union. The national turnout for European elections had been low for years and European officialdom in Brussels was considered too remote from the issues that mattered to the public. Despite the irritation of the 'Remain' lobbyists, who blamed a 'Little Englander' mentality, British sentiments had always been far more expansive and global. There was an inherent dislike of a large European bureaucratic bloc, which the public associated with entities like the Soviet Union, while the inherently protectionist (and agrarian) cartel within the EU sat uneasily with a country that was wedded to free market economics and consumerism. In contrast to the Commonwealth, the EU seemed less of a 'free association' of nations than a system that would apply punishments for non-compliance, as Ireland and Greece experienced over two decades. Moreover, the British still identified more closely with Americans, despite the unpopular wars, because of economic systems, language and culture. Above all, the majority of the British public in favouring Brexit were establishing a claim to their identity, based on a sense of history, and rejected a series of integrationist, multicultural neo-Liberal mantras. Yet the public was divided. The minority felt strongly that Britain's future lay in Europe. The left, which had long struggled to accept an EU it associated with big business, concluded that European courts might provide a mechanism to defeat British laws that curbed the power of Trades Unions. Others saw kindred spirits in Europe that prioritised rights over economic performance. But, in essence, both sides were projecting onto Europe much older British political and ideological divisions: between free markets or socialism; rights or responsibilities; and freedom or regulation. British Grand Strategy cannot remain immune from these debates, although it is striking that NATO, including collective defence in Europe, has remained central to British strategic thinking.

Prime Minister David Cameron's claim to be 'international by design' and Boris Johnson's 'Global Britain' agenda raised more questions than they answered. The phrases implied that small nations might look to internationalise any dispute in order to obtain Britain's, and, by extension, America's backing. This was certainly the view in Scandinavia and the Baltic states, because they felt that, militarily, they could not survive without British and American intervention.[15] The key question was about Britain's capability: how could it possibly manage all its global commitments if more than one was challenged at the same time? Defence personnel questioned the ability of Britain to 'do another Falklands' given years of defence cuts.[16]

Challenges and Opportunities

There are both challenges and opportunities for the United Kingdom's Grand Strategy.[17] The most serious threats to the UK itself derive from subsurface and missile threats from Russia, although its global interests are challenged equally by China, North Korea, and Iran, as well as terrorist organisations. The greatest opportunities lie in its close association with its allied Western nations, in the technological prowess it possesses, and its economic potential. In this sense, the principles of the UK's Grand Strategy still apply: it still has an enduring geographical setting, global interests, and long-standing practices to uphold.

The subsurface threats to the UK's critical national infrastructure, both in terms of energy and communications are the responsibility of its air, maritime, and intelligence services. Attacks on the architecture of the UK's energy and commercial systems are not exaggerated: the destruction of Nordstream II in the Baltic, the severing of Norway's cable in the Arctic, and Russian targeting of Ukraine's ports, grain, energy, electronic networks, and civilian communications have underscored their importance. The UK possesses excellent early warning systems, surveillance capabilities in the air and beneath the sea, and the capability to surge resources to any threatened point. Yet none of these can be taken for granted. An attack would cause significant damage. The destruction of a major commercial port, such as Immingham, London, or Felixstowe, would disrupt British imports and exports very badly indeed.[18]

The UK has to protect the public from acts of terrorism. The most serious weapons that terrorists could utilise would almost certainly originate from overseas, such as hijacked airliners or improvised explosive devices brought in by sea or the Channel Tunnel. Nevertheless, the broad-based effects of terrorist attacks tend to be short-lived. Transport systems recover quickly, financial losses are addressed, and the British public, who are familiar with such attacks since the 1970s by the IRA, exhibit a phlegmatic defiance. That is not to diminish the existence of panic and fear during incidents, but it is remarkable that the British public tend to reach for icons of defiance and resistance, like Winston Churchill's rhetoric, when they are confronted such challenges.

Another challenge, and an opportunity, is global interconnectedness, particularly when it comes to the supply chain of information and technologies. The private sector plays a key role in the development of defence and security technologies, from the software of detection and cyber penetration to the aerial development of platforms of surveillance. The burden on government resources, particularly after the economic crisis of 2008, has added to the pressure to engage with and subcontract to the private sector for a range of defence needs, from real estate to research. Maintaining the operational security of future developments will certainly be more challenging for Britain. Like many Western countries, it expects that it will possess a leading technological edge for only a short period, although new breakthroughs are widely anticipated. The opportunity therefore lies not in over securitising technologies, but their embrace in order to foster the flow of resources, informational and commercial, on which the UK's prosperity depends.

There is a significant opportunity in the UK's nuclear capability. The Dreadnaught class of submarine will be equipped with the new generation of nuclear weapons and these have already demonstrated that even a hostile state like Russia will hesitate before challenging nuclear-armed countries directly. The nuclear arsenal is also a major contribution to NATO, which, alongside its maritime and air power means it does not need to maintain a large land force on the continent itself. The growth of land forces in Europe, in response to Russia's aggression against Ukraine, has created an opportunity for the UK to deploy its forces, which are by their nature expeditionary, to contest Russia and other hostile actors in global settings.

The most important challenge is the shift in the global strategic balance of power. The United States remains the pre-eminent world superpower, but China's rapid economic development has created a significant challenge for the Americans, generally in terms of Chinese aspirations to reshape in global affairs and specifically in the Chinese view of their exclusive sovereignty in the South and East China Seas. China has threatened Taiwan and other regional states, and the UK, while acknowledging Beijing's claim, does not recognise its sovereignty beyond the borders it established in 1949. It does not accept, for example, China's claim to the 'nine-dash line'. The United Kingdom is not immune from American-Chinese rivalry, seeing commercial opportunities with Beijing but clearly unwilling to sacrifice any part of its strategic relationship with Washington. The opportunities are once again significant. The United States is eager for the UK to play its part in the Indo-Asia-Pacific region, there are commercial export and technology openings, in areas such as the GCAP (Global Combat Air Programme) programme for next generation air power with Japan, and the AUKUS (Australia, UK, and United States) nuclear propulsion for submarines development programme. For Britain, there are vast civil commercial opportunities in areas such as artificial intelligence, financial services, and manufacturing across south and south-east Asia.

Indeed, there are significant opportunities for the United Kingdom amongst the emerging states of the world. Alongside its close relationship with the Commonwealth countries, the UK may well be an important partner of a new Atlantic regionalism, which would include numerous countries including the United States, Canada, Brazil, and Nigeria. Moreover e-commerce, which Britain champions, may well address many of historical and geographical restrictions, and gradually prise open the authoritarian states of Russia and China regardless of their attempts to prevent it. The economic liberalism which the United Kingdom has championed could again prove to be a much more successful model of global influence.

As an island nation, the UK recognises the need to keep enemies at arm's length, and this has been the traditional role of the Royal Navy and the Royal Air Force, but the UK's global interests mean that it cannot afford to look only to the protection of its immediate borders. Fighting at home would be damaging. Defence is therefore projected forward, across the continent of Europe, and through its regional allies in the Middle East, Africa, the Caribbean, South Asia, South-East Asia, and the Pacific. This means that Britain's partners can anticipate a continued forward posture as it constitutes an integral part of its enduring Grand Strategy.

An assessment of British values, ends, ways and means indicates that the British have been compelled to make significant adjustments over time to preserve their interests. They have moved to a position of working more closely with coalitions and allies to preserve the UK's influence. The UK has adjusted its posture according to the global situation, and several inflexion points have highlighted when its Grand Strategy was applied, and when it was neglected, the most prominent of which were the world wars, the Suez Crisis, decolonisation, and the Cold War, and, in the more recent decades, the changing relationship with Europe, responses to global terrorism, and Russian military aggression.

Setbacks in the UK's Grand Strategy occurred when its strategic principles were ignored: relative decline in economic power; periodic lack of balance in the posture of the armed forces, and episodic weaknesses in coalition strength. Yet British strategy has long recognised the limits to national power and adjusted to avoid catastrophic failure. Decision-making has been scrutinised by committees and cabinets, the Chiefs of Staff have accepted committee decision-making, and civil primacy in strategic design, the country has recognised the importance of building coalitions to augment its strength. In economic terms, the UK has the installations, factories, capital, trained workforce, education and training it require.[19] What the UK cannot afford to do is neglect its maritime strength, because its infrastructure, its prosperity, its businesses, and the public are utterly dependent on it. In the two world wars, it was this vital lifeline that Germany targeted. It will certainly be the target of future threat actors.

Taken together, The UK is a country that has a strong thread of pragmatism, and thus a willingness to adapt, but it has some enduring and immutable features in its Grand Strategy. The test for the success of that strategy is whether, in the long term, and globally, it can continue to uphold its strategic advantages and protect that which is most vital.[20]

1. UK trade in goods, year in review - Office for National Statistics (ons.gov.uk)

2. UK trade in numbers (web version) - GOV.UK (www.gov.uk)

3. The UK registered trading fleet was the 23rd largest in the world by DWT in 2022. The UK alone has a gross tonnage of 10.3 million. Container ship capacity is measured in 'twenty-foot equivalent units' (TEU), and container ships can move 24,000 TEUs. https://www.gov.uk/government/statistics/shipping-fleet-statistics-2022/shipping-fleet-statistics-2022

4. Paul Kennedy, *The Realities Behind Diplomacy: Background Influences on British External Policy, 1865-1980* (London: Fontana, 1981).

5. John Charmley, *Splendid Isolation? Britain and the Balance of Power* (London: Hodder and Stoughton, 1999), pp.397ff.

6. *A Strong Britain in an Age of Uncertainty: The National Security Strategy* (London: Crown Copyright, 2010), p. 5.

7. David French, *The British Way of Warfare, 1688-2000* (London: Unwin Hymen, 1990), p.148.

8. Turkey and France have more aircraft than the UK, although the Royal Air Force is increasing and possesses more 'next generation' strike platforms. The Royal Navy has 38 vessels, including 2 aircraft carriers and 11 nuclear submarines. The surface fleet also possesses numerous warships, including 13 frigates and 6 destroyers.

9. French, *The British Way of Warfare*, pp. 206-207, 216; D. Reynolds, *The Creation of the Anglo-American Alliance, 1937-41: A Study of Competitive Cooperation* (London: Europa, 1981); Henry Kissinger, *Diplomacy* (New York: Simon and Schuster, 1994), p. 532; John Lewis Gaddis, *The Cold War* (London: Allen Lane, 2005), p. 127; Hugh Thomas, *The Suez Affair* (London: Weidenfeld and Nicolson, 1957).

10. Kennedy, *Realities Behind Diplomacy*, p. 376.

11. *A Strong Britain in an Age of Uncertainty: The National Security Strategy* (London: Crown Copyright, 2010); see also the *National Security Strategy and Strategic Defence and Security Review* (London: Crown Copyright, 2015).

12. *National Security Strategy and Strategic Defence and Security Review* (2015), p. 49.

13. Desmond Browne, 'The Political-Military Relationship on Operations' in Bailey, Strachan and Iron, *British Generals and Blair's Wars,* (London: Routledge, 2014), p. 273.

14. 'Netanyahu Angrily Cancels Dinner With Visiting Briton', *New York Times*, 18 March 1998, http://www.nytimes.com/1998/03/18/world/netanyahu-angrily-cancels-dinner-with-visiting-briton.html (accessed December 2017).

15. Authors interviews in Sweden, Finland, Norway, and Estonia.

16. 'Royal Navy could lose "beach-landing" ships in next round of defence cuts', *The Telegraph*, 6 October 2017, http://www.telegraph.co.uk/news/2017/10/06/royalnavy-could-lose-beach-landing-ships-next-round-defence/ (Accessed December 2017).

17. Julian Lindley-French, 'Could Britain respond strategically to Russian aggression', in Janne Haaland Matlary and Tormod Heier, (eds), *Ukraine and Beyond: Russia's Strategic Security Challenge to Europe* (Basingstoke and New York: Palgrave Macmillan), p. 112.

18. Felixstowe handles 48 per cent of Britain's containerised commerce.

19. G.C. Peden, *British Rearmament and the Treasury, 1932-39* (Edinburgh, 1979).

20. Kennedy, 'Grand and Less-Than-Grand Strategies', op cit., p. 238.

21st Century Maritime Britain in Context – 100 years on

Dr Matthew Heaslip

The 21st century is increasingly framed by the pace at which our lives are changing, most commonly in conjunction with what has been framed as the fourth industrial revolution. Discussions of the impact are almost cliched in their emphasis upon the speed of that process. Against that urge to focus upon the present, our immediate pasts, and potential futures, there is a need to step back and consider the bigger picture. To fully understand Maritime Britain in the 21st century, we need to review the past century and consider what has changed, what has remained the same, and what insights the past yields for what we could do better. While there is often a temptation to explore the post-1945 world to understand the present, the interwar period or 'violent peace' 1919-39 offers a better recent guide to the contested and challenging environment the UK faces in the 2020s. Failing multilateral structures, global pandemics, broken disarmament conventions, proxy conflicts, disruption from new technologies and energy sources, and economic sparring between weary incumbents and tentative challengers all feature to greater or lesser extent. For all the change over the past century, the parallels between the two eras should not be understated. However, do those similarities match Britain's maritime connections, its ability to deter potential adversaries, and the aspirations of its communities to treasure Britain's maritime spaces?

Britain remains indelibly linked to the sea for its economy, environment, cultural development, and its defence, but it should not be assumed to be a maritime nation purely through being a kingdom of islands. Too often there is an immediate linear leap that an island nation <u>must</u> be a maritime nation and, by extension, it is therefore by default a global nation. The resulting discourse is then focused almost purely upon global challenges. While Britain is a global maritime nation, it is not only global or maritime and neither element should be taken for granted. Maritime Britain is a multi-faceted entity that is as much local as global. As a result, this chapter will focus upon three key related, but separate zones, starting in-shore with 'riverine' aspirations, sailing via 'coastal' or regional challenges, before voyaging out to 'blue water Britain'. Given the range of global issues, the latter section will feature greater discussion, but the key point is that Maritime Britain is not synonymous with Global Britain and this chapter intends to highlight that wider context.

Rather than a purely naval definition, this chapter uses 'riverine Britain' to explore that large segment of the UK associated with the water by identity, the connectedness enabled by maritime transit, or as a leisure pursuit. If you will, the sizable segment of the country whose employment is not directly associated with the sea. While maritime culture was deeply embedded in the nation's collective psyche over the 18th, 19th and 20th centuries, to what extent do its blue arteries still define Britain's identity and global aspirations as we move into the 21st? Little over a century on, to what extent does the nation still believe that 'there is nothing, absolutely nothing, half so much worth doing as simply messing about in boats'?[1]

We will then explore 'coastal Britain' and the challenges for its communities, environment, and the defence of the British Isles. At the junction between those who depend on the sea, those who live in proximity to the sea, and Britain as a whole – that coastal world has always played a pivotal role in defining maritime Britain. Bridging both the littoral gap and the siloed groups operating in that space, this section will explore how passionate discussion about that coastal world has long struggled to translate into clear, considered courses of action.

Finally, the chapter will sail over the horizon to blue-water Britain and consider how its commitments and maritime links are exposed to vulnerabilities both old and new. Trade, knowledge exchange, and diplomatic commitments have long tied Britain to the wider world, but looking back from our rapidly changing lives we might be surprised by the extent to which core aspects remain the same.

Riverine Britain

The framing of Britain as a 'Maritime Nation' has been a core feature in political discourse over much of the past century.[2] That rhetorical identity has evolved, however, from a dual patriotism for the UK at the centre of a maritime empire, to an imagined unique national maritime sense of self. Thankfully, it has also shifted from what was a racialized and at times racist division of who could and should contribute to that 'Empire of the Sea', to a more embracive and helpful view that Britain's maritime nature connects it with communities all around the world, although one still dogged by legacies of the past.[3]

Offering some continuity between those eras, the Royal Navy remains central to that national identity, whether via HMS *Hood's* 'Empire Cruise' in 1923-24 or Carrier Strike Group (CSG) 21 at the heart of 'Global Britain'.[4] The Navy's ties extend beyond the political arena to deeper cultural perceptions across British society of its maritime-ness, given the continued popular appeal of naval inspired literature, film, and music. There is perhaps no better example than C.S. Forester's Hornblower, widely available in print almost 90 years from his first appearance and the television adaption still drawing significant appeal after 20 years. Alternatively, and less obviously, there is the endearing nature of JMW Turner's artwork, many of which featured naval themes. His paintings have drawn lasting audiences both in their own right as well as indirectly, whether the 2014 biopic *Mr Turner*, or via the different symbolic interpretations by 'Q' and Commander Bond of *The Fighting Temeraire* in *Skyfall.*

In addition to the sustained popular appeal of naval culture, it is clear that British society also retains a broader love for 'messing about in boats'. Fourteen per cent of domestic tourism trips in the UK are made to the coast, with marine leisure contributing over £25bn to the UK economy in 2014.[5] Heading out onto the water, approximately two million cruise journeys are taken from UK ports each year.[6] Back on land, maritime heritage retains its appeal. The National Museum of the Royal Navy with roots dating back to 1911, the Royal Museums Greenwich created in 1934, and Merseyside Maritime Museum founded in 1980, are all among Britain's most visited tourist attractions.[7] The precise nature of tourism may have changed, but this is broadly comparable with the four million visitors to the 1909 naval review in London or the golden age of seaside holidays during the 1920s and 1930s.[8] While jetting off for the Mediterranean sun has changed how Brits interact with many coastal destinations, Blackpool's 23.5 million visitors in 2022 is just as impressive as its own four million annual visitors in 1910.[9] Even away from the coast, the popularity of Richard Attenborough's *Blue Planet* (I and II) and the 'Freshwater' and 'Ocean' episodes of the recent *Wild Isles,* highlight the degree of passion felt for the maritime environment.

This all paints a rather rosy picture of Britain's attitude towards the sea, but it masks a degree of superficiality that has grown over the past century. Evocations of 'Maritime Britain' have become cliched and while possibly meant with genuine passion and meaning, too often mask a complete failure to appreciate the centrality of the sea to British life. Whether it is the 99.9% of the British population who do not know that over 90% of imports arrive by ship, government ministers who "hadn't quite understood" how important the Port of Dover is, or everyone else who overlooks that their emails, work data, and entertaining cat videos are largely delivered by undersea cables.[10]

This raises two questions. The first is, how did it get this bad? While the full explanation requires a book of its own, the problem can be partly explained by two trends over the past 70 years – containerisation and decolonisation. The introduction of the first shipping container in 1958 cut the cost of shipping goods between Europe and the United States by roughly half within a decade, largely through cuts in the number of required dockworkers. As a result, there were only 10,000 registered dock workers in Britain by 1989, compared to 60,000 just 20 years earlier.[11] Moreover, rather than ships docking in 'Port Cities' (pre-1950s), container trade increasingly ties into 'Port Regions' (post-1950s), exemplified by the decline of London's Docklands and the rise of London Gateway and its rival Felixstowe.[12] As a result, Britain's vital maritime trade now takes place largely away from major population centres and directly employs comparatively few people – ashore and afloat. The same is true of the fishing industry, another important part of maritime Britain, whose direct workforce declined by approximately 76% between 1948 and 2022.[13] When combined with the drop in the number of warships in service and a resulting 60,000 fewer service personnel in the Royal Navy and Royal Marines, as Britain's global commitments declined – maritime workers are now 'out of sight, out of mind'.[14] This extends far inland and through generations beyond immediate years of service. We can compare Portsmouth and Chatham, for example, which both have deep historic links with the Royal Navy. Forty years on from the closure of its naval base, Chatham no longer has a significant veteran community, in contrast to Portsmouth that has one of the highest concentrations in the UK.[15] It is therefore not just the direct loss of hundreds of thousands of employed mariners and dockers, but potentially millions of people who no longer have previously been employed in working with the sea. As a result, rather than seablindness – an inability to see how important the sea is – Britain suffers from sea sensory-deprivation; a lack of lived experience of how important the sea is.

The second question will be left open as a somewhat philosophical one. Is Britain still a 'Maritime Nation', if British society and decision-makers have lost sight of what actually makes Britain a maritime nation?

Whatever the answer may be to that question, one of the most significant problems resulting from that worsening awareness of how important the sea is to Britain, is that it hampers the willingness of the public and politicians to commit sums towards addressing maritime challenges or exploiting its opportunities. One of the easier elements for historical comparison here is in naval funding. If we look back at the great successes of the Royal Navy during the Napoleonic Wars and over the 19th to early 20th centuries, the British public were willing to be taxed for, and the government was committed to spending more on, its navy than France and then Germany, and not just during times of crisis.[16] Defence cuts were a regular source of debates, but public and politicians alike were willing to maintain sizable and potent naval and maritime capabilities.[17] Without better public appreciation of the importance of the maritime environment, economy, and critical infrastructure for main-taining their day to day lives, it seems unlikely there could be similar commitments to long-term spending to address challenges in all those areas. This is even more critical during times like the present when there are so many demands on already stretched household and government budgets and so maritime Britain needs to emphasise it is not just a luxury for good times.

Coastal Britain

Flowing from Britain's inland waterways, meandering through its towns and cities, we reach its coasts where the passion for maritime spaces and the aspirations of those in habitants to be part of a maritime country meet a harsher reality. Whether we consider 1923 or 2023, we find that clash between what the British public perceive or wish the coast to be, and the reality of what exists in that littoral zone. Returning to the coastal community of Blackpool, we find the first example of this schism and one that also reveals a stark contrast over the past century. While the city still draws vast numbers of visitors, as it did a century beforehand, it is now England's 3rd most economically deprived local authority.[18] In the 1930s, Blackpool's popularity resulted in a 'vast modernisation' with a mixture of middle and working-class amenities, which added to a steady flow of previous investments between 1870-1914.[19] Contrasting recent fortunes highlight a wider issue of Britain's coastal communities, which tend to be more economically deprived, worse connected, and receive less investment – public and private – with Blackpool joined by Hastings, Great Yarmouth, Liverpool, Hartlepool, and many others. Given that demand for tourism and leisure activities in those coastal communities appears as strong as it was a century ago, something is clearly amiss in 21st century maritime Britain.

Turning to coastal manufacturing, we again find curious clashes between perceptions and the actual state of British shipbuilding. After a surge in wartime and immediate post-war ship construction, much of the interwar period was framed by significant underemployment of British shipyards and unemployment for their workers. Indeed, at its worst in 1933 the unemployment rate among shipbuilding and repair workers in Scotland hit 77%.[20] And yet amidst that gloomy picture for workers, the top 14 British shipbuilders built 1,244 ships totalling over 7.5 million tons (1920-39). While badly affected by 'boom and bust' cycles, Britain comfortably outbuilt its competitors, with a much younger and more efficient merchant fleet than its comparable rivals.[21] Likewise, while many historians have lamented a lack of new capital ships during this period, British shipyards completed 345 warships totalling almost 1 million tons and the Royal Navy entered the Second World War with a large and comparatively youthful fleet.[22] It was a clash between the degree of wartime construction capacity that the UK wished to retain and a lack of global demand for substantial quantities of new ships. Fast forward to 2023 and British shipbuilding is now a niche player in the global market, but capacity remains to furnish the government with all the ships it is willing and able to pay for, employing tens of thousands of workers in the process.[23] Whereas 20th century Scotland was the worst hit by the glut in interwar capacity, in the first half of the 21st century the Glasgow and Rosyth yards will be busy producing warships just on present commitments – just so long as they remain within the UK.[24] The somewhat more difficult question is whether Britain retains sufficient spare potential capacity should global events take a further turn for the worse. Underutilized yards in the 1920s and 1930s were neither politically popular nor economically efficient, but they proved incredibly valuable by the end of that decade.

After the luxury of three decades where threats were seen to be somewhere 'over there', Britain has recently been reminded its front line is its coast and has been for centuries. While there is always the hope to push hazards as far away as possible, threats to Britain's defence, to its health or biosecurity, and to its environment, all present challenges in its coastal spaces. Air travel does now dominate the flow of passengers compared to 100 years ago, but a long-term average of 22-23 million passenger movements occur to and from UK ports each year and most imports arrive by ship. As a result, countering potential pandemics and invasive species remains a major maritime challenge.[25] Post-2020, the risk posed by pandemics is now widely appreciated and is predicted to only get worse. Comparisons to the 1918-19 'Spanish Flu' influenza pandemic should be made cautiously, but one of the responses in subsequent years was an effort to develop a network for monitoring healthcare in ports, as the primary path of international transmission. Unfortunately, mirroring the later response to the 2002-04 SARS outbreak, those efforts were largely limited to the 'Eastern Bureau' of the League of Nations Health Organisation (a forerunner of the World Health Organisation) and so restricted to East Asia.[26] Similar challenges exist from plastic pollution, sewage releases, and many other threats to our maritime environment and health. If we just consider aquatic non-indigenous/invasive species, the threat posed by resulting biodiversity loss and environmental change is currently serious, under monitored, and also expected to 'surge' over the coming years.[27]

Improving Britain's maritime monitoring and defences for containing a range of those threats over the coming years will likely feature similar changes to those seen during the interwar period, although one would hope with greater realisation about the need for international cooperation. Moreover, with the 2021 Integrated Defence Review suggestion that a serious CBRN attack is likely by 2030, those security preparations tie into Britain's coastal defences.[28] While a biological attack by a terrorist group is still relatively unlikely, some international states are now regularly breaking vital taboos surrounding the direct or indirect use of such weapons.[29]

This brings us to the theme of coastal naval defence, which has come full circle over the past century. In the previous 'competitive age' of the 1930s, the British government was fully aware how vulnerable its energy supplies were in coastal waters, particularly the exposed collier routes from Tyneside to London. There were plans to shift some shipments onto the railways and canal networks, but they offered limited spare capacity to reroute substantial flows.[30] As a result, from 1937 greater focus was placed upon defending coastal and not just oceanic shipping, particularly on the exposed North Sea coast.[31] To highlight the scale of the challenge, 85 ships were lost on those coastal routes in just nine months of 1941.[32] While the sources of energy and means of transporting it have changed to windfarms, high-voltage undersea cables, and gas pipelines, the same vulnerability remains from surface, sub-surface, and aerial threats, once again most evident in the North Sea. Indeed, it is remarkable that challenges of increasing capacity on land once again mean that critical flows are being directed via the east coast, although admittedly now beneath the waves. Failure to secure those supply lines in either era could soon result in the lights going off in British cities. Amplified by Russia's invasion of Ukraine, the 21st century challenge has triggered a similar scramble to 'relearn old tricks' with RFA *Proteus* entering service and discussion of regenerating coastal forces capacity.[33] While many of the same challenges for coastal Britain therefore exist a century on, the magnitude and complexity of the issues has only been magnified over recent decades.

Oceanic Britain

Charting a course beyond those coastal zones, like much of Northern Europe's merchant shipping we must transit through the Western Approaches. While 21st century Britain might underappreciate how important global shipping is for its trade and economy, the safety of those sea lanes has been a key part of British defence planning for centuries. After numerous false births, this was first clearly 'articulated and thoroughly developed' with the reestablishment of the Western Squadron in 1746 under Admiral Anson.[34] These sea lanes have remained as a significant lifeline and a key vulnerability for maritime Britain and as a result their protection has been a core mission of the Royal Navy ever since, including throughout the past 100 years. However, the nature of global trade has changed during that timeframe. Given all too frequent references to the Battle of the Atlantic, we should review precisely what the situation was prior to 1939 and where Britain is in the 21st century.

As demonstrated during the Covid pandemic lockdowns, the first and most important trade priority during a crisis is to feed the population. While over the past century globalisation has generally led to Britain becoming more reliant upon imports, conflict and agricultural advances mean that this has not been true of core food supplies. Entering the First World War, Britain relied upon 18.1 million tons of food imports, including 80% of its cheese, 79% of its cereal grains, 73% of its fruit, and 60% of its meat. Many of these were imported at significant distances and often from outside of the British Empire, notably the USA, the Russian Empire, and Argentina, although Canada, India, and Australia were all vital sources.[35] Despite great industriousness in that earlier conflict and during the interwar period, Britain still relied upon imports for 70% of its food in 1939. Considerable hard work in wartime was therefore required to increase domestic yields and to voluntarily or legally restrict consumption of some produce, leading to the wartime British public being sufficiently fed, even if via a rather 'dull diet'.[36] As a result, contrary to popular assumptions, German consumers were forced to limit their consumption of food and other goods to a greater degree and from earlier in the conflict than their British counterparts. Benchmarked against 1938, British aggregate consumer spending was down by 14% at its weakest in 1944, although food purchases only dropped by 11%. In contrast, German consumer spending had dropped by 18% even by 1941 and, in some areas, it was down by a third by 1944.[37] For all its vulnerability as a maritime nation, Britain fared better than its continental adversary through good planning, and both governmental and voluntary controls. In contrast, one of its biggest challenges throughout the conflict was in maintaining sufficient exports to pay for the war.[38]

In contrast, looking to 2023 the UK's food security is much improved, at least on the surface. It is largely self-sufficient for eggs, cereals, and moderately self-sufficient for potatoes, sugar (from beet) and oil seeds, in addition to long-standing strengths in milk and meat production. However, the system is now far more complicated with imports of fertilizers, veterinary products, food preservatives, seasonal produce, farm equipment, farm labour, or the exchanges of specific meat cuts, among others, all important parts in the resilience of the overall food system that require reliable trade flows. The most maritime of foods – fish – is the perfect example, with British consumers favouring cod, haddock, prawns, and tuna that are largely imported, whereas domestically landed herring, mackerel, salmon, and langoustines are all heavily exported. Moreover, fruit and vegetable supplies are now more exposed, with the proportion grown in Britain dropping from 27% and 74% respectively in 1913, to just 16% and 54% in 2022. The saving grace in the 21st century is that threats do not come from Britain's immediate neighbours, who instead now provide many of the missing elements. If we then include vegetables grown in countries with relatively safe, short-distance links to the UK, then 93% of UK supplies are relatively secure. In light of experience gained during the Covid pandemic, the challenge for 21st century Maritime Britain may therefore be one of network and public resilience to highly disrupted diet in times of crisis. Seen again in the case of fuelling the nation after the 2022 Russian invasion of Ukraine, the primary challenge for Britain was attempting to keep energy prices under control, as far as possible within global markets. Countries do not need to be at war to face wartime inflation, particularly following existing inflationary pressures from a resurgence in global demand post-pandemic. For all the change of the past century, good planning, and the ability of society to implement changes required in difficult times, appear in common with earlier periods.

Looking beyond the defence of trade to delivering effective naval power as part of Britain's foreign policy, introduces a more direct link between the past and the present. One of the challenges CSG21 encountered during its global tour came from comparisons with earlier imperial enterprises.[39] Similar criticisms were levelled against the Johnson-era approach towards 'Global Britain', particularly in its discourse surrounding Africa, that was reminiscent of earlier imperial 'civilising' approaches.[40] Britain faces the unfortunate legacy of having built a vast empire at the expense of many, if not most, of the populations that came under its rule, and one that affected further areas beyond its formal boundaries. Informal imperial influence was no less threatening whether it involved gunboats in Chongqing deep inside China, battleships off Istanbul and marines on its streets, or the use of naval searchlights during neutral port calls to make unsubtle hints at the ability of naval guns to bombard targets miles ashore. Addressing that legacy is a challenge and one that forces 21st century Maritime Britain to be mindful of how its actions and language may associate with that past. It is a past that Britain has largely forgotten, and which some of its popular press attempts to deny. Even at its peak power, the British Empire was vulnerable to boycotts, strikes, riots and other forms of protest against its use of heavy-handed gunboat diplomacy. In the present, such organic challenges combine with the weaponized use of History via 'wolf warrior' style diplomacy or engineered social-media outrage. With economic growth in Asia continuing to outstrip most developed nations, many countries that were on the receiving end of European imperialism now have significant global influence.[41] National self-flagellation or retreat from the world is not the answer, but Maritime Britain does require an improved awareness of the unintended consequences that can arise from missing uncomfortable historical parallels.

This is all the more important as effective naval power in violent or contested peacetimes requires an appreciation of the role that recipient communities play, whether allied, neutral, or potentially hostile, in maritime interactions. The primary uses of naval power outside of conflict, whether soft power 'flying the flag' or harder 'gunboat diplomacy' style operations, require goals that the 'other' parties may be able to accept. This is easier for the former, with humanitarian assistance and disaster relief (HADR) deployments delivering relatively uncontroversial ways of securing modest benefits to regional relationships, often beyond the direct value of the assistance provided.[42] Naval HADR can also deliver potential secondary strategic gains, although this may be more challenging to accomplish. While not the primary purpose of Admiral Leveson's order to send all possible assistance to Japan in the aftermath of the 1923 Great Kanto earthquake, it helped repair some of the damage done by the non-renewal of the Anglo-Japanese Alliance in 1921.[43] This may have helped extend the period in which Japan and Britain were able to cooperate on common challenges, before the dramatic breakdown in the relationship from 1927. Whether the direct use of naval power or indirect value of maritime culture, they both made and continue to make a significant contribution to Britain's place as the second ranked country in global soft power.[44] Soft power only works, however, if it appeals to the audience and they are willing to listen, attend educational institutions, or pay attention to a naval display and that they subsequently interpret the outcome of in a positive way. Moreover, it needs to be part of a coherent long-term strategy as flying the flag in itself only delivers limited and temporary benefits.

The use of naval power in a more threatening capacity to achieve foreign policy outcomes outside of war has always been far more controversial. Whether or not it meets the definition of gunboat diplomacy, these operations feature a vital and often underappreciated element, which is that they need to be coercive, and the recipient needs to be able to accept the consequences. That recipient may be a state, but it may also be a sub-state group, such as pirates, bandits, or warlords in a civil conflict. The act can range from a subtle performative threat of potential violence, even via something seemingly harmless like a musical display, to the employment of weapons to cause harm.[45] Indeed, an important point of emphasis is that historically the most effective and least controversial examples usually did not require physical violence to occur, even if violent cases have subsequently tended to attract the most attention and define popular understanding of what gunboat diplomacy involves. This is a vital difference to the more 'antagonistic' Big Stick Diplomacy adopted by Theodore Roosevelt, which has had a lasting if inconsistent influence upon US foreign policy.[46]

Coercive displays are where the Royal Navy has long demonstrated its core peacetime value to Maritime Britain, as naval theatre can be performed with a greater degree of subtlety and in a wider range of circumstances than other service branches are normally capable of. Whether conducting firework displays during Asian port calls in the 1920s or as the ship just over the horizon during the latter stages of the Sierra Leone civil war, naval power can impress and intimidate without being explicitly threatening.[47] In most of those cases, positive outcomes have been achieved without the need to deploy large expensive formations, such as a carrier air group. Crucially, such displays tend to lack the negative headlines and direct perception of violence associated with their aerial counterparts: fighter jets and military drones. Even if we just consider their names: 'Typhoon', 'Tempest', or 'Reaper' and its predecessor 'Predator' are ill-suited to subtlety, in comparison to HMS *Spey* or *Lancaster*. Where the naval approach struggles, it is often a result of not considering whether the coercive behaviour can and is likely to be accepted, and whether the scale of resources used is appropriate. Too much or too little threatened force, or excessive and undeliverable demands, often leads to direct violence or one side having to make an embarrassing submission that simply complicates further interactions.

This is where effective communication with a range of civilian bodies in the past proved vital, whether coordinating with diplomats or seeking the advice of business experts, academics, or even charities. If we look back to the early 20th century, it was not uncommon for the British government to order the Royal Navy to defend certain national or imperial interests, but usually based upon allusions from public commentators that something was at stake. In practice, in some cases it was subsequently discovered that the assets in question, such as factories or mines, were not actually financed with significant amounts of British money. Instead, the shareholders or creditors came from around the world, via a process of syndicated imperialism.[48] By the 1920s, British businesses themselves increasingly protested against threatened violence or violent acts by British forces, as they felt it caused far greater economic harm through resulting boycotts of British goods.[49] After all, 'trade requires willing buyers and willing sellers.'[50]

Which brings us then to Britain's maritime connections with the world and the role of naval power in its foreign policy. After a relatively short period of global European dominance in the second half of the 19th century, the First World War accelerated a slow shift of relative power to the Americas and then to Asia. The impact on the European empires was profound, including on how Britain attempted to defend both its formal Empire and those informal interests beyond its borders. The interwar period then offers some context for current debates about 'East of Suez'.

Britain's strategy for deterring Japan, or defending against it, did not fail because it was a particularly unsound strategy. As the officers who developed the strategy knew, even at its peak relative power the Royal Navy was a two-ocean navy, and after 1941 it was trying to fight a five-ocean war. Britain lacked the luxury of choosing to be either European or Global, and with war established against Germany and then Italy its overstretch was obvious, which Japan duly exploited. This does not mean that Britain performed as well as it might have done, just simply that there was no 'right' strategy in those circumstances. While the scale is clearly different, after decades of decolonisation and so with a much smaller Royal Navy, Britain still faces that challenge of having to be both European and Global, or perhaps in the context of this chapter, of being riverine, coastal, and blue water, all at the same time. Moreover, it is unlikely to field sufficient resources to cover all those priorities. Whether dealing with peacetime trade or wartime conflict, it has never been a binary dichotomy. Moving beyond the divisive absolutist legacy of 2016 may be the only solution for recreating an effective geostrategic plan for juggling Britain's various maritime priorities. The effective implement-ation of new technologies can help, whether radio as a force multiplier in the interwar period, or potential flotillas of Uncrewed Surface or Underwater Vehicles operating in conjunction with mother-ships in the near future.[51] However, technology has rarely provided the 'golden bullet' to solve similar underlying challenges in the past. As Britain's interwar planners appreciated, no one nation can deliver effective naval power everywhere all the time and so resources must be prioritised. However, they also identified that a global maritime nation still needs to maintain the flexibility to make friends and influence people around the world, wherever the wind and waves will take it.

Conclusions

What does the past 100 years then tell us about Maritime Britain in the 21st Century, how it has changed, and what this might mean for the future? Returning to popular culture, the evolution of Commander Bond illustrates many of its struggles and the challenges ahead. While fictional, faithful, and most certainly flawed, through 27 films the character has faced Britain's evolution from the collapsing third power trying to compete with the USA and Soviet Union, through decolon-isation and Cold War, adapting to a post-1991 world, and finally a period of rebirth and facing up to problematic legacies. While often through a nostalgic and sometimes rose-tinted lens, this has reflected real changes and challenges in Britain, as well as how it has been seen by the world[52] – myth and reality intertwined. Present day Maritime Britain is therefore reflected in its own way in Daniel Craig's interpretation of Bond: a weary titan, facing up to an uncertain place in the world and hiding from mental scars with a legacy of great achievements as well as a trail of collateral damage and broken hearts. While no-one should aspire to copy Bond, if we step back and consider what positives are highlighted by the films, then working together as part of a coordinated and increasingly diverse team is not a bad lesson. For all Bond's mistakes and heroics, at his best he was part of an effective team led by the incisive and analytical 'M', supported by the cynical and tough 'Moneypenny', equipped with the latest technology by 'Q' ('the latest thing from Q branch – called a radio!'), along with many other supportive figures whether British, allied, or even potential adversaries.

As the various chapters in this book highlight, Maritime Britain needs to work as a coordinated team, bringing together all its expertise and strengths, while also acknowledging and addressing its weaker elements. It can build from a base support in the population for the maritime world that is deep and vibrant, and that ties into so many parts of British life, but one that clearly suffers from a growing practical detachment from the sea. Over the past century, the coast and the sea have become far more temporary and transient spaces that the British public visit, pass through, or fly over, rather than experience as core to their lives. That then clashes with the reality, which is that the maritime is just as important to Britain in the 21st century as it was during the 20th.

Britain is a global maritime nation, but its maritime strength flows from the riverine arteries of its green(water) and pleasant land, through its coastal zones and communities, before reaching the wider blue waters of the global oceans. Each of those three areas faces significant challenges that become clear when placed in context. Improving ocean literacy, if it is to be achieved, needs to consider communities from all around the UK. Trying to force feed them the memorization of facts about the maritime world, or Britain's naval history, only engages surface learning at best and will not address the superficiality of bonds with that heritage. People may only remember 10% of what they read, 20% of what they hear, 30% of what they see, but 70% of what they discuss with others and 80% of what they use in real life.[53] As a result, thought should go into how communities might better experience the maritime and how to generate discussion about its significance, so that they can better appreciate its value for the communities themselves, as well as the wider nation.

If improving ocean literacy will help boost the UK's aspirations to not just talk about being a maritime nation, but to develop and secure its maritime future, the coast offers many opportunities to guard against key challenges as well as to unlock Britain's full potential. The sustained decline of many coastal communities, including those that retain an appeal as strong as a century ago, represents a significant drawback on the wider British economy. Moreover, it highlights a neglect for the coast that reflects and reinforces the underlying issue of poor ocean literacy among decision makers. Encompassing far more than just economic and social issues, this ties into environmental, health and defence issues that need to be addressed through a single cohesive, non-political national strategy. Rather than being seen as the extremities of the British Isles, the coast should be seen more accurately as the connective space between Britain and the wider world, in much the same way as politicians regard its airports. Whether via undersea cables, holidays, ferry journeys, cultural depictions, or even the classic British 'fish and chips', the coast is what helps make Britain global.

At its peak power, 1920s Britain could build from stronger riverine and coastal spaces, but faced many of the same challenges around the blue planet as it does in the 21st century. Once again, we encounter a contested global environment, containing states that are willing to launch sustained violent campaigns to achieve expansionist and maximalist military goals. Operating in that world requires a better appreciation of unfortunate parallels for Britain as a former imperial power, but one that can be made easier through better knowledge of the context in which events are occurring. This may be the history of a country or region and its former interactions with Britain, but looking to the past we find those examples that highlight the importance of rich economic data and a nuanced appreciation of local cultures and how best to positively engage with them. Vitally, the role of human interactions is fundamental and that for all the value of technology, people still do business with people. Building deep trading or diplomatic relationships takes sustained engagement between groups of individuals, and while automated warfare might provide military solutions, conflicts only end when the two fighting communities are willing to stop fighting. Not only does the maritime link Britain to that world, but the effective use of its naval and wider maritime power offers the means to deliver all those key elements, with the due subtlety that is often required for success.

A century on, Maritime Britain looks very different, but it remains central to British life, its economy, its defence, and its links to the communities around the globe. While there is a wealth of challenges present across the various interlinked elements, spread from deep within Britain to the wider world, there are numerous opportunities to unlock a great potential to do better. The challenge looking ahead to the rest of the 21st century seems to be how best to coordinate the process of ensuring that in another century, historians will be able to report significant successes in navigating a more prosperous, healthier, less polluted, and safer path.

[1.] From Kenneth Grahame's *The Wind in the Willows* first published by Methuen in 1908.

[2.] As a broad indicator, 'Maritime Nation' and similar expressions appear regularly in Hansard entries 1920-2023, although at a reduced level between 1996 and 2008. This hit a peak in July 1981, with 16 references to 'Maritime Nation' that month, in the aftermath of the June 1981 *The United Kingdom Defence Programme: The Way Forward* white paper that outlined significant cuts to the Royal Navy.

[3.] John Mitcham, *Race and Imperial Defence in the British world, 1870-1914* (Cambridge: Cambridge University Press, 2016), pp.129-157.

[4.] Ralph Harrington, ''The Mighty Hood': Navy, Empire, War at Sea and the British National Imagination, 1920-60', *Journal of Contemporary History*, 38/2, (2003), 171-185; Press release by British Embassy Tokyo 'UK Carrier Strike Group will sail to Japan on its maiden deployment', 27 April 2021, https://www.gov.uk/government/news/uk-carrier-strike-group-will-sail-to-japan-on-its-maiden-deployment, last accessed 08 November 2023.

[5.] Emily Stebbings, Eleni Papathanasopoulou, Tara Hooper, Melanie C. Austen, and Xiaoyu Yan, 'The marine economy of the United Kingdom', *Marine Policy*, 116, (2020).

[6.] Data set: All UK international short sea, long sea and cruise passengers, 1950-2022, UK Department for Transport, SPAS0101.

[7.] Coherent comparable data is difficult to come by, but that available from Visit Britain (https://www.visitbritain.com/en), Visit England (https://www.visitengland.com/), Visit Scotland (https://www.visitscotland.com/), and the museum websites confirm their place amongst the top 10-25 destinations in the UK.

[8.] Jan Ruger, *The Great Naval Game: Britain and Germany in the Age of Empire* (Cambridge: Cambridge University Press, 2007), pp.12-33; V. Richter, "Seaside Resort Blues: The English Seaside in the 1930s" *Hungarian Journal of English and American Studies* (HJEAS) 27/1 (2021), 33–48.

[9.] Gary Cross, "Crowds and Leisure: Thinking Comparatively across the 20th Century" *Journal of Social History* 39/3 (2006), 632.

[10.] 'Brexit secretary Dominic Raab says he 'hadn't quite understood' importance of Dover-Calais Crossing, *Independent,* Thursday 8th November 2018, last accessed 1st November 2023; *The Maritime Barometer*, Nautilus International, February 2022, p.3.

11. André Vigarié, "From Break-Bulk to Containers: The Transformation of General Cargo Handling and Trade", *GeoJournal* 48/1 (1999), 6.

12. For more about the impact of containerisation on port dynamics see: Cesar Ducruet and Hidekazu Itoh, "Regions and Material Flows: Investigating the Regional Branching and Industry Relatedness of Port Traffics in a Global Perspective." *Journal of Economic Geography*, 16/4 (2016), 805–30.

13. E. Uberoi, G. Hutton, M. Ward, and E. Ares, *UK Fisheries Statistics*, 11 October 2022, House of Commons Library, p.13.

14. Allowing for the distortions of the two world wars, Royal Navy / Royal Marine personnel numbers have dropped from just under 100,000 in the 1920s, to 38,770 in April 2023. See: Cabinet Committee on Reduction of Naval Expenditure, January 1923, the National Archives (UK), Cabinet Files (CAB) 24/160/72; Quarterly service personnel statistics, 1 April 2023 (updated 14 September 2023), UK Ministry of Defence.

15. ONS 2021 Census: https://www.ons.gov.uk/releases/ukarmedforcesveteranscensus2021inenglandandwales

16. Jonathan Dull, *The Age of the Ship of the Line* (Barnsley: Seaforth Publishing, 2009), pp.179-182; Roger Morriss, *The Foundations of British Maritime Ascendancy: Resources, Logistics, and the State 1755-1815* (Cambridge: Cambridge University Press, 2010), pp.399-401.

17. Andrew Lambert, 'Economic Power, Technological Advantage, and Imperial Strength: Britain as a Unique Global Power, 1860-1890.', *International Journal of Naval History* 5/2 (2006); Philip O'Brien, 'The Titan Refreshed: Imperial Overstretch and the British Navy before the First World War', *Past & Present*, 172 (2001), 146-169; David Edgerton, *Warfare State: Britain 1920-1970*, (Cambridge University Press; Cambridge, 2006), pp.16-37.

18. Indices of Deprivation 2019, UK Ministry of Housing, Communities and Local Government, last accessed online 01/11/2023.

19. Cross, 'Crowds and Leisure', 639.

20. Hugh Murphy, "Labour in the British Shipbuilding and Ship Repairing Industries in the Twentieth Century", in *Shipbuilding and Ship Repair Workers around the World: Case Studies 1950-2010*, edited by Hugh Murphy et al., (Amsterdam: Amsterdam University Press, 2017), 59.

21. Phil Banks, "Emaciated', 'Withered', 'Emasculated' and 'Crippled' – A reappraisal of the decline of British Sea power in the interwar years', unpublished MA Dissertation (University of Portsmouth, 2020), pp.81-102.

22. Edgerton, *Warfare State*, pp.32-33; Robert Chesneau (ed.), *All the World's Fighting Ships 1922–1946*, (London: Conway, 1992).

23. *National Shipbuilding Strategy*, UK National Shipbuilding Office, March 2022.

24. George Allison, 'Military Shipbuilding in Scotland – A quick look', *UK Defence Journal*, 4th June 2022, last accessed online 02/11/2023.

25. Sarah Manchester and James Bullock, "The Impacts of Non-Native Species on UK Biodiversity and the Effectiveness of Control", *Journal of Applied Ecology* 37/5 (2000), pp. 855-857; Cascade Sorte et al, "Ocean Warming Increases Threat of Invasive Species in a Marine Fouling Community", *Ecology* 91/8 (2010), 2198–204.

26. Tomoko Akami, 'A Quest to be Global: The League of Nations Health Organization and Inter-Colonial Regional Governing Agendas of the Far Eastern Association of Tropical Medicine 1910–25', *The International History Review*, 38:1 (2016), 1-23; Martin Gorsky et. al., "The 1918/19 Influenza Pandemic & COVID-19 in Ireland and the UK." *Historical Social Research* 33 (2021), 215-217.

27. Sarah Bailey, et al. "Trends in the Detection of Aquatic Non-Indigenous Species across Global Marine, Estuarine and Freshwater Ecosystems: A 50-Year Perspective." *Diversity and Distributions* 26/12 (2020), 1780–97.

28. *Global Britain in a Competitive Age: The Integrated Review of Security, Defence, Development and Foreign Policy*, UK Cabinet Office, March 2021, p.32, https://www. gov.uk/government/publications/global-britain-in-a-competitive-age-the-integrated-review-of-security-defence-development-and-foreign-policy, last accessed 09 November 2023.

29. Oliver Mihell-Hale, "Desperate and Opportunistic: CBRN Terrorists and Civilian Radiological Material" *Journal of Strategic Security* 16/2 (2023), 60-61.

30. Christopher Savage, *History of the Second World War: Inland Transport* (London: HMSO, 1957), pp.31-42.

31. Stephen Roskill, *Naval Policy Between the Wars, Volume II: The Period of Reluctant Rearmament, 1930-1939*, (London: Pen & Sword, 2016), pp.345-350.

32. Savage, *Inland Transport,* p.654.

33. 'A guide to RFA Proteus – the UK's new seabed warfare vessel', 10 October 2023, Navy Lookout, https://www.navylookout.com/a-guide-to-rfa-proteus-the-uks-new-seabed-warfare-vessel/, last accessed 09 November 2023; R. Skelton and A. Young, '(Re)Learning Old Tricks: The Royal Navy's Coastal Forces Squadron', *RUSI Journal* 25 (2023), https://www.rusi.org/explore-our-research/publications/rusi-defence-systems/relearning-old-tricks-royal-navys-coastal-forces-squadron, last accessed 09 November 2023.

34. Nicholas Rodger, 'Sea-Power and Empire, 1688-1793', in *Oxford History of the British Empire*, (Oxford University Press: Oxford, 1998), pp.174-177.

35. A. Peters, 'Lecture on the Economic Aspects of War', 1930, National Maritime Museum, PET/7.

36. Richard Overy, *Blood and Ruins: The Great Imperial War 1931-45,* (London: Allen Lane, 2021), p.411.

37. Overy, *Blood and Ruins,* p.407. The figures are adjusted for inflation.

38. Jamie Martin, 'The Global Crisis of Commodity Glut During the Second World War', *The International History Review*, 43:6 (2021), 1273-1290.

39. For example: 'China warns UK as carrier strike group approaches', 30 July 2021, BBC News; Z. Hui and Z. Yusha, 'UK tilting toward Indo-Pacific to counterweight China 'immature' decision', 16 March 2021, China Global Times, last accessed 09 November 2023.

40. Juergen Haacke and John Breen, "From Benign Neglect to Effective Re-Engagement? Assessing British Strategizing and Policies Towards Southeast Asia Since 2010." *Contemporary Southeast Asia,* 41/3 (2019), 329–63.

41. E.g. World Bank's Fall 2023 Regional Economic Updates, 4 October 2023, https://www.worldbank.org/en/news/press-release/2023/10/04/world-bank-fall-2023-regional-economic-updates, last accessed 28 November 2023.

42. E.g. HMS Spey offering disaster relief in Tonga, 20 January 2022, https://www.royalnavy.mod.uk/news-and-latest-activity/news/2022/january/20/220120-spey-heading-for-tonga-disaster-relief, last accessed 28 November 2023; HMS Medway and RFA Tideforce offering disaster relief in Turks and Caicos Islands, 27 September 2022, https://www.royalnavy.mod.uk/news-and-latest-activity/news/2022/september/27/220927-royal-navy-delivers-disaster-relief-in-the-wake-of-hurricane-fiona, last accessed 28 November 2023.

43. Matthew Heaslip, *Gunboats, Empire, and the China Station: The Royal Navy in 1920s East Asia,* (London: Bloomsbury Academic, 2022), pp.20 and 171.

44. E.g. Brand Finance Global Soft Power Index 2023, 3 March 2023, https://brandirectory.com/softpower/, last accessed 29 November 2023; Higher Education Policy Institute 2023 Soft-Power Index, 22 August 2023, https://www.hepi.ac.uk/, last accessed 29 November 2023.

45. Heaslip, *Gunboats, Empire, and the China Station*, pp.152-158 & 206.

46. Serge Ricard. "The Roosevelt Corollary." *Presidential Studies Quarterly*, 36/1 (2006), 17–26.

47. E.g. James Dobbins et al. *Europe's Role in Nation-Building: From the Balkans to the Congo* (RAND Corporation, 2008), p.38; Gerald Dickens, Unpublished Autobiography, Captain Sir Gerald Dickens Papers, Liddell Hart Centre for Military Archives, London; Admiral Hugh Tweedie, *The Story of a Naval Life* (London: Rich & Cowan, 1939), p.263.

48. Ian Phimister, 'Foreign Devils, Finance and Informal Empire: Britain and China c. 1900-1912', *Modern Asian Studies* 40/3 (2006), 759.

49. Jürgen Osterhammel, 'Imperialism in Transition: British Business and the Chinese Authorities, 1931–37', *China Quarterly* 98 (1984), 267-280; Heaslip, *Gunboats, Empire and the China Station,* pp.101-103.

50. Philip Pugh, *The Cost of Seapower* (London: Conway, 1986), p.67.

51. Heaslip, *Gunboats, Empire and the China Station,* pp.171-173.

52. Christopher McMillan, 'Broken Bond: Skyfall and the British Identity Crisis', *Journal of British Cinema and Television*, 12/ 2, 191-206.

53. John Biggs and Catherine Tang, *Teaching for Quality Learning at University: What the Student Does* (3rd Edition), (McGraw-Hill Education: 2007), pp.21-98.

Seapower Culture

Looking to the Sea – the 'Art of Admiralty', and the Maintenance of Naval Power

Lore and Legend: British Maritime Heritage through the Arts

Culture and the Coast in 21st Century Britain

Looking to the Sea – the 'Art of Admiralty', and the Maintenance of Naval Power

Prof Andrew Lambert FKC

Let me begin with a definition: while the 'Art of the Admiral' concerns the leadership of navies, in war and peace, the 'Art of Admiralty' is the sustained effort to place the maritime dimension at the heart of national economic, strategic and cultural life, to foster the conditions that sustain a seapower state, one that privileges the oceanic and outward facing vision over the terrestrial and domestic. This 'Art' is a national project, and it depends on a dedicated support system at the heart of the state.

Selling seapower identity, and the need for powerful navies, has never been easy. As Sir Julian Corbett observed a century ago 'since men live upon the land', they naturally assume that it is the more important element. However, there have been, and still are, states which deliberately chose to emphasise the sea in all aspects of their policy, exploiting geography, opportunity and offshore energy to be different, and harvest the rewards of an asymmetric approach to politics, economic activity, strategy and international relations.

In Britain such messaging was sustained and delivered for four hundred years by the Admiralty, a great department of State, presided over by a senior Cabinet Minister. The Admiralty was far more than a Government department to direct and administer the Navy. The Admiralty was the national centre that linked the Navy to Government, economics, trade, science, identity and culture. Seapower messaging was created by Admiralty Civil Servants, a dedicated cadre who spent their entire careers inside naval administration, and came to identify with it. They, rather than seagoing personnel, were the guardians of the seapower state. The Admiralty interacted with key stakeholders in Government and the City of London, sustained seapower messaging and co-ordinated all aspects of the state's presence at sea.

The synergy of trade and security prompted Oliver Cromwell's

Navigation Acts, which encouraged English seafarers and English shipping by protecting them from unfair foreign competition. British merchant shipping grew to dominate global trade, and remained the world's largest fleet down to 1945. Today Scandinavian states use their tax and legal systems to promote seafaring enterprise, in return big companies secure influence with Government, leading to improved maritime security – a virtuous circle. In today's unstable world maritime security is a precious commodity, in troubled regions like the Persian Gulf and Red Sea. British flagged ships can call for naval support, and this should give UK registers an advantage. Political decision-makers appear to have forgotten that the Royal Navy is first and foremost a maritime security organisation, the everyday mission, and equally capable of war-fighting. Raising the standards of merchant shipping is an ongoing process, one the ecological turn will hasten. Britain has the chance to take the lead on these issues, and shape a coherent cross-departmental approach to global shipping and security.

A revival of British ship-building, ship-owning and operating is long overdue. It would require a coherent cross-government maritime policy and strategy to link all aspects of sea use and dependency, presence and influence. It is the only option if Britain wishes to remain globally significant. While the future is uncertain, the centrality of sea communications to global economic activity is not. China is trying to dominate global shipping, a prospect that should alarm the rest of the world, because such dominance would be a powerful tool of coercion, at the very least. It could crush the economic basis of the liberal international order, isolate any nations that resisted and redirect global trade without firing a shot.

The 'Art of Admiralty', the sustained development and promotion of a coherent, positive and holistic long-term approach to a nation's engagement with the sea, is a cultural concept that extends far beyond any calculus of warships, trade, diplomacy or seafarers. It has under-pinned the creation and promoted the maintenance of seapower states for millennia.[1] Seapower states, necessarily small, agile polities that depend on the sea for security, prosperity and even basic foodstuffs, combine inclusive political and economic systems under the rule of law, with the promotion of high levels of maritime commercial activity and the necessary naval strength to secure the nation, its extended interests, allies and partners. They emphasise the maritime in national strategy, using sea dependence to shape force levels in all dimensions. The seapower combination of progressive/inclusive political systems and maritime power shaped the western world, and it still frightens the closed political and economic systems of contemporary autocratic empires, which remain vulnerable to internal dissent and maritime economic coercion.

The British 'Art of Admiralty' was neither novel nor unique to Britain. It can be traced back to ancient Athens via medieval Venice and the seventeenth century Dutch Republic, states that relied on the sea to secure and promote their interests, celebrate identity, and define culture. They also relied on fleets for security and deterrence.

Having established a language of global power Britain maintained the peace with other major powers by publicly announcing the assembly of a fleet to meet emerging diplomatic crises. The necessary publicity was handled by the Admiralty, exploiting long standing connections with the full range of contemporary media outlets, conveniently located within half a mile of the Admiralty building. Long before nuclear weapons and the Continuous at Sea Deterrent Britain maintained a Royal Navy that could deter great power rivals, back British diplomacy, support allies, and deliver the necessary messaging.

When Henry VIII made a decisive break with Europe he expanded the standing Royal Navy to provide strategic security, establishing a Department of Government to manage it, the Admiralty. Henry understood the visceral power of great warships, displaying images of his fleet beside his throne to impress rivals. In 1546 his fleet persuaded France that the Channel was 'English'. In 1588 the defeat of the Spanish Armada made naval glory the foundation myth of the English nation, and a critical link between the state and the City of London, which provided many of the ships. Little wonder Shakespeare's English was suffused with sea words, and sea stories. He and his seafaring clientele brought the sea into popular culture, turning ships and voyages into a field of dreams for rising generations. To see the world meant boarding a ship, and taking a risk. This impulse generated a large and rich literature of the sea, so rich that many stories have been transposed into space, another domain where ships traverse great distances.

Other monarchs developed Henry's legacy, notably Charles II and James II, who commanded the Navy in battle. George IV deployed pictures of great naval victories, the Glorious First of June and Trafalgar in the ante-room at St James' Palace, images that emphasised the world changing impact of naval glory.[2] Trafalgar replaced the English victory of 1588 with an inclusive British success, with Nelson as a suitable hero for the new nation.

Trafalgar was celebrated with a universally recognisable classical motif of imperial dominion. Nelson's column, modelled on those of the Augustan Temple of Mars in Rome, proclaimed Nelson's deity, and the creation of a sea empire that would endure. The column and the square, key elements in the 'Art of Admiralty' were shaped by Admiralty officials.

It was fitting that Nelson's mortal remains began their final journey in the Admiralty Building on Whitehall, where the body had rested overnight. He would be buried by the City of London, which had worshipped him in life, under the crossing of St. Paul's Cathedral, at the epicentre of a pantheon of British heroes. The 'Art' was a synergy of fleet, strategy, politics, economics and culture, negotiated with the Nation. The naval defence of floating trade in war and peace secured the City of London's support for the Navy, enabling the state to mobilise the political and economic strength to sustain long term sea control strategies that prevented the emergence of a pan-European empire, and maintained access to overseas markets. Providing naval support for merchant ships in troubled regions has a very long history. Beyond the commercial sector heroic images, notably at the annual Royal Society of Arts exhibition, along with popular prints, ballads, books and newspapers, promoted the cult of naval glory, as a pillar of national identity.

In peace and war the Admiralty sustained the message, raising and lowering the level of implied threat to match the emerging situation. Statesmen who served on the Admiralty Board acquired unrivalled strategic expertise, among them Winston Churchill. That expertise enabled Britain to win three total wars.

At home the seapower state was preferable to absolute monarchs and standing armies, leading to the 'Glorious Revolution' of 1688 that established a partnership of Crown and Parliament. The 'Art' worked because it was developed and sustained by the Admiralty, a great department of State, located on Whitehall. at the centre of political power. The Admiralty engaged widely across British society, supporting the science of the sea, ships and navigation. Charles II founded the Royal Society to advance navigation and shipbuilding. The King understood the cultural value of his Navy, hiring the world's best marine artists to paint English naval glory. The Royal Society shared members with the Admiralty, not least Samuel Pepys, and used naval voyages to promote ocean science, of which Captain Cook's Pacific ventures are only the most familiar. Cook took scientists and Admiralty funded artists on his voyages, to gather information and images. In the 1810 and 1820s both Admiralty Secretaries sat on the Board of the Royal Society, which oversaw research on astronomical and terrestrial magnetic phenomena, improved navigation, tidal phenomena, improved ship-building, and new voyages of discovery.

While the Admiralty provided strategic guidance, managed the Navy's finances, and harnessed science across four hundred years, it also sustained the messaging that promoted the case for a seapower state and a dominant Navy through a dedicated Civil Service, entirely separate from those serving in other departments of state. Admirals and Captains might spend a few years working at the Admiralty, but they relied on Civil Servants to shape and deliver the naval messaging that sustained the fleet's domestic political base. To that end Admiralty officials created modern naval history: Admiralty Secretary Samuel Pepys used naval history to explain current policy. He understood that history had a critical role in capturing and digesting naval experience and explaining why the Navy was essential to national security and prosperity. Pepys also used history to justify his own actions. His long serving successor Josiah Burchett went further. His massive text of 1720, *A Complete History of the Most Remarkable Transactions at Sea*, developed a powerful case for the primacy of naval power in British policy from the history of naval warfare since the ancient world. In a striking introduction Burchett boldly instructed the new German King, George I, on his duties and responsibilities as a British ruler of the seas. George understood: using naval display to block Russian expansion into northern Germany and Scandinavia.

The 'Art' also handled threats to national icons. In 1816 Admiralty Secretary John Wilson Croker bought Lord Nelson's letters to Lady Hamilton, and hid them for forty years, to prevent a hint of scandal from tarnishing the image of the national hero. His colleague Second Secretary John Barrow crafted biographies of other famous Admirals, Anson and Howe, to situate current policy choices, and blamed the 'Mutiny on the *Bounty*' on Captain Bligh's lowly origins. Outside the office Barrow managed naval publishing, both history and exploration, and created what would become the Royal Geographical Society. Both Burchett and Barrow held office for 40 years, emphasising the critical importance of continuity in sustaining the seapower state.

There were other cultural outputs, the Admiralty collected seapower art, constructed imposing classical buildings, buildings that spoke the language of power, in London and in the Royal Dockyards. It created and celebrated the launch of iconic ships of state, (it is believed that 200,000 people attended the launch of HMS *Trafalgar* at Woolwich Dockyard in 1841. The Admiralty also communicated directly with key stakeholders in the private sector, including Lloyds of London, trade associations, shipbuilders and other maritime organisations.

By 1900 the Admiralty had expanded: it managed the global strategy of a world girdling empire, mastered new technology, and improved critical connections. The submarine telegraph cable made the Admiralty a global seapower centre, while the first telephone line into the building linked it with Lloyds of London, recognising the critical partnership that had protected convoys in 1793-1814, and would do so again in 1914-18, and 1939-45. At the same time the Admiralty supported and encouraged the emergence of a new naval history, a partnership between the Navy's need to understand past experience, and an emerging academic discipline.[3] The Admiralty had supported naval history in Pepys' day, by 1900 history had become an integral part of strategic planning, tactical doctrine, international law and policy choices. The Admiralty hired Julian Corbett to teach strategy to mid-career and senior naval officers. Corbett's book *Some Principles of Maritime Strategy*, the definitive analysis of the 'British Way of War', appeared in 1911, having been read and approved by the First Sea Lord. It was the contemporary national strategic doctrine primer. Corbett went on to direct the national Official History of the First World War project, working with the Admiralty Naval Historical Branch.

The vital need to sustain and develop the essential naval messaging across the centuries meant that an enduring Admiralty, rather than any individual, was critical to the maintenance of the seapower state. The abolition of the Admiralty in 1964, and the loss of its' dedicated civil servants, occurred at a time of economic stress, decolonisation and Cold War nuclear anxiety. Scare funds were focussed on securing the Inner German Border. The Ministry of Defence provided the Treasury with an endless supply of hostile briefs against major naval projects, leading to the temporary and misguided abandonment carrier aviation. Without an obvious home within Government seapower messaging faltered, slowly replaced by the British condition of 'sea-blindness'. This dangerous condition emerged because the state, deliberately or carelessly, forgot to repeat the old seapower agenda, or add new stories to engage the rising generation. This failure meant the sea became yesterday's story. The mid-1960s naval messages were dismal, withdrawal from 'East of Suez', increasing irrelevance in a world view circumscribed by the limits of

NATO. Naval deployments outside the original NATO boundaries were marginalised as 'Out Of Area'. Without the Admiralty there was no locus for the seapower case, and no organisation charged with explaining the need for a Navy.

By 1980 it seemed the sea was about to disappear from national culture. Prime Minister Margaret Thatcher closed shipyards, while Defence Secretary John Nott, the Cabinet Minister responsible for the Navy, planned a naval future confined to the North Atlantic. Those of us old enough to remember 1982 may recall just how quickly the old messages were revived, not least by First Sea Lord Admiral Sir Henry Leach. The fact that the Argentine Navy was an 'Armada' exerted a peculiar influence over the media: suddenly naval history was a matter of the fist importance for an anxious nation. The brief Falklands conflict provided a potent demonstration of why these messages were necessary. While some progress has been made tackling 'Sea Blindness' in the absence of an Admiralty is a national issue, far beyond the reach of academics (my own profession has been strikingly uninterested), think tanks and policy fora. All armed services engage in messaging – but the Royal Navy's approach since 1967 has been unnecessarily modest. Despite having the unique advantage, for a Navy, of being the Senior Service, it has become the 'Silent Service'.

Ultimately the 'Art of Admiralty', sustaining a seapower identity in times of peace as well as war, was lost with the Admiralty. The challenge we face is to ensure that the next international crisis does not meet the same unreflective response as the last. Why did the Secretary of State for Defence conclude that Russian aggression on land in 2022 should be addressed by soldiers. There are more than enough NATO troops between the Polish/Ukrainian border and the English Channel to render such that unnecessary. Applying maritime pressure on Russia's exposed coastal flanks would be consistent with the 'British Way of War', the subtle, elegant and effective strategic concept developed for the twentieth century. For close on three hundred years Britain has restrained Russian aggression by applying pressure at and from the sea, combining economic sanctions with support for local actors and, when necessary, sea-based offensives targeting the weakest points, as naval strategist Alfred Thayer Mahan explained in 1900.[4] Russia remains vulnerable to pressure exerted through sea control.

The 'Art of Admiralty' sustained seapower messaging at the heart of British Government through to the 1960s, when the Admiralty was abolished. Since then seapower messaging has been uneven at best, and often dangerously inadequate. No alternative locus for the 'Art of Admiralty' has emerged. While a unified, essentially terrestrial and local approach to defence may be appropriate for most nations, it does not work for those that must necessarily prioritise the ocean.

Looking ahead some form of the 'Art' will be essential to sustain any notion of 'Global Britain', along with key alliances and regional partnerships like NATO and AUKUS. It is not an especially difficult message to frame, but it needs sustained, committed central direction to ensure it reaches the key audience – the British public. We have much to learn from our predecessors.

Recovering the 'Art' would require a renewed emphasis on the maritime dimension across all aspects of Government, the conscious shaping of economic, industrial, strategic and cultural policy to locate it at the heart of our modern identity. History indicates that Seapower states do not 'just happen', they have to be consciously constructed in the minds of national leaders, politicians, intellectuals and artists, to shape and integrate all aspects of state policy. So much of what we take for granted in the contemporary United Kingdom, including the Royal Navy, is a legacy from an older seapower state, created centuries ago. The connection with the ocean needs to be refreshed and revitalised. It is no accident that Trafalgar Square, the centre of London, links naval power with national identity, while the Admiralty Building still stands close by in Whitehall. In three total wars between 1793 and 1945 the Royal Navy saved Britain from invasion and starvation, defeated all rivals, and opened the way for ultimate success. Today we remember inconclusive skirmishes on land and in the air when the existential Battle of the Atlantic, waged across al three dimensions on every single day of the Second World War determined the outcome of that conflict. That so few recall or understand those realities is a standing indictment of our education system, our public discourse, and our limited horizons. At the political level there has been a signal failure of ambition and comprehension, the sea is overlooked in the constant clutter of daily news – until the *Ever Given* blocked the Suez Canal, and threatened to cancel Christmas.

Ultimately recovering the 'Art of Admiralty', recognising our dependence on the sea, **and** going forward the immense economic, strategic and cultural opportunities that flow from being different would transform the nation. Britain did not invent seapower identity, the concept was borrowed from a long line of relatively small, dynamic, agile states that took to the sea to gain an edge in trade and war against larger, more populous rivals. There are examples that suggest how a 21st seapower state might be constructed. This would be a long game, best conducted by strong durable political, economic and strategic structures, blessed with deep institutional memories. There is still hope: many of our friends around the world still see Britain as a profoundly maritime entity. Perhaps the task is not beyond us…

1. Andrew Lambert *Seapower States: Maritime Culture, Continental Empires and the conflict that made the Modern World.* Yale University Press, London 2018

2. These pictures were created by Philippe Jacques de Loutherbourg and J M W Turner, using the artistic language of contemporary 'Apocalyptic Sublime', they emphasise Britain's triumph over Revolutionary and Napoleonic France, rather than any literal truth.

3. Andrew Lambert, *The British Way of War: Sir Julian Corbett and the Battle for a National Strategy.* Yale UP, London 2021 pp 123-243.

4. Alfred T Mahan, *The Problem of Asia.* Sampson Low & Marston, London 1900.

Lore and Legend, British Maritime Heritage through the Arts

S/Lt Joseph Reindler

Lore and Legend – British Maritime Heritage

The American naval historian Alfred Thayer Mahan once wrote glowingly of the Royal Navy that: 'Those weather-beaten, storm-tossed ships, which the grand army never saw, stood between it and dominion of the world.'[1] He was of course writing about the power wielded by absolute control of the sea, which in this case was instrumental in limiting the reach of Napoleon's armies beyond continental Europe. But the statement might also befit the perception of the British public. For all the centuries that Britain has exploited mastery of the seas, it would be easy for the casual observer to be remiss of what actually happens there and what it affords the country, its dominions and allies at home. From the endless toil of the blockading squadrons of Nelson's time plying their way off hostile shores, to the watch and ward of convoy escorts during the great wars, to the protection of sea lines of communication and continuous deterrence still active to this day, our maritime influence extends unseen beyond vast horizons.

Fortunately for the Royal Navy, beyond dispatches and records and demonstrations of purpose and exploit, there exists another link of interest endearing itself toward the public imagination. The wonderful aesthetic of the warship has captivated the minds of many for generations. It is true that ships of state have always been designed not only for warfighting function, but also for their artistic form. After all, what better device to impress and influence the political discourse of other nations, or to deter a foe, than a magnificent ship in fighting trim? The poet Robert N. Rose once wrote that 'Ships are the nearest thing to dreams that hands ever made.'[2] He was probably right. Perhaps most Naval service personnel have thought similarly at some point, and perhaps this has influenced many of us to pursue a career at sea. Visually impressive, and having meanwhile leant themselves as decisive instruments to some of the most desperate, glorious, and crucial points of our history, warships have also attracted the attention of generations of artists. Hence the discipline of maritime art, which has evolved in step with our history at sea to tell its stories. And as histories go, in ours there are many stories to tell.

The Tale of HMS *Lion*

The battlecruiser *Lion* (1912) led a storied life. As Admiral Sir David Beatty's flagship of the First Battlecruiser Squadron of the Grand Fleet during the First World War, she was heavily engaged at both the Battle of Dogger Bank on 24 January 1915, and later at the Battle of Jutland on 31 May 1916. She was so heavily damaged on both occasions that the Imperial German Navy was convinced she would have been sunk. Yet, like some restless ghost, she would always appear again to haunt them in battle. Indeed, *Lion* probably would have been lost at Jutland, had not the actions of Major Francis Harvey VC RM saved the ship. For ordering a 13.5" shell handling room to be flooded to prevent explosion as he lay trapped inside it, dying from his injuries, he was posthumously awarded the Victoria Cross.[3] It is said that at the surrender of the German High Seas Fleet on 21 November 1918, as that vast and formidable naval formation steamed solemnly into the confines of incarceration as a war prize, the German sailors manning the rails stood in stone silence, appalled at the humiliation now inflicted upon their once magnificent fleet. Yet as the grizzly procession steamed passed *Lion*, ship by ship, those forlorn sailors manning the rails all snapped to attention and saluted her; the ship for which they held the unusual reverence of a former foe whose sting they knew only too well.[4]

Such stories are mere threads of the vast tapestry of history upon which three centuries of pride and tradition are inscribed. Our history is important, because as naval officers and service personnel we are charged to uphold the standards of our forbearers, and to act in their stead. Where in death a voice to tell a story is denied to him who would have told it, it is through the arts that great deeds of heroism and sacrifice are celebrated, and great tragedies memorialised. The cultural significance of maritime art also reaches far beyond the naval service. Our ships bear relation to countless thousands whom have connection to them by family members in active service, or through family history; or, by interests which might provide inspiration for seafaring careers yet to be realised, or which otherwise encourage appreciation for maritime affairs, and for the precious and vast domain of the world's oceans and coastlines that encompasses them all. As illustrious as is our history at sea, it also follows that without artists to record its events and bring them to light, they might otherwise be given to obscurity. The cumulative wealth of written record falls short of properly conveying the complete human experience of these events without artists' illustration to augment it. Yet beyond merely augmenting record of events, maritime art has elevated our collective memory of them into physical treasures of national and cultural significance.

The celebrated British maritime artist William Lionel Wyllie RA lived in Portsmouth and practiced throughout the Great War at sea. He knew our stories well. They are echoed in the wealth of his life's work, his paintings of His Majesty's ships, both in the ferocity of battle, and in its aftermath. His '*Bringing in the Wounded Lion*' is spectacular in both its detail and its ambience. Following the Battle of Dogger Bank the heavily damaged battlecruiser *Lion*, the flagship of Admiral Sir David Beatty, is portrayed being eased back into Rosyth for repair. With a heavy list to Port she limps under tow from the battlecruiser *Indomitable*, with myriad other vessels on hand to render assistance and escort. The loss of *Lion* would have had disastrous effect on morale by this stage of the war. This being considered, the time and place for illustrating the cost of war is sometimes not during war itself. The first studies Wyllie made of this scene, painted from life, were in fact censored from wartime publications.[5] By this, if nothing else, the motif commands authenticity through Wyllie's honest statement of what he witnessed. One can only imagine what the conclusion of the events of battle would have inspired in the minds of those who witnessed it. Perhaps the dormancy of contemplation is conveyed in this vignette. The badly damaged flagship, ferocious in battle, is now vulnerable in its aftermath. Her decks still strewn with splinters, wreckage and human remains where enemy shellfire had taken its effect. The Forth rail bridge, the backdrop of the painting, features prominently silhouetted by the glow of dusk. Towering above the ships humbly plying their way it beacons as an emblem of British Industrial might, antithesis to the humility of the foreground scene. The Firth of Forth being a familiar setting to the Royal Navy of the time, the soldiers standing guard on the Forth bridge would often call down to these ships as they passed beneath it. It is told that in the aftermath of Jutland they hailed to the battlecruiser *Tiger* asking: '*where's the Queen Mary?*' to which none had heart left to labour a reply. *Queen Mary* had met with the fate which *Lion* had so narrowly avoided. As

'Bringing in the Wounded *Lion*' the battlecruiser *Lion* under tow into Rosyth, following the Battle of Dogger Bank. Oil painting by WL Wyllie RA.

statements go the painting is indifferent as to glorification of war; yet is defiant and unashamedly proud. *Lion* even mauled, greets the viewer with the fine and handsome lines characteristic of the battlecruiser type. Echoing perhaps elements of Joseph Mallord William Turner's *Fighting Temeraire*, the wounded *Lion* glides calmly under tow beneath a now peaceful sky, bathed in the golden light of it, after the noise and violence of battle has passed. Home again to Rosyth, the Scottish shipwrights who built so many of her ilk will yet put her right to sail again.

By quirk of fate, *Lion* would bear blood relation to one of her arguably more famous successors. When the ship was stricken in 1920, the veteran battlecruiser a victim of the newly imposed Washington Treaty limitations, many of her ship's company would pay off and immediately help form the first compliment for the new battlecruiser *Hood*, which was by then just working up into commission. The story of *Hood* is one already well told and will not be expounded needlessly. The story of the name 'Hood' however, merits some further telling.

HMS *Hood*

VENTIS SECUNDIS, 'with winds favourable', was originally the motto of the 1st Viscount Hood, Admiral Sir Samuel Hood the elder, for whom the battlecruiser *Hood* was named. The ship's crest, depicting a Cornish Chough grasping an ancient pattern sheet anchor, was also that of the 1st Viscount. But the name Hood carried well-earned notoriety in the Royal Navy – and several important historical figures, Admirals all, bore the same name. Admiral Sir Samuel Hood the younger, KB, the 1st Viscount's first cousin once removed, formerly one of Admiral Horatio Nelson's distinguished captains, was another especially brilliant naval officer in his own right. In January of 1794, whilst in command of the 32-gun 5th rate frigate *Juno*, then Captain Hood, attempted to put into the inner roads of Toulon which he assumed was still a friendly port controlled by French Royalists. Having had no way of receiving news of the matter, he was unaware that the British had left and that the White French had fallen to the Jacobines. The French promptly opened fire. At this critical juncture *Juno* struck rudely upon a shoal, abruptly losing all way, and presenting herself an easy prize. The French, so sure of the outcome reasonably expected of the situation, sent a prize crew aboard to assert custody of the British frigate as a war prize. Captain Hood, meanwhile, nonchalantly braced his mizzen boom hard to weather, backing that sail so that he could sail backwards off the shoal – sounding just enough tide to clear it – and slipped the inner roads of Toulon, under the guns of the fort, while returning its fire, with the French prize crew themselves taken as prisoners![6]

But the fame of the Hoods was not limited to those Admirals of Nelson's Navy. Rear Admiral Horace Alexander Lambert Hood KCB DSO MVO, a descendant of the 1st Viscount, served in the Royal Navy a century later during the Great War. As officer commanding the Third Battlecruiser Squadron at Jutland, his exploits are befitting of the highest traditions of the Royal Navy. Amid the confusion and calamity of that major fleet action, his squadron arrived to save Admiral Sir David Beatty's battle-weary First Battlecruiser Squadron from what might have been its end, during the closing moments of what became known as The Run to the North. Cheers rang out aboard Admiral Beatty's battlecruisers as Admiral Hood's ships appeared out of the murk; a welcome sight of relief for which they were in desperate want. Admiral Hood had brought his ships into the action despite navigation being as woefully hindered as it was by gathering dusk, thick coal smoke and deteriorating visibility. By incidents illustrating the fragility of early wireless signals communication, Admiral Sir Hugh Evan-Thomas' Fifth Battle Squadron had failed to receive its order to engage – thereby otherwise leaving the First Battlecruiser Squadron to the open jaws of the German High Seas Fleet. The battlecruisers *Indefatigable* and *Queen Mary* had already been blown up with near absolute loss of life; and *Lion* had also very nearly been lost, as already told. Admiral Sir Henry Pelly KCVO CB, then Captain of the battlecruiser *Tiger*, would later lament that he had played a round of golf

'The Final Sacrifice' His Majesty's British Battlecruiser *Hood*, engaged off Iceland at the Battle of Denmark Strait. Oil painting by S/Lt Joseph Reindler RN.

with Captain Cecil Irby Prowse RN of *Queen Mary*, just 24 hours prior to watching the ship be torn to pieces and sunk.[7] But Admiral Hood had in his charge some of the finest gunnery platforms in the Grand Fleet; something for which he himself had taken personal responsibility by rigorously enforcing high standards of gunnery training. This was an exception rather than the rule; the relentless burden of tasking for the Royal Navy being what it was at that time. The weight of his ships' fire was immediately felt. The Imperial German Cruiser *Weisbaden* and battlecruiser *Lützow* were engaged and reduced to sinking condition within minutes, the latter having been struck as many as eight times by 12-inch shells from Admiral Hood's flagship *Invincible*. It was sadly, however, by these same actions that Admiral Hood was killed when *Invincible* was lost. Visibility had suddenly shifted rendering *Invincible* silhouetted against the setting sun – whereby she came under fire from two German Battlecruisers and was destroyed, the conflagration being the result of another magazine explosion. The great naval arms race of the turn of the last century had progressed with such voracity that many ships, *Invincible* included, were by now terribly under-protected in a major fleet action. The widowed Lady Hood would later christen the new battlecruiser *Hood*, pennant number 51. By these same events the ship's bell, a family heirloom, was also presented to the ship. Now resting with the National Maritime Museum of the Royal Navy in Portsmouth, it was salvaged from the wreck in 2016 having still been carried aboard at her loss, the subject of the painting illustrated on the facing page, which is my own.

Here, His Majesty's battlecruiser *Hood*, Captain Ralph Kerr CBE RN, the Flagship of Vice-Admiral Lancelot Ernest Holland CB, together with His Majesty's battleship *Prince of Wales*, Captain John Catterall Leach DSO MVO RN, are seen heavily engaged at the Battle of the Denmark Strait off Iceland, on Empire Day 24 May 1941. *Hood* is depicted at the instant she received a straddle of 38cm shellfire resulting from the German battleship *Bismarck*'s fifth salvo – with the signal "Two-Blue" for "Turn Together Two Points To Port" still streaming and the slightest inclination of a roll to Starboard, indicating that she is just initiating her final turn. In the seconds that would follow, a series of catastrophic events unfolded whereby a magazine explosion engulfed the ship. *Hood* would be lost, with a toll of 1,415 lives. *Prince of Wales* would continue alone in the fight, inflicting serious damage to the enemy, but in doing so receiving serious damage herself. A further 13 lives would be lost in *Prince of Wales* during the action – with one more dying of his wounds the following day.

These stories are told and retold again through the imaginations of generations of artists, and always by different individualistic means. The time of completion of this painting marked the 80th anniversary of the event, and the combined loss of 1,429 lives from both ships. The disaster of *Hood*'s loss represented the worst loss of life from a single ship ever suffered by the Royal Navy. Referencing Cecil Spring-Rice's poem 'I Vow to Thee My Country', the glow of the boatdeck fire on *Hood* reflects a holy cross in her maintopmast and yard, giving title to the painting *"The Final Sacrifice"*. The foreshadowing red glow of the fire and its long reflection, echoing J.M.W. Turner's "Peace – Burial at Sea", lead the eye toward deliberate symbolism. Three additional aspects of the environment illustrated help to tell the story and convey meaning from within the work. Firstly, is the statement of the restless deep, the cold black darkness by which the ship will be consumed; the foreground heavily shaded, reminding the viewer that the sea will never give up its dead. Striking opposite balance to this is the hope of salvation suggested in the backlit warmth of the murky sky; the harmony chosen being romantic, which in this case was deliberately warmer than real. Lastly, between the relentless pull of both, is the terrible violence by which the ship is now overwhelmed.

In fine art, realism must temper romance. Such is the balance I tried to strike within this painting. The probable smoke from what would have been the only salvo from *Hood's* Y-turret curls over and obscures the air-warning aerials further aloft at the maintopgallant mast, as two last rounds of 15-inch armour-piercing ammunition are flung down range toward the enemy. This last detail is merely suggested to the viewer. There is obviously variance across eye-witness accounts concerning whether either of *Hood's* X or Y turrets' firing arcs managed to lay on the enemy and engage at all before the ship was lost. Some accounts suggest that an aft turret did engage; while others are suggestive of either a misfire, or nothing having been fired at all. The artist is always at pains to only illustrate what is certain, and never to contradict an individual first-hand account. With both ships between salvoes the rest of the British heavy-calibre guns were at this moment silent, before the deafening and horrible drone of incoming enemy shellfire. *Hood's* displacement hull-form heaps tens of thousands of tonnes of seawater into mounds of foaming wake as 144,000shp are transmitted into the cold depths of the North Atlantic Ocean. Admiral Holland had limited the speed of his formation to 29 knots, which was the best speed at which the new battleship *Prince of Wales* could keep up. *Hood's* turbines scream as the ship's stokers coax nearly every available knot from the complex and delicate machinery from deep within the ship. A pressure safety fitted to one of the ship's 24 Yarrow Small Tube Boilers blows and a long jet of steam curls into the sky – a further indication that her machinery is being pushed hard. Herewith, a specific device in classical painting has been employed to help illustrate her speed; whereby placing an object in motion between two stationary objects, in this case the plumes of water heaved upward by exploding shells, aids in drawing the eye to that fact. Four shell splashes are erupting – with that furthest astern having been the result of a likely dud. The enemy was ripple firing his eight main guns; thereby more ordinance is still on the way. The likelihood of observing fall of shot over to *Hood's* Port side was approached with caution; the ship obviously having been engaged and hit on her Starboard side – and the trajectory of enemy fire being relatively flat given the range. It was reckoned that the ship's own speed, coupled with her observably low freeboard, as well as the time it would normally take for the plume to grow, might have permitted a window by which a shell has fallen to Port without hitting the ship, or at least has clipped and skipped off the ship before exploding in the sea causing the observed effect. It was difficult to reconcile obscuring any part of *Hood's* elegant lines from the viewer; but individual vantage points are seldom afforded everything in plain sight. Thereby this was also reckoned to add some realism to the scene.

That tired old maxim of pictures' worth in words aside, there is much more detail to explain. The sea state and conditions on the day were cold and bleak, yet fairly calm. The engagement was actually fought at 2:00AM – with ships' clocks being set four hours fast. This being said, night hours are few and the midnight sun lights the sky in these extreme Northern latitudes during the month of May. The orb of the sun traverses a low arc across the horizon, offering an endless early dawn light that never waxes fully to the broadness of day. The keenly eyed viewer might also note the black or dark grey antifouling paint in the trough trailing *Hood*'s bow wave. An obscure reference to dockyard paint manifests was produced in recent years, contradicting what was commonly held belief that all HM capital ships' bottoms were painted red. In fact, many were painted black or dark slate grey, from the First World War and the interwar years right up until wartime paint supplies ran low during the Second World War and cheaper more plentiful red oxide became widely used. The British artist and Army veteran, John Hamilton MC, certainly seemed to know this all along, probably having recourse to information relayed to him by those who knew, whom are long since now lost. In his well-known painting of *Prince of Wales* steering desperately out of line to get clear of the wreckage of *Hood*, which was published in his self-illustrated 'War At Sea' volume, he has very clearly painted her undersides black. How easily information is lost to common memory if not for the arts to lend to its preservation.

The Role of Maritime Art

With our history vastly rich as it is with pictures to imagine, we shall return to its relationship to the artist. Foremost in its earliest conception, maritime art was a means by which information about a maritime subject or event might be recorded; the intended audience being invested parties, shipwrights, owners, naval officers and admiralties. Indeed, maritime artists were at times embarked aboard warships and commissioned as war artists to record major events and battles in real time. Willem Van Der Velde the Elder provides the classical example, being present at the Battle of Schooneveld in 1673, and at five preceding actions under King's commission with the Royal Dutch Navy prior to his emigration to England. Two centuries later William Lionel Wyllie RA would become a frequent sight, sitting with his easel on the Admirals' stern walks of His Majesty's Ships, or with brush in hand working quietly amidst a busy

'The Old Atlantic Fleet In Line Ahead' – Sketched from the stern walk of HMS *King Edward VII*. Watercolour by WL Wyllie RA.

Royal dockyard. Montague Dawson would also be present to record the Surrender of the German High Seas Fleet in 1918. Rowland Langmaid, then serving as a Lieutenant Commander, would join Admiral Cunningham's staff as Admiralty Official War Artist, recording the work of the Royal Navy's Mediterranean Fleet while at its busiest during the naval war of that theatre.

The origins of fine art obviously being long before the advent of the camera. It followed that maritime paintings of the earliest genre would show us information about their subjects rather than deliberately provoke emotional response or convey ideology by design. Gradually, however, representational painting digressed from catalogue of what information was known about a subject to what would actually be seen of it, and by extension of this, what the observer might feel if witnessing the event. To this end, a far greater attention would be paid toward the elements comprising the marine environment, to inflection and to mood. There might be some debate as to when this first pronounced itself within the genre. Perhaps it was in the more spirited expressions to have been made by the Dutch painters of the golden era of the seventeenth century, or perhaps it would transpire more fully with Turner and his contemporaries of the romantic movement. Perhaps works of the post-impressionism movement and what came afterward are the most relatable to modern eyes; with the events of history contemporary to it standing fresher to living memory. The style and devices employed by the post-impressionists also lending themselves more keenly to the way we have learned to see things.

Either way, fine art represents an artefact of our earlier culture which has remained relevant and useful to us despite having changed only by nuances with the tidings of the centuries. Techniques and materials have largely not changed, with the only differences measured with progression of manufacturing technology, which has very slowly improved the tools to which the artist has recourse. Yet these advances have not altered how paintings are made; rather only prolonged lightfastness and improved conservation quality. Few or none other products of human creation benefit, as fine art does, from its physical value increasing with age. Cinema, by comparison, has historically been outpaced by the development of its own techniques and production special effects over the decades; although it is another matter for subjective debate as to whether its artistic merit has actually improved. Eclectic interest groups aside, a cinema piece produced with the most advanced techniques available in the 1950's might be unwatchable to an audience of today. Maritime art, meanwhile, has scarcely had to change. The language of it is as readable today as it was then.

Maritime artists have quite usefully been alive and practising their trade for long enough to witness and record centuries' worth of important history, capturing as they did, visual information which is at times seldom ever detailed in written texts. Of course, as reference materials are concerned, some might question the candour of artwork made by artists during wartime years, where romanticism and in fact nationalism might have pervaded or even obfuscated fact. It is an easy argument to make, however, that having some visual record of history is a richer thing than having none. The German maritime artist Claus Bergen lived and practiced during both World Wars. Being appointed by the Kaiser as official war artist for Germany's naval war, he also held the very unusual distinction of going to sea in the U-Boat U-53 on active war patrol to observe and record. He was later employed as a propaganda artist for the Third Reich. Despite this, his illustration of the German side of both conflicts, and especially of the First World War at sea, stand as an invaluable and culturally significant contribution to the record we have of these events, for which photographic record was at times scarce or none. Through his works, unapologetic statements of grim reality are often more palpable than undertones of nationalism. To this end, his representations both of Jutland and of Germany's submarine war in the Atlantic are particularly deserving of mention. His works have since found their way into official state collections on both sides of the Atlantic. Notably, his '*U-Boat On A Mission*', a 180 x 320cm oil painting hung in the Flag Officers' mess at COMSUBLANT, the United States Navy's Commander Submarines Atlantic Fleet in Norfolk Virginia, until its repatriation to Germany in 1978.[8]

The Challenge of Representational Maritime Art

The reader with even casual experience of the creation of fine art will understand the vast difficulty of producing the stuff, let alone asserting mastery of it. The maritime genre is furthermore complicated by the environment it represents. Of all the myriad challenges posed by natural subject matter to representational painters, those posed by painting realistic water are perhaps the most severe. Water behaves very specially, and painterly representation of it completely separates the maritime genre from the myriad other disciplines in fine art. For centuries, classical painting has evolved around practices of compositional design and paint-handling which are completely at odds with what is normally required to execute works in the maritime genre. Tightness and accuracy of drawing and painterly freeness are perpetually at odds. A painting executed freely is usually correspondingly loose in drawing; and conversely, a painting emphasising tightness of drawing and detail is normally too pains-takingly composed for the brush to have moved freely. Critically however, the maritime subject matter requires both intricacy of drawing and painterly freeness; and beyond trading in compromise, an effective piece of maritime art will pull these elements, normally at odds, together into an unlikely sort of harmony. It is a very difficult balance for the artist to strike. The distraction of detail at expense of mood or feeling within a painting is always cause for caution. A living master once warned me: "focus less on the detail and more on the feeling of what you are painting." He went on: "Suggest detail more softly, and do this only once the mood of your work is compelling."

With fine art also having evolved as a method of recording information, many of its accepted techniques are tailored toward either copying from a subject or transposing information from studies, themselves executed from life, into the fully worked piece. This is something scarcely afforded to the maritime artist. Seascapes fold and writhe endlessly; and the events of actions and incidents evolve too quickly to be recorded into fully-finished paintings executed in real time. The treatment of water in maritime painting also demands particular techniques which are contrary to, or even ill regarded, in classical painting. This owes largely to classical and *Alla Prima* painting strongly discouraging overworking of paint.[9] The commonly held belief is that a lesser extent of work evident to accomplish a finishing stroke is the hallmark of better paint-handling and control, and understanding of the subject, compared with over-finishing or piling up overpaint. A painting overworked is the equivalent of a story told in stilted or contrived language. The complexity of how fluids move, however, usually results in considerable work and overpainting to capture the natural detail of a seascape. This is the case even when only softer forms of realism are sought.

To digress gently, it is also important to mention the importance of softer representation of realism. Underworking the finishing strokes of a painting, and stopping well short of hard realism, is generally considered to better engage the imagination of the viewer, and to involve the viewer more in the determination of intelligent emotional response to the piece. Its freeness also better assumes the complex and constantly changing forms of the natural elements, suggesting perhaps the natural propagation and flow of the scene rather than seizing sharply upon a sudden excerpt of it. The opposite applies with photography as a visual medium, which albeit very useful and now abundantly available, leaves very little to the inference of the viewer. To suggest a representation of nature more softly than photo realism is to induce the imagination of the viewer to more vivid conclusion. It is a normal state of the human condition for us to wonder at what we look at. By this, elements of human experience are projected and resonate with the viewer. It is through such devices that maritime painting still retains its relevance in a world now dominated by photography and film as visual mediums.

Having expressed the difficulty of emulating the detail and mood of the marine environment in painting, ships meanwhile are very intricate subjects unto themselves. Hullforms' lines are nuanced. Naval architecture is complex. Ships can be vastly large. Shipboard equipment and machinery and its uses are furthermore complex. The same is to be said for sail, which is even further complicated by the technology of it having evolved significantly across the centuries. A ship might appear subtly different on some evolution of seamanship from how she appears upon the next. Ships' appearances also change subtly – or sometimes completely – within a given context. Refits and reconstruction, or changes in paint schemes, especially where wartime camouflage is considered, can be very easily misunderstood. And then there is the vastness of information either lost to time, or to which substantial research is still constantly at work and changing what is known.

The illustration of historical subject matter being so important and sought after, artists meanwhile do not copy, except from life. When the vantage point of witness to a subject is not possible, which is usually the case with maritime scenes, the artist invents his composition from what is known. A comprehensive understanding of history is required, as is criticality of what may have been embellished in record. Inference is obviously paramount, because even eloquent anecdotal evidence of an event will mostly not furnish the wealth of detail in a painting. By this a painter must determine both *what to paint*, and also *how to paint it*. Recreating a scene in painterly form, threading the very fine lines of almost compromise between freeness and detail, all the while being carefully considerate of the wealth of information being conveyed, and being further humble to not state too nakedly what is either not known or is too contentious or too easily contradictable to state, is not easy work. Artistic license and historical fact all too frequently act in opposition. So the imagination of the artist must be carefully tempered. To this end the working of accuracy into the flow of a maritime artwork demands very particular skill. By this, we demonstrate the rarity of the finest maritime art and, by as much, its physical value.

The Cultural and Physical Value of Maritime Art

In *The Doors of Perception*, Aldous Huxley wrote that: 'I personally should like to renounce speech altogether and, like organic Nature, communicate everything I have to say in sketches.'[10] The irony of the statement and its maker is not lost. Huxley was a brilliant writer. Yet in his humility he is able to reconcile that the capacity of information conveyed by languages and systems of arbitrary symbols is less than what can be expressed in pictures accurately emulating nature. Organic nature being the highest reservoir of information; thereby the interaction of the physical with the intelligence perceiving it is theoretically the richest possible mode of communication. Huxley would go on to muse his lament at the volume of non-representational artwork then being produced. It is not the place of this author to evaluate that topic;

however, on the apparent economy of effort within non-representational painting techniques, we are in agreement. But as for economy, at the time of its invention many had wondered whether the photographic camera might have made representational painting obsolete. Brushing aside the necessary skill and practice of the painter, anybody with a lens would now be afforded the ability to record accurate images of reality with relative ease.

Yet the camera, being a simple recording device, is confined to see only where a photographer can take it. It cannot travel backwards in time, nor take vantage in events which would have been too dangerous for the photographer to attend. A painter's imagination, meanwhile, can overcome these restrictions. To do so however, the painter must not only have ideas vivid enough to compel an audience, but also the skills to transpose them effectively. The latter can only be obtained very painstakingly through practice. To borrow an anecdote, the British maritime painter Roy Cross RSMA was once asked how long it took him to complete a picture; to which he bluntly answered 'about forty years.'[11] The human lifetime being finite, the experience to be afforded to pursuit of any skill is limited. The distractions of life and simple necessity also take a habit of displacing creative pursuits. This is to be lamented. Although there exists an economy for the sale and exchange of fine art, it is a very difficult place to forge a career. A great many skilled represent-ational painters never stand a chance of success. Part of the reason for this is the decoupling of skill and reputation. As artists develop and improve, their works do not necessarily always become better known or more sought after. Inject elements of luck, or lack thereof, and the relative fortunes of painters become widely disparate. To this end, the investment value to be realised of underpriced artwork has fuelled speculation in its market. The late Anglo-American master maritime artist John Stobart would start out selling his paintings for mere hundreds, and ultimately make sales for millions.[12] Although he was an exceptional painter, his fortune was probably the exception and not the rule. But that an economy exists for the trade of fine art is something to be celebrated. Few paintings would ever have been made without patrons to pay the artists who made them. The irony of learning any fine art discipline and trying to build a career from it however, is that one must be prolific to succeed, and one must meanwhile be successful to be prolific. Failure may reward the individual with personal development and learning, but seldom with financial gain. This contributes to the rarity of maritime art. Of all the disciplines of classical painting it is perhaps the most difficult to learn. When we admire the fruition of it, through the works of Wyllie or Wilkinson, or Dawson etc, we enjoy contributions to our culture made in spite of innumerable factors not encouraging, rather acting against them ever being made.

Maritime Artists in the Royal Navy

Some historians would argue the reason why we won wars at sea against the French was that they sent artists to war and not the fighting sailors we did. To steal another old vernacular, it is after all better to be a warrior in a garden than a gardener (or an artist!) in a war. But the intellectual is a very useful seafarer and the combination of the creative imagination and the analytical mind is a powerful one. The fate of nations and the outcomes of future wars will very likely pivot upon incorporation of new thinking. Meanwhile the ability to understand physical nature and engineering and simultaneously the individual is especially useful in the naval context, where ships and personnel are so mutually dependent and so indispensable. Despite appearances, in the military context there is always something to be said for the softer side of human endeavour. Nelson, by example, would never have invested his confidence in his captains, and afforded them the freedom to dispense what tactical autonomy they did, had he lacked the empathy to understand and know the capabilities of his team.

It also follows that despite apparently vast differences between the professions of seamanship and artistry, there is actually some overlap. Attention to detail, knowledge and understanding of the maritime environment, and of naval architecture and engineering, are all heavily pervasive in the genre, as is the empathy to understand how an audience thinks. The latter being critical to a painter's understanding of a target market. Both the constructions of perspectives within pictures and certain evolutions of seamanship and navigation are also given to mathematical reasoning. Although not all naval officers or sailors need to be artists, pictures of ships meanwhile would be of little value if the artists executing them never understood how ships were used or why, and how they would have looked during specific evolutions of seamanship or the context of why they were doing them. It is not a common mix of professions, but naval officers and sailors have become known maritime artists. The number however is admittedly few.

Thomas Buttersworth was both a maritime artist and a British sailor of the Napoleonic wars. He went on to capture a brilliant and important historical record of the events which he witnessed, or to which he had the

'The Captured American frigate *President*, lying at Bermuda' – oil painting by Thomas Buttersworth. NMM Collection.

benefit of first-hand accounts. In some cases, details far too obscure to have survived in written account are presented to us in his paintings. Buttersworth's *The Captured American frigate President, lying at Bermuda* is characteristic of his talent and is laced with a wealth of obscure information. As depicted by the facing plate Commodore Stephen Decatur's broad pennant still flies on the captured *President*, displaced by the British blue pennant streaming further aloft. As a point of curiosity the white broad pennant is marked with the text *"President"*. It was common practice for mottos or phrases to adorn the pennants and hoists of American warships of the time. The classical examples being Captain James Lawrence's *'Free Trade and Sailors' Rights'* in the frigate *Chesapeake*;[13] and after him, Admiral Oliver Hazard Perry's *'Don't Give Up The Ship'* at Lake Erie. But as not all of these flags were preserved or even recorded, especially those captured; so record of them by any means is invaluable. The British frigate at centre right is the *Endymion*, visibly missing her foretopmast, which was lost in the preceding action. Sailors' eyes have particular keenness for detail, especially with respect to understanding the workings of sailing men of war. This is especially so with Thomas Buttersworth, and warrants particular credibility in his works.

Admiral Richard Brydges Beechey might have been the most senior figure in the Royal Navy to have held both King's commission and the distinction of known maritime artist. Serving into the middle of the 19th century, his paintings are highly illustrative of evolutions of seamanship in our old sailing navy, carrying valuable qualification. Montague Dawson also served in the Royal Navy during the First World War. Later becoming perhaps the most celebrated maritime painter of the last century. At the height of his career he was the second most highly paid living master of any genre of fine art in the world; only Picasso out earned him. In fact, Montague Dawson along with Norman Wilkinson, another of his artistic contemporaries, had worked together on the design of dazzle camouflage schemes for the Admiralty during the war.[14] As such, his paintings of His Majesty's ships in 'warpaint' are likely trustworthy as historic record. Oscar Parkes OBE held multiple qualifications; a naval officer surgeon, historian and writer, and a distinguished maritime artist. He served in the Royal Navy during the First World War, being commissioned until 1919 and was also editor of Janes Fighting Ships.

Rowland Langmaid, also aforementioned, served as an officer in the Royal Navy during the Second World War. Then holding the rank of Lieutenant Commander and attached to Admiral Andrew Cunningham's staff as Admiralty official war artist to cover the Mediterranean theatre of the war. Many of his works were signed with the rank he wore at that time. These were published via Admiralty official wartime publications and various other titles, namely *The King's Ships, Through the Ages*', '*East of Malta West of Suez – the Admiralty Official Account of the War in the Mediterranean*', and later '*The Mediterranean Fleet – From Greece to Tripoli*'. Derek Gardiner RSMA, another Second World War veteran and officer in the Royal Navy, was deaf in one ear after injury resulting from damage to the destroyer *Broke*, in which he served and survived the sinking. He garnered an impressive following during a career which spanned many decades after the war until his passing. His pace of work, it seemed, could never quite keep pace with strong demand for his paintings.

The list of contemporary practising maritime artists who have served or are serving in the Royal Navy is short. Captain (Ret'd) Richard Cosby LVO RN formerly commanded the destroyers *Cardiff* and *Manchester*.

Across the Atlantic, Victor Mays served in the United States Navy as an intelligence officer, painting throughout the rest of his life. His final exhibition at the Annual International show at Mystic Seaport in Connecticut would also be my first. To this end, I am probably also obliged to write as author to this chapter that I am myself both a maritime artist and a serving Royal Naval officer. The former pursuit stemmed from the latter at its periphery; having always seen works of maritime art during a boyhood spent fascinated with ships and the sea, and ultimately with a naval career. The final part of this chapter shall introduce one more of my works, befitting in its subject the British public interest in events at sea.

The Battle of North Cape

We are a maritime nation. A poignant reminder of this fact sits proudly alongside on the Thames to this day in the form of the former Second World War cruiser *Belfast*. 26 December 2023 marked the 80th anniversary of the Battle of North Cape, at which *Belfast* was present. That engagement is the subject of the final painting of this chapter.

As told from the German side, the engagement took place against impossible odds amid driving snow and a howling Force-8 gale in the frozen polar dark, some 60 nautical miles North of the Northern most tip of Norway. Here the German battleship *Scharnhorst*, flagship of Vize-Admiral Erich Bey, is seen engaged on both broadsides; fighting Admiral Sir Bruce Austin Fraser GCB KBE's flagship battleship *Duke of York* to starboard less than 12,000 yards distant (hence the relatively flat elevation of the German guns), as medium and small calibre shells from British cruisers and British and Norwegian destroyers are still arriving from the obscured murk off her Port Quarter, to Northward. A medium calibre shell skips off *Scharnhorst's* sloping turret armour and fragments into a hail of shattered metal as the tortured seascape writhes in both heaving Arctic swell, as well as sprays of splinters from all manner of naval ordinance being flung at the German ship.

The first salvoes of radar-laid fourteen-inch shellfire from the British King George V-class battleship told with immediate effect – punching deep into the ship and knocking the forward triple 28cm super-firing turrets, 'Anton' and 'Bruno', out of action. Turret 'Bruno' was later brought to bear, albeit at a lesser rate of fire – however by this stage of the action fire and smoke, as well as emergency flooding carried out in the forward magazines for these turrets, had precluded their use. As par the course for night actions, British and German accounts differ significantly

'The German Battleship *Scharnhorst* Engaged At The Battle Of North Cape' Boxing Day, 26 December 1943. Oil painting by S/Lt Joseph Reindler RN.

in detail; interpolating these however it seems that whilst turret 'Anton' had seized amidships in travel position, barrel elevation was still possible as hydraulic power was presumably still supplied. turret 'Bruno' would likely have been trained to Starboard shortly after the first British heavy-calibre shells arrived but is seen here silent. German accounts of this action paint a harrowing tale of hope slowly eroded as it became more obvious with every wound inflicted that they would not be going home. For lack of flashless propellent charges, the incandescent heat of turret 'Caesar' answers defiantly into the night, cheering the hopes of the German crew; but firing furiously throughout the running fight it ultimately fell silent, having expended its last shell. It was with admirable industry that as the action wore on, the forward magazine was again pumped out so that ammunition could be carried aft to turret 'Caesar' when both forward turrets eventually became unusable. Basked in the light of starshell, the flashes of gunfire, and the glow of fires burning across the ship are observed dancing flurries of snow.

The ship was constantly lit from stem to stern by British starshell, with what Dr Fritz-Otto Busch would later write to describe as 'pitiless clarity' in *The Drama of the Scharnhorst,*[15] his famous work which was since translated and republished for the English-speaking world. The contrast of light, warm and cold, echoes the themes of war and peace, and the ebb of defiance into atonement. The elements would claim many lives that night – with only 36 of 1,968 souls being picked out of the water. None of the officers of the ship's company would survive the sinking. Admiral Sir Bruce Fraser GCB KBE would later debrief his officers following this action, advising them that if ever they found themselves facing a fight of such impossible odds – that he expected them to conduct their ships exactly as per the example set by the crew of *Scharnhorst*. The gallantry of the German officers and men cannot be overstated, notwithstanding sides of history. Although the German Ensign has been unapologetically hidden in this composition, the placement of the Vize-Admiral's flag at the fore, rather than the main, where it could feature more prominently, is a deliberate nod to him.

That we are a maritime nation is etched into our culture by the invaluable wealth that is the accomplishment of generations of maritime artists across the centuries. As we live further into the 21st century and the memory of our past grows ever more distant, the contribution of artists will remain a steadfast illustration of who and what we are. It will remind us of our seafaring roots and inspire by examples what our nation and our forebearers accomplished before us, especially during some of the greatest struggles yet written into human history. This could not be more relevant as we stray further into the uncharted territory of an increasingly interconnected and ever more volatile world. It seems a sober inevitability that more wars will yet be fought at sea. More history will yet be recorded. The final point to note, as to the continued purpose and relevance of maritime art into the 21st century, is its utility as a device for reconciliation between nation states, previously at war and now at peace. For example the last painting of *Scharnhorst* is heavily based on Dr. Fritz-Otto Busch's written work, a former German naval officer and veteran of both world wars. Contemporary Japanese maritime artist Hiroyuki Sugano is renowned not only for his drawings of the Imperial Japanese Navy of the Second World War, but also for his works depicting our ships, and those of our allies. British artist Kenneth Grant made himself known for his depictions of American frigates during the War of 1812, notably during single-ship actions against Royal Navy ships, which were not always decided in our favour. Claus Bergen travelled to Great Britain during the interwar years, also painting our ships and coastlines whilst our respective nations were struggling to foster peace. By as much we demonstrate that as nations cooperate in shared prosperity, maritime artists bring our common connection to the sea as nations into light. The common connections we find with our allies and partner nations will be vitally important given the challenges we have yet to face this century. Finally, through the arts we tell each other's stories and mourn the tragedies of a shared past. In this, perhaps, is a device for peace.

[1] Alfred Thayer Mahan (2016). "*The Influence of Sea Power upon the French Revolution and Empire 1793-1812* (Complete)". p.427, Library of Alexandria.

[2] Robert N Rose (Year Unknown). *"Clipper Ships"*, Poem.

[3] W.D. Kirkpatrick, C. Owen, WL Wyllie RA (1919). *"More Sea Fights of the Great War"*, p.116, Cassell, London

[4] Victor Hayward (1977). *"HMS Tiger at Bay, A Sailor's Memoir 1914-18"*, p.173, William Kimber, London.

[5] www.MaritimeOriginals.com

[6] Roger Knight (2007). *"The Pursuit of Victory – the Life and Achievement of Horatio Nelson"*, p.165. Allen Lane, Penguin.

[7] Henry Pelly, Admiral Sir (1938). *"300,000 Sea Miles – An Autobiography"*, p.166. Chatto & Windus, London.

[8] Jorg_M. Hormann, Eberhard Kliem, (2002). *"Claus Bergen Uber Vier Epochen"*, p.127. Koehlers Verlagsgesellschaft mbH, Hamburg.

[9] Richard Schmid (1998). *"Alla Prima – Everything I know about Painting"*, p.183. Stove Praire Press LLC, Vermont: "Many collectors prefer "photographic" highly detailed art, particularly wildlife art fans and others who collect for authentic renditions of specific subject matter. "Western" paintings in particular are popular (cowboys, Indians, the U.S. Cavalry), also aviation, military and war stuff, automobiles, old sailing ships, etc. This demand tends to encourage the use of photos because the market, however naïve, is very lucrative. However, it has nothing whatsoever to do with Art.

[10] Aldous Huxley (1954). *"The Doors of Perception"*, p.73. HarperCollins, New York.

[11] Roy Cross, Derek Gardener, John Groves, Geoff Hunt, Mark Myers (2005). *"Clippers, Packets and Men O' War – The Tall Ship in Art"*, p.11. Non Basic Stock line.

[12] John Russel Jinishian Gallery, Fairfield CT, USA, www.jrusselljinishiangallery.com

[13] C.J.H. Snyder (1923). *"The Glorious Shannon's Faded Blue Duster – and Other Faded Flags of Fadeless Fame"*, p.4. McClelland & Stewart, Toronto.

[14] Ron Ranson (1993). *"The Maritime Paintings of Montague Dawson"*, pp.7, 11. David & Charles, London.

[15] Fritz Otto Busch (1956). *"The Drama of the Scharnhorst"*, p.136. Robert Hale, London.

Culture and the Coast of 21st Century Britain: A Review of Maritime Heritage in Action

Daisy K E Turnbull

Introduction

It is often said that in the UK you are never more than 70 miles from the sea.[1] However, this proximity to the coast does not guarantee the predominance of *maritimity* in national culture.[2] In recent years there has been a notable concern raised, within academia, business, military and governmental circles, over a decline in national awareness of maritime space's importance to 21st century Britain.[3] Despite this apparently waning familiarity, as an island nation we remain dependant on the sea, faced with new pressures on our use, control and understanding of the marine. Observing this, elements within the cultural sector are generating sustainable, holistic, and positive promotion of engagement with the sea to effectively improve national 'ocean literacy' and refute a 'sea blindness' within society. This chapter argues for further integration between functions of industry and government with cultural heritage modes as a way of 'sustaining a seapower identity', providing a 'long-term approach to the nations engagement with the sea' in the 21st century.[4]

Case studies within this chapter offer a range of current and recently concluded heritage projects, that promote mindful and tactile engagement with coastal space. Such cultural encounters with the seashore can bring greater awareness of the marine economy and ecology, geopolitics, climate change, and personal wellbeing, by reflecting on the past use of maritime spaces via their modern interpretations. As such, this contribution asks how Britain engages with its maritime legacy and what impact our relation to the modern *anthropocenic* sea is having on British cultural identity.[5] Furthermore, it argues that our relationship between identity and the maritime environment has recently been reshaped in the wake of 'Brexit' and the Covid-19 pandemic, resulting in a significant cultural turn towards the coast in recent years. Furthering such an argument, this chapter focuses its discussion on a review of 'heritage in action', exploring the value of holistic engagement with littoral cultural space in the construct of a British maritime identity in the 21st century.

In Defence of The Coast

Since the foundation of state, the geographic security of the English coast has been a cause of near constant political and social anxiety. However, in recent years it has been increasingly threatened by both human and non-human actors that have reframed historic discussions over our national maritime border and how it should be defended. Although the stealthy crossing of the English Channel by heavily loaded small boats today is ideologically, politically and contextually disparate to those that undertaken by *Operation Nightingale* 80 years ago, both crossings of the English Channel hold significant impact on national attitudes towards the same maritime space. They also lay foundation for popularised rhetoric's concerning the security of the British Isles and its role in Europe. With full sovereign control over the defence of our border being a key argument in debates favouring 'Brexit', how can history help us understand Britain as a post-EU Island? A coastal history of the Kentish border, for example, exposes the longevity of a national anxiety over the Channel crossing and its historic weakness.[6] Since the inauguration of the Confederation of the Cinque Ports in the 12th century, the south-eastern coastline of Britain has been a geo-political cornerstone in national defence and historically reflects the political and social unease formed by the questionable security of its *Maritime Cultural Landscape*.[7] An unease that was once managed under the direction of its own branch of the Admiralty.[8] However, this historic anxiety is not exclusive to the Kentish coast and was well understood to the British population in the previous century.

Following the course of modern history, UK coastal spaces have arguably adapted threefold. Firstly, as the leisure beaches and spa resorts of the late 18th and 19th century.[9] Secondly, as a militarised border, responsive to the threat of large-scale maritime and airborne invasion during the World Wars and to some extent the technological advance-ments of the 'Cold Wars'. To now reshaping as a 21st century borderland, threated by rapid climate change and influenced by a tide of govern-mental instability, retaining important cultural position. Few have addressed the potential societal impact incurred between each of these phases. Yet, each turn has influenced our national relationship with the sea and been instrumental in our current inward-facing national attitude.

In the second of these adaptations, the rush to defend Britain's coast in the 1940's saw the rapid militarisation and dramatic reshaping of the nation's maritime border that rendered it largely inaccessible to potential invaders but also civilians. The social and cultural impact of former 'pleasure beaches' and coastal spas of the inter-war period being hurriedly fitted with lines of barbed wire, designated as minefields, shielded by defensive outposts and anti-tank structures during the Second World War, has had little focused study yet occurred on the edge of current living memory.[10] In the span of only a few generations our national experience of the coast has been dramatically reshaped to reflect global geo-political pressures. The domestic cultural and social ramifications of this change to the coastal experience is little understood.

Some 28,000 pillbox structures were built in 1940 alone and many of those concrete structures remain recognisable in the British landscape, sometimes covered in layers of graffiti spanning from those soldier ready to 'fight them on the beaches' to the spray painted 'tagging' of modern-day youth.[11] However, these structures were but part of a larger and more hazardous line of defence where British beaches were reshaped to be used, if necessary, as killing fields. For example, Roly Evans recently highlighted that there exists a lack of awareness surrounding the existence and extent of Britain's historic coastal minefields; the tragic difficulties in their construction but also of the significant casualties sustained in their clearance post-war.[12] Trimmingham beach in Norfolk marked the last mined beach to be released back to the public in 1972 after extensive operations to clear the site that claimed the lives of 26 Royal Engineers that was only publicly memorialised in 2004.[13] Britain's clearance of coastal landmines runs well into living memory and continues to have impact today with possible WWII coastal landmines found almost every year on British beaches and the post-conflict policy replicated in on the beaches of the Falklands for example. It remains vital for long-term military communication and involvement with associated historical initiatives to mitigate long term-impact on the cultural landscape. How many people visiting the coast of Britain today think about these places as 'battlefields' and recognise the cultural significance, if not hazardous potential, of these seaside spaces now enjoyed as recreational places?

CITiZAN 'Solent Harbours' Programme

The work of the Coastal and Intertidal Zone Archaeological Network's (*CITiZAN*) (2015-18) has explored opportunities for sustainable public engagement with maritime heritage in England. It has successfully developed an understanding of lesser-known modern historic remains within a *Maritime Cultural landscape* of 21st century Britain. The 'Solent Harbours' initiative is one of six regional discovery programmes instated by *CITiZAN* across the country, each fitting within wider research frameworks and overarching thematic agendas as outlined and funded by national heritage bodies such as Historic England, the Lloyds Registry Foundation and the Council for British Archaeology, amongst others.[14] Across each of the regional divisions the principal aim of *CITiZAN* was to develop a coherent digital mode of reporting that build upon pre-existing networks of interest groups whilst also recruiting further local volunteers as 'citizen scientists'.[15] Encouraged through in-person training and on their online platforms, *CITiZAN* created a standardised recording and monitorisation system of at-risk archaeological features on the coast, used by members of the public via a freely downloadable mobile app. As well as meeting the agenda of long-running research initiatives the practical application offered reflection on local historic environments and added personal knowledge and experiences to the national archaeological record.[16]

The abundance of archaeological features on the historic seafronts of the Solent offers an ideal vantage point for urban populations to re-engage with their port-town heritage.[17] As such, the 'Solent Harbours' programme worked with community groups in Portsmouth, Langstone and Chichester Harbours, as well as areas of Gosport and Lee-On-Solent. It has added considerable value to previous surveys undertaken by *The Defence of Britain Project* (1995-2002)[18] and the *Defence Area Project* (2002-2004)[19] in the region, registering current conditions of historic military remains, including a large number of 1940's infrastructures, and enriched records with further information from personal archives, private researchers and individuals' experiences. For example, a programme led survey, that introduced the wider public as well as local students to the initiative, developed a digitally accessible low-tide trail of Hill Head. The unremarkable concrete slabs half covered by shingle at Stones Bay, as part of this trail, are understandably 'hard to imagine' as once part of a temporary harbour site for the embarkation of vehicles that played a vital rose in the preparations for D-Day landings [See Figure 1a&b].[20] The response of volunteers who undertook this survey highlighted the potential to overlook such features.[21] Bringing together new and previous research the trail encourages the public to reflect on the changing use of this cultural space, re-entering elements of relatively recent coastal

Fig1a *Top left* & b *Top right*: Site surveyed by CITiZAN at Stokes Bay, Hampshire, photographed in 2020(a) and under construction as a temporary harbour site in c.1943-4. (Image credit: *CITiZAN* & Friends of Stokes Bay) (MacDonell, James, 'D-Day's Secret Harbours', *CITiZAN*, 24 Feb 2020. <https://www.citizan.org.uk/blog/2020/Feb/24/d-days-secret-harbours/> [accessed 29 Nov 2023]).

history back into every-day comprehension.[22]

Not only looking at dry coastal sites but intertidal and partially submerged remains, *CITiZAN* has also been instrumental in bringing modern ship and boat remains back into the cultural fold.[23] The 'Solent Harbours' programme has re-contextualised a collection of deliberately abandoned historic 'hulks' in Gosport and around Chichester Harbours. At Fornton Lake the remains of at least 13 different vessels, ranging in date from the 1800's to the 1960, form a 'ship-graveyard' that was repeatedly surveyed by *CITiZAN* volunteers [See Figure 2]. Close to Portsmouth's Naval Dockyard on its western bank, the inlet once housed a number of boatyards but became a 'temporary' holding for small vessels prior to their sale for scrap; at least 9 former military vessels never left. Amongst the metal skeletal remains in the intertidal lake, three Assault Landing Craft (LCD) vessels possibly used during the D-Day landings, a possible Motor Gun Boat (MGB) and a rare RAF ferry boat all add into

a wider record of Post-war disarmament and the gradual disuse of coastal spaces left to re-enter a civilian context.[24]

Similarly, remains to the east of Portsmouth, close to the narrow channel of Langstone harbour a Mulberry Harbour has been left in perpetuity with its 'back-broken', never to leave the waters it was made in. It remains as a local landmark and a monument to the former construction site of these strategically vital concrete structures, surrounded by other 'drifted materials' of the post-war.[25] From the *CITiZAN* blog it is evident that the 'Solent Harbours' programme has had significant impact on locals in this area who have 'simply not paid enough attention' to otherwise mundane and weathered concrete structures or historic hulks who now 'reflect and research what other secrets' their local coastline holds.[26] In this example, *CITiZAN* has offered the re-entry of this military detritus, of the 'forgotten rejectma' of past strategic defences into modern cultural comprehension, its programme

Fig 2: Areial image of the 'boat graveyard' at Fornton Lake, Gosport, Hampshire taken by drone during survey in 2020. (Image credit: *CITIZAN*).

offering local solutions to a national and self-sustaining recording of at-risk archaeology from the neolithic to the modern age.

Facing The Threat of Sea Level Rise

The overarching aim of the *CITiZAN* project, although community dependant, aligns with a series of other projects across the UK and Ireland that recognise the imminent threat posed by climate change and sea level rise to Britain's coastal heritage in the 21st century.[27] This threat is well known to the public, however, the scale of our national coastal heritage's vulnerability is rising, with major storms becoming more frequent and severe, despite large scale civil engineering projects and a national annual expenditure for coastal defences in excess of a billion Pounds.[28] For instance, the collapse of wall at Hurst Castle in February 2021 gathered widespread news coverage and became 'emblematic of the huge challenge posed by climate change to our heritage'; archetypal of the significant foreseeable losses to coastal heritage the country now faces despite multiple grants and millions of pounds spent on its reinforce-ment.[29] However, not all sites are afforded such investment in their protection and the historic coast has once again become one of strategic defence, now against the sea itself.

Sites such as Cuckmere Haven on the Sussex coast, that once held significant prominence in nationalist iconography during the Second World War, has seen the recent withdraw of active intervention and state funding.[30] Local landowners and volunteers have self-fund work to protect local heritage coastlines as their own 'home-front'; they have sought value in documenting historic features in the process and attracted inter-national attention hosting annual arts, music and heritage events.[31] Whether undertaken by national policy or local initiative, the reshaping of these littoral spaces as a response to climate change and sea level rise, also irrevocably changes the *Maritime Cultural Landscape* of many seafronts, including sites of previous strategic or cultural importance.[32] Altering how most of the British population personally experiences the sea, reducing its liminality and altering its accessibility by installing large concrete fortifications; rendered similar in appearance to the military defensive structures of the last decade, particularly around urban coastlines.[33] The incremental threat of sea level rise has thus diminished the timeframe within which coastal archaeological sites' importance to the national maritime consciousness can be effectively realised and opportunities for coastal history's role in 'sustaining a sea-power identity' in 21st century Britain can be acted upon.

Developing A Regional Response – *SCAPE*

Established in 2001, the ongoing Scottish Coastal Archaeology and the Problem of Erosion project (*SCAPE*) aims to work with the public to 'explore, interpret and celebrate eroding archaeological sites' on the coast of Scotland.[34] Supported by research institutes such as the University of St Andrews and funded by the Historic Environment Scotland's Partnership Fund, Heritage Lottery Fund, Local Authorities and Research Councils, the project has been recognised internationally for its innovative community involvement. It has been championed for its approach in fostering long-term stewardship of local at-risk coastal heritage whilst adding considerable knowledge to the national record.[35] Rapid site surveys have mapped and photographed the condition of hundreds of sites on the Scottish coast, entered via a freely downloadable mobile app to create a consolidated and updatable record of historic features in the 'coast-scape' of 21st century Scotland. As a predecessor of the English *CITiZAN* project amongst others, *SCAPE* pioneered this digital means of public survey, empowering pro-active local volunteers in

research projects, field surveys and pragmatic discussions of future coastal change, granting the public a considerable degree of agency. Identifying areas of priority for monitoring in the next decade, *SCAPE* has utilised data from the 2016 coastal erosion susceptibility model and the 2021 'Dynamic coast' initiatives, as well as their own observations, to determine which sites will be under greatest threat by 2030 within their remit.[36] Undertaking site survey under a priority-based structure has established a sustainable methodology, and quantitative scale, for the physical prioritisation of at risk archaeology on the British coast that has not yet been effectively replicated outside of Scotland.

SCAPE has not only successfully brought attention to sites at greatest risk but is also credited with the creation of new knowledge including the registration of previously unrecognised heritage sites. The project's most recently published survey, of the Aberdeenshire coastline between Cullen to Milton Ness, between May of 2022 and 2023, documented 323 archaeological and built heritage sites, 77 of which were not previously entered in heritage records.[37] The most frequently recorded feature types

Fig 3 *Top left*: Decorated anti-tank block dated 1940 with banner reading 'Hitler's Graveyard', Newburgh, Aberdeenshire (Photo Credit: Jim Lister, March 2021). (Boyd, Sarah and Hambly, Joanna. '*Coastal Zone Assessment Survey Aberdeenshire & City of Aberdeen: Cullen to Milton Ness*', The *SCAPE* Trust and University of St Andrews, (2023), Figure 17, p.22).

Fig 4 *Top right*: Split apart pillbox feature in the wave zone at Balgownie Links, City of Aberdeen, photographed as part of *SCAPE*'s 2022-3 CCZAS of the Aberdeenshire coast. It is recorded on their online database <https://scapetrust.org/sites-at-risk/site/15044> (Boyd, Sarah and Hambly, Joanna. 'Coastal Zone Assessment Survey Aberdeenshire & City of Aberdeen: Cullen to Milton Ness', The *SCAPE* Trust and University of St Andrews, (2023), Figure 5B, p.10).

reflect the significant military presence that was held there during the Second World War.[38] For example defensive remains at Foveran Links including intact sections of anti-landing scaffolding, gun emplacements, rare pill-box variations and 'Hitler's Graveyard' decorated anti-tank cube [See Figure 3], are now at significant risk of loss by 2030. Images of features from the survey show the typically decrepit state of the WW2 structures in the Aberdeenshire coastline, as broken, topped, even split in half, ever closer to the wave zone [See Figure 4]. Nationally set guidelines acknowledge that it is hard to justify the conservation of these former defensive remains, thus emphasis is placed on their in-situ rapid recording before being lost to the sea, however, they are also at risk from human action such as 'souvenir hunting' and relies on community safeguarding in this regard.[39]

The aim of *SCAPE*'s survey of the Aberdeenshire coast was to characterize and assess the vulnerability of the archaeological record there, having not already been subject to a Community Coastal Zone Assessment Survey (CCZAS) under the project's direction. The majority of existing heritage records from the area otherwise being 'over-whelmingly related' to these WW2 defences, project organisers were conscious that the 'visibility of any other heritage is very poor' despite having a rich and deep history of maritime culture and being equally at risk of disassembly by coastal erosion.[40] The survey, despite its brief nature, lays the groundwork for an extensive understanding of the *Maritime Cultural Landscape* of the eastern Scottish mainland. The structural remnants of features, including former fishing and mining industries, agricultural boundaries and settlement remains, are testament to the past cultural and economic importance of this coastline. Rare surviving examples of 'bodlin' apparatus and other largely disused equipment, structural elements, even the boats, now stand as the relics of 'traditional' economic uses of the sea, namely a salmon fishing industry, that declined in the years preceding the Second World War. The survey tells a vivid tale of the cultural turns to the coast in recent history, but also hints to the habitation of landscape in prehistory with the discovery of lithic scatter and shell midden at Forvie Nature Reserve.[41] The sites recorded by volunteers during this walking survey, add a rich layer to the inter-pretation of the modern coastline's wider context in the history of Britain and further demonstrates the potential of research-orientated recreation to promote understanding of past, current and potential future sea-dependency of cultures of the British Isles whilst features remain visible and accessible to the public.

This long-running programme understands the need for rapid regional development of community infrastructure that is responsive to the threat of the sea on our heritage coastlines, withstanding of national policy changes, funding allowances and cultural governing structures. For example, the division between Scottish, English, Welsh and Northern Irish heritage organisation limits the opportunity for an amalgamated approach to public engagement with coastal history. For instance, a single unified body would struggle to mitigate differences in research frameworks and funding; an obstacle not historically faced by the Admiralty in its 'Artistic' capacity.[42] However, meaningful collaborative research and public engagement initiatives with the coastal and maritime in the 21st century is possible across politicised borders.

Collaboration Across Political Borders – *CHERISH*

One of the principles of the 'New Coastal Historiography' school of thought is that opposing coasts have more in common culturally than their hinterland counterparts; this historic cultural link implores

Fig 5: *CHERISH* outdoor engagement activity at the site of Dinas Dinlle in North Wales, 2019, excavations at the site at the time attracted over 400 visitors but public tours of the surrounding coastscape were also given, as pictured, to smaller groups. [Image Credit: *CHERISH*] (<https://cherishproject.eu/en/> [Accessed 02/12/2023].

connection across maritime space in the generation of research.[43] The work of *CHERISH* (Climate, Heritage and Environments of Reefs, Islands, and Headlands) embodies this concept, bringing together four key partners across Wales and Ireland in a transnational project that reached across the Irish Sea, seeing a commonality not just in the *maritimity* of coastal inhabitants but also in the issues affecting maritime cultural heritage in the past, present and near-future.[44] The project was enabled by €4.9 million in financial support from the European Regional Development Fund between 2017 and June 2023, taking the learnings from projects like *CITiZAN* and *SCAPE*, to develop a nine-point objective that included the development of joint good practice guidance, training for citizen scientists and collaboratively formed open access digital data depositories.[45] In the pursuit of best practice, *CHERISH* has successfully developed a 'toolkit' for recording the impact of climate change on heritage on land, sea and places in-between, that, despite its technical focus, maintains the development of strong community connections via volunteer training and programmes of outreach are vital for sustainable and long term monitoring of at-risk heritage sites.[46]

Only recently concluded, the legacy of the *CHERISH* project is yet to be determined. What is certain is that the rescinding of Britain's status as a member of the European Union will make future trans-national funding for maritime heritage projects with neighbouring states difficult to acquire. It will require the reconsideration of Britain's maritime space and wider public acknowledgment of its importance for the expenditure to be politically justified. In the strategic development of our maritime space, and as national dependency on offshore renewable energy grows, it will be vital to reconsider our 'watery connections' in future policy discussions.[47] Looking to our current and future use of the North Sea, for example, this premise my well yield interest in the near future with the Orkney Islands becoming test bed for potential new tidal stream net-zero energy production for the UK by 2050.[48] We must reconsider how we conceptualise and culturally interact with our maritime borderland in the 21st century, seeing not as the coast-'line' but something more fluid.

Reconsidering 21st Century Coastal Space

Arguably the development of coastal tourism was the first significant reconsideration of coastal space in Britain, where individuals were encouraged to experience the sea at its shore. Since the late Georgian period, a British population keen to escape the urbanising and industrialising 'heartland', has turned to the seaside as a resort, a leisure beach or coastal spa. 'Once quiet fishing villages', places such as Brighton, Great Yarmouth, Blackpool and Scarborough became fashionable and popular retreats, with people drawn there for the 'clean' sea air and 'medicinal' waters, staying to enjoy the pleasure gardens, piers and pavilions of the rapidly developing towns.[49] Recent studies have detailed the geographic and economic impact of this coastal turn on English and Welsh coastal resorts over the last 300 years and the enduring legacy of the seaside leisure industry that continues to shape our nation's connection to the sea and fuels domestic tourism.[50] The research highlights conflict that occurred between 'polite society and the commercial realm' as the tensions between leisure-seeking hinterlanders and maritime-dependent coastal communities altered the function of these coastal spaces seasonally.[51] The history of the British seaside has subsequently been marked by the rise and fall of these industries and the profitability of the port and 'traditional' maritime industries coming into conflict with the development of domestic tourism; a dynamic that remains evident.

One of the most significant driving factors behind the rapid popularity of the coast as a place of wellbeing was the cholera epidemic, a 'deluge of pestilence', that raged through mid-19th century urban England.[52] Instances such as the 1854 Broad Street Pump outbreak, the 'Great Stink' in 1858 and the Aldgate Pump Epidemic of 1876 in London demonstrated the favourable condition of urban Britain to transmit contagion in the 19th century. The diseased traveling to coastal retreats in search of ailment and restoration, adding to further tension between often economically disparate communities. Comparison can be drawn to much more recent history. During the Covid-19 pandemic a 'new' understanding and importance has been given to coastal spaces as places of mental restoration and reflection as many flocked to the coastal perimeter for daily exercise and relief from 'lockdown' protocols.[53] Subsequent recent studies have shown the benefits of coastal visits in the relief of stress, reduction of depression and its restorative and therapeutic qualities.[54] The elimination of a 'sea-blindness' in society offers potential relief from an ensuring public mental health crisis. With the charity MIND reporting over 17,000 serious incidents, two every hour, between April 2022 and March 2023, there is due concern about the public's loss of confidence in mental health care across in the UK.[55] Many have instead turned to the 'green' or 'blue' environment in search of mindfulness and personal reflection. In a post-covid context, has the coast once again become a place of physical and mental wellbeing?

'Coasts in Mind'

Across the world maritime archaeologists have long recognised the benefit of the 'citizen scientist' to the management of heritage sites above and below water and their valuable contributions to research.[56] However, projects also recognise the positive impact on the health and wellbeing of their regional participants. With the conclusion of funding and research timelines for projects like *CITiZAN*, will future community orientated iterations encourage maritime mindfulness? Stemming from the aforementioned project, a pilot initiative, backed by the National Lottery Heritage Fund and managed under the directive of MOLA (Museum of London Archaeology), launched in 2023. The 'Coasts in Mind' project aims to co-create a national 'Community Archive' that traces coastal change over the past 100 years, developing a framework for local groups to engage with policy makers and be given agency in discussions as

Fig 6: 'Coasts in Mind' participants recording audio and collecting materials to contribute towards a sensory box display as part of initial trial of the project at Herne Bay, Kent, 2023. [Image Credit: *CITiZAN*] Tyson, Rebecca. 'Introducing Coasts in Mind, a new *MOLA* project exploring community-centred approaches to coastal change'.
CITiZAN, <https://www.citizan.org.uk/blog/2023/Jul/17/introducing-coasts-mind-new-mola-project-exploring-community-centered-approaches-coastal-change/#:~:text=Participants%20were%20encouraged%20to%20explore, of%20value%20to%20their%20communities.> 17 July 2023. [Accessed 02/12/2023].

Britain continues to respond to the impact of sea level rise.[57] The remit of the proposed project, if further explored, would enable insight into the value of at-risk coastal heritage sites to individuals, as places of maritime interaction. For instance, the first 'Creative Session' run by the initiative in East Kent brought youth supported by the charity MENCAP to Hearne Bay to collect items as part of a sensory box, recording experiences via audio during the beach walk and proving the potential of the scheme to explore multi-sensory modes of engagement with the coast [See Figure 6].[58] Such exploration breaks down barriers and perceptions between people and places and invites discussion into our place as European island inhabitants.

Aiming to be a 'people-powered' project, this new initiative recognises the past focus on data collection by heritage bodies and that more action towards a 'creative placemaking' approach could instil further benefit; as has been shown in a series of studies in the UK and Europe.[59] The develop-ment of freely downloadable interactives, self-guided tours, context displays, artistic instillations and other engagement materials are only of value if information is absorbed into a wider cultural fold, particularly if used to refute a 'sea-blindness' in society. Britain must not let its coastal heritage become 'forgotten rejectma' in the 21st century but find new ways of engaging with it mindfully, finding individual benefit from it.

Conclusion

The facilitation of future physical interaction with the coast, as impactful on a national scale, requires a governing body that works collaboratively with a range of state partners and adjacent organisations to circum-navigate complexities in the current system of heritage organisation. Contemporary heritage projects have made significant impact on the perception of individuals, communities and policy makers by enabling the re-contextualisation of Britain's historic coastline with modern day issues, most namely of climate change and its direct impact on the physical remains of our maritime heritage. However, regional division of research agendas and funding has inhibited impact on national identity and limited the wider recognition of the *Maritime Cultural Landscape*'s importance to 21st century.

Despite argument that there exists a maritime vacuum in national consciousness, there are evidently those actively seeing to address the generational gap in 'ocean literacy' within the heritage sector by working within communities, valuing the contribution of individuals, to secure a national depository of information for future generations to utilise as record of our past, present and future maritime dependency. They are developing realistic capabilities, that are globally replicable, to re-integrate and re-interpret coastal spaces once peacefully enjoyed, heavily defended, now to be fortified again by sea walls and other emplacements to prevent maritime incursion. As the place of geographic interaction and as a marine environment, the coast will play a significant role in further development towards a 21st century national maritime consciousness as it is re-shaped and re-altered, creating new meaning as mindful space, a borderland, and as anxiety over its security increases. It falls upon institutions of heritage and art to foster sustainable cultural exchanges on our domestic shore to repair our national relationship with the maritime and understand this new cultural turn towards the sea.

1. 'Hull to London', *Coast*, BBC2, 1 September 2010, 20:00pm.

2. The concept of *Maritimity*, developing primarily from geographic thought, can be defined as the binding relationships between society and the sea that results in marine-orientated policy economy, landscape, settlement, lifestyles and culture. See: Péron, Françoise and Jean Rieucau (dir.). La maritimité aujourd'hui. (Paris: L'Harmattan, 1996).

3. This concern is not exclusive to the British coast. See: Robert, Samuel. 'What can sea-related associations reveal about a coastal region's maritimity? A case study in southern France'. *Maritime Studies,* 23:4 (2024).

4. As was recently called for by Professor Lambert, recognising the vacuum left in the decline of the admiralty's historic role as a cultural entity in the last century; Andrew Lambert, 'The art of Admiralty: How to mobilise naval power', Britain's World, 23/05/2023, <https://bit.ly/3qrELgD> [Accessed:16 Nov 2023].

5. The impact of humans on the planet has been marked with its own geological epoch as the 'anthropocine', in relation to the sea it includes the impact of climate change, pollution, acidification and other chemical changes, and as well as changes to bio-diversity.

6. Worthington, David, ed. *Introducing the New Coastal History: Cultural and Environmental Perspectives from Scotland and Beyond.* (Springer International Publishing, 2017); Land Isaac. 'Tidal waves: The new coastal history'. *Journal of Social History.*40:3 (2007), p.731-43.

7. Westerdahl, Christer. "Conclusion: The maritime cultural landscape revisited." *The archaeology of maritime landscapes.* (New York, NY: Springer New York, 2011). P.331-344.

8. The Admiralty of the Cinque Ports came to function as protector of the state and as cultural director to potentially fickle medieval populations in a manner defined by Professor Lambert's as the 'Art of Admiralty'. In the decline of the Cinque Ports as a constitutional authority in the 19th and 20th centuries, state understanding and order over the unique *Maritime Cultural Landscape* has been lost within a modern centralised authority at Westminster that is now struggling to manage the same 21st century British coast as a political front.

9. Walton, J. K. 'Seaside Resorts and Maritime History'. *International Journal of Maritime History*, 9:1 (1997), pp.125-147.

10. Evans, Roly. 'World War II Coastal Minefields in the United Kingdom', *Journal of Conventional Weapons Desctruction.* 21:1 Article 9 (2017).

11. 'Military Structures, Listing Selection Guides', *English heritage* (2011), p.15.

12. Evans, Roly. 'World War II Coastal Minefields in the United Kingdom', *Journal of Conventional Weapons Desctruction.* 21:1 Article 9 (2017).p.9.

13. *Ibid,* p.6; In the immediate aftermath of the war the inaccuracy in record keeping, and the ill factored consideration of the materiality of the coast in the shifting and drifting of intertidal materials, lead to time consuming and hazardous programs of clearance undertaken principally by divisions of the Army who employed terrestrial methods on shifting sands despite petitions to utilize local coastal knowledge.

14. CITiZAN, <https://citizan.org.uk/> [accessed 20 Nov 2023]. Other areas of study include Humberside, Liverpool Bay, South Devon Rivers, Mersea Island and East Kent Coast.

15. *Ibid.*

16. Band, Lara. "CITiZAN 2015-2018 and 2019-2021, a community archaeology project past and future: successes, challenges, potential solutions." *European Journal of Post-Classical Archaeologies* 9 (2019), p.399-409.

17. Gale, Alison. *The Story Beneath the Solent: Discovering Underwater Archaeology.* (Southampton, Hampshire & Wight trust for maritime Archaeology, 2000).
      Beaven, Brad, Karl Bell, and Robert James, eds. *Port towns and urban cultures: international histories of the waterfront, c. 1700-2000.* (London: Palgrave Macmillan; 2016).

18. Council for British Archaeology, '*Defence of Britain Archive*'. York: Archaeology Data Service, (2006). <https://doi.org/10.5284/1000327> [Accessed 02 Dec 2023].

19. William Foot, Council for British Archaeology, 'Defence Areas: a national study of Second World War anti-invasion landscapes in England' *York: Archaeology Data Service,* 2009. <https://doi.org/10.5284/1000032> [Accessed 02 Dec 2023].

20. MacDonell, James, 'D-Day's Secret Harbours', *CITiZAN*, 24 Feb 2020. <https://www.citizan.org.uk/blog/2020/Feb/24/d-days-secret-harbours/>[accessed 29 Nov 2023].

21. *Ibid.*

22. The trail uses research by the Nautical Archaeology Society (NAS), Friends of Stokes Bay and other local interest groups, as well as data from an original survey undertaken in the Autumn of 2018. See: 'Solent Harbours: Hill Head', *CITiZAN,* <https://citizan.org.uk/low-tide-trails/solent-harbours-hill-head/> [Accessed 02 Dec 2023].

23. Studied as a 'hauntology' Rich argues that only through investigation, excavation or curatorship that the remains of a vessel can evoke a cultural memory and re-enter the cultural fold, otherwise being left as 'forgotten rejectma' for archaeologists to uncover. See: Rich, Sara. *Shipwreck Hauntography.* (Amsterdam University Press; 2021).

24. CITiZAN South West, '*Incredible hulks & where to find them?*', 30 June 2021. <https://www.citizan.org.uk/low-tide-trails/solent-harbours-forton-lake-gosport/> [accessed Nov 2023].

25. Turnbull, Daisy K,E. "A 'drift' in the Anthropocene: A case study of urban maritime materiality." *Coastal Studies & Society* 1.2-4, (2022) p.156-179.

26. MacDonell, James, 'D-Day's Secret Harbours', *CITiZAN*, 24 Feb 2020. <https://www.citizan.org.uk/blog/2020/Feb/24/d-days-secret-harbours/>[accessed 29 Nov 2023].

27. Milne, Gustav, et al. "Citizen Science in Coastal Archaeology." *Citizen Science in Maritime Archaeology: The Power of Public Engagement* (University of Florida Press; 2023), p.140-143.

28. Hughes, Regan. 'Investment in flood defences, UK: May 2023', *Office for National Statistics*, 17 may 2023. <https://www.ons.gov.uk/economy/ economicoutputandproductivity/output/articles/investmentinflooddefencesuk/ may2023#:~:text=Central%20government%20is%20the%20largest, billion%20in%202021%2C%20current%20prices> [Accessed 02/12/2023]; 'UK and Global extreme events – Wind storms', *MET Office*, <https://www.metoffice.gov.uk/ research/climate/understanding-climate/uk-and-global-extreme-events-wind-storms.> [Accessed 02/12/2023].

29. 'Hurst Castle – Collapse of Section of East Wing Wall', *English* heritage, 27/02/2021, <https://www.english-heritage.org.uk/about-us/search-news/pr-hurst-castle-statement/> [Accessed 02 Dec 2023]; Despite considerable investment, with Hurst Castle recognised by the Environment Agency as one of the country's most at risk historic sites receiving over £2,000,000 since 2017, sites like this are increasingly instable in the wake in more frequent storm and heightened flooding risks resultant of global climate change.

30. Hibbs, Peter. 'Why Cuckmere Haven is of national importance', 30 may 2011. <http://www.pillbox.org.uk/blog/216684/>[Accessed 02/12/2023].

31. Hibbs, Peter. 'Why Cuckmere Haven is of national importance', 30 may 2011. <http://www.pillbox.org.uk/blog/216684/>[Accessed 02/12/2023].

32. Westerdahl, Christer. "Conclusion: The maritime cultural landscape revisited." *The archaeology of maritime landscapes.* (New York: Springer New York, 2011), p.331-344.

33. Turnbull, Daisy K. E. "A 'drift' in the Anthropocene: A case study of urban maritime materiality." *Coastal Studies & Society* 1.2-4, (2022) p.156-179.

34. SCAPE <https://scapetrust.org/> [Accessed 02/12/2023].

35. Dawson, Tom. "Eroding archaeology at the coast: How a global problem is being managed in Scotland, with examples from the Western Isles." *Journal of the North Atlantic,* 9:9 (2015), 83-98; Graham, Ellie, Joanna Hambly, and Tom Dawson. "Scotland's eroding heritage: A collaborative response to the impact of climate change." (2017).

36. Fitton, J. M., Hansom, J. D. and Rennie, A. F. 'A national coastal erosion susceptibility model for Scotland'. *Ocean & Coastal Management,* 132, (2016), p.80-89; Hurst, M. D., Muir, F. M. E., Rennie, A. F. and Hansom, J. D. 'Dynamic Coast: Future Coastal Erosion. CRW2017_08.' *Scotland's Centre of Expertise for Waters* (CREW), (2021). <https://www.dynamiccoast.com/reports> [Accessed 9 Jan 2023]; Boyd, Sarah and Hambly, Joanna. 'Coastal Zone Assessment Survey Aberdeenshire & City of Aberdeen: Cullen to Milton Ness', *The SCAPE Trust and University of St Andrews.* (2023).

37. Boyd, Sarah and Hambly, Joanna. 'Coastal Zone Assessment Survey Aberdeenshire & City of Aberdeen: Cullen to Milton Ness', *The SCAPE Trust and University of St Andrews.* (2023).

38. *Ibid,* p.3; 33% of records in Aberdeenshire (and 72% of records along the short stretch of coastline surveyed within the City of Aberdeen) are related to the defense of Britain's coasts, making up over 30% of recorded sites and over 80% of newly entered features to the SCAPE database.

39. *Ibid*, p.37. See also; 'Military Structures, Listing Selection Guides', *English heritage* (2011).

40. Boyd, Sarah and Hambly, Joanna. 'Coastal Zone Assessment Survey Aberdeenshire & City of Aberdeen: Cullen to Milton Ness', *The SCAPE Trust and University of St Andrews*. (2023), p.2.

41. *Ibid*

42. See; Andrew Lambert, 'The art of Admiralty: How to mobilise naval power', Britain's World, 23/05/2023, <https://bit.ly/3qrELgD> [Accessed:16 Nov 2023].

43. Worthington, David. *Introducing the New Coastal History: Cultural and Environmental Perspectives from Scotland and Beyond*. (Springer International Publishing, 2017); Land Isaac. 'Tidal waves: The new coastal history'. *Journal of Social History.*40:3 (2007), p.731-43; Gillis, John. R. *The human shore: Seacoasts in history*. (University of Chicago Press, 2015).

44. 'Climate Change and Coastal Heritage.' *CHERISH*. <https://cherishproject.eu/en/> [Accessed 02 Dec 2023].

45. Corns, Anthony, et al. "CHERISH: Development of a Toolkit for the 3D Documentation and Analysis of the Marine and Coastal Historic Environment." *3D Imaging of the Environment*. Taylor & Francis, (2024); Shotton, Elizabeth. "Coastal Heritage, Communities & Climate Change." *Documenting Maritime Heritage at Risk*. (Routledge; 2024), p.1-11.

46. 'Investigating heritage and Climate Change in Coastal and maritime Environments. A Guide to the CHERISH Toolkit', *CHERISH,* (Aug 2023), <https://cherishproject.eu/en/sharing-our-practice/> [Accessed 02 Dec 2023], p.144.

47. For example, the incorporation of 'Archipelagic' thinking into policy making, recognising the impact of maritime space on mainland interactions and national relationships to reform a 'watery connection'. See Stephens, Michelle and Martinez-San Miguel, Yolanda, eds. *'Contemporary Archipelagic Thinking, Towards New Comparative Methodologies and Disciplinary Foundations'*, 1st edn (Rowman & Littlefield; 2020).

48. Frost, Ciaran. 'Quantifying the benefits of tidal Stream Energy to the wider UK energy system; A 2050 case study'. *CATAPULT Offshore Renewable Energy.* (June 2022).

49. Berry, Sue. "Pleasure Gardens in Georgian and Regency Seaside Resorts: Brighton, 1750-1840." *Garden History*, 28: 2, (2000), p. 222–30; Jarratt, David. 'Sense of place at a British coastal resort: Exploring 'seasideness' in Morecambe', *Tourism: An International Interdisciplinary Journal,* 63:3 (2015), p.351-363; Hassan, John. *'The seaside, health and the environment in England and Wales since 1800'*. (Routledge, 2016).

50. Borsay, Peter. "From port to resort: Tenby and narratives of transition 1760-1914." Resorts and ports: European seaside towns since 1700 (Channel View Publications; 2011): 86-112; Gale, Tim. "Modernism, post-modernism and the decline of British seaside resorts as long holiday destinations: A case study of Rhyl, North Wales", *Tourism Geographies*, 7:1 (2005), p.86-112; Tunstall, Sylvia M., and Edmund C. Penning-Rowsell. "The English beach: experiences and values." *Geographical Journal*, (1998), p.319-332.

51. Brodie, Allan. 'Leisure and Commerce: Seafront Rivals in England's First Seaside Resorts', *Tourism and Innovation*, 12:1 (2019), p.13-22.

52. Andrews, Gavin J., and Robin A. Kearns. "Everyday health histories and the making of place: the case of an English coastal town." *Social Science & Medicine* 60:12 (2005), p.2697-2713.

53. Jellard, S., & Bell, S. L. 'A fragmented sense of home: Reconfiguring therapeutic coastal encounters in Covid-19 times.' *Emotion, Space and Society*, 40, 100818. (2021); Earl, Joseph, et al. "Best day since the bad germs came': exploring changing experiences in and the value of coastal blue space during the COVID-19 pandemic, a Fylde Coast case study." *Coastal Studies & Society* 1:1 (2022), p.97-119; Lamers, Machiel, and Jillian Student. "Learning from COVID-19? An environmental mobilities and flows perspective on dynamic vulnerabilities in coastal tourism settings." *Maritime Studies* 20:4 (2021), p.475-486.

54. See: Driver, Felix. "Moral geographies: social science and the urban environment in mid-nineteenth century England." *Transactions of the Institute of British Geographers* (1988), p.275-287.

55. MIND, 'Mind reveals true extent of crisis in mental heathcare with more than 17,000 reports of serious incidents in past year alone' <https://www.mind.org.uk/news-campaigns/news/mind-reveals-true-extent-of-crisis-in-mental-healthcare-with-more-than-17-000-reports-of-serious-incidents-in-past-year-alone/> Tues 10th October 2023. [Accessed 02/12/2023].

56. Wragg, Eliott, et al. "Community recording and monitoring of vulnerable sites in England." Public Archaeology and Climate Change (2017), p.44-51; Band, Lara. "CITiZAN 2015-2018 and 2019-2021, a community archaeology project past and future: successes, challenges, potential solutions." *European Journal of Post-Classical Archaeologies* 9 (2019), p.399-409; Milne, Gustav, et al. "Citizen Science in Coastal Archaeology." *Citizen Science in Maritime Archaeology: The Power of Public Engagement* (University Press of Florida, 2023).

57. Tyson, Rebecca. '*Introducing Coasts in Mind, a new MOLA project exploring community-centred approaches to coastal change*'. CITiZAN, <https://www.citizan.org.uk/blog/2023/Jul/17/introducing-coasts-mind-new-mola-project-exploring-community-centered-approaches-coastal-change/#:~:text=Participants%20were%20encouraged%20to%20explore, of%20value%20to%20their%20communities.> 17 July 2023. [Accessed 02/12/2023].

58. *Ibid.*

59. Nettley, Amy, et al. "Visualising sea-level rise at a coastal heritage site: Participatory process and creative communication." Landscape Research 39.6 (2014), p.647-667; Haraldseid, Thomas. "Exploring social creativity in place-making: A case study from a coastal town in Northern Norway." *Norsk Geografisk Tidsskrift-Norwegian Journal of Geography* 73.5 (2019), p.257-272; Stevens, Quentin, and Mhairi Ambler. "Europe's city beaches as post-Fordist placemaking." *Journal of Urban Design* 15.4 (2010), p.515-537.

People and Communities

Maritime People: Valuing Seafarer Good Health

From Deep Waters into the Light: Locating Seamen's
Women in Naval Social History

Maritime Women

Blueing Maritime Britain: the need for a Transformative
Blue Governance Agenda

Maritime People: Valuing Seafarer Good Health

Dr Joanne L. Fallowfield and Cdr Matthew Court RN

Introduction – Seafaring People Challenges

The United Kingdom (UK) maritime sector provides an important link between British business and the rest of the world. Economically, it contributes over £55bn in direct business turnover (and a £116bn total aggregate turnover), being responsible for over 95% of UK trade by volume – including 40% of the UK's vital food supply.[1] From a people perspective, the sector provided 227,100 jobs in 2022, where every job directly employed *circa* five jobs in the wider UK economy. However, the maritime sector faces significant people challenges, including:

- worldwide sector shifts from permanent to temporary employment models;[2]
- increasing international competition for trained and experienced seafaring talent;[3]
- extended time away from home, with seven-day working weeks and lack of internet connectivity whilst at sea (significantly impacting a connected generation entering the workforce);[4]
- health hazards and specific occupational safety risks, both for shore-based workers employed in shipbuilding and maritime maintenance trades, as well as seafarers;[5]
- and issues related to under-recruitment of trainees in the face of an aging and retiring workforce.

All these factors have contributed to a downward trend in workforce numbers over the early 21st century, decreasing more markedly during the COVID pandemic and remaining below 2018 levels in 2022 despite a modest recovery.[6] The International Chamber of Shipping has asserted that recruitment and training must markedly increase to mitigate projected significant workforce shortages. These shortages will create strategic staffing gaps, especially in technical and management seafaring roles.[7]

The historic attraction of the maritime industry were the opportunities to travel the world whilst working in well-paid, high-skilled jobs. However, transport developments over the last fifty years make international travel for leisure accessible and affordable. Moreover, industrial and commerce globalisation has provided many more opportunities to travel for work without the hazards or austerities associated with seafaring. The future vision for the British maritime sector is one of an inclusive, vibrant and technologically advanced workplace, with high standards of workforce safety, health and welfare. To achieve this vision, there must be: investment in attracting the necessary talent; knowledge-development and skills-training; action to realise a cultural shift in the workplace; as well as interventions to support and promote the health, wellbeing and performance of the UK's maritime workforce.

Government Support for Maritime Training (SMarT) was initiated in 1998 to fund approved courses for seafaring ratings, officers and officer cadets across the Maritime and Coastguard Agency (MCA) and Merchant Navy Training Board.[8] This programme has proved to be good value in terms of public money investment based on the Benefit to Cost Ratio (BCR).[9] For every Government pound invested in SMarT, there is an estimated £4.8 BCR return to UK Gross Domestic Product.[10] Moreover, the through-career benefits have also been recognised, with maritime workers – specifically those in seafaring roles – demonstrating higher levels of productivity relative to non-maritime occupations. As one strategy to arrest the year-on-year decline in seafarer numbers, SMarT funding was doubled in 2018; the subsequent SMarT Plus programme has targeted both increasing the number of cadets starting training as well as supporting the transition of trainees into seafaring careers.[11] Nevertheless, more is required to restore pre-pandemic seafarer numbers with the requisite knowledge and skills, and indeed to grow the workforce to meet 21st century maritime Britain requirements.

To link potential training funding with candidates, a coordinated cross-sector approach to raising awareness in schools and colleges of maritime sector career opportunities has been identified. Ahead of attracting new-entrants, the sector also needs to address its workplace culture, which is generally viewed as *traditional* and *male-orientated*. A current lack of diversity in age, gender and ethnicity further reduces the maritime sector's attractiveness to a more diverse workforce – and so the issues are compounded. The proportion of women in the industry is very low,[12] and this is even lower in sea-going roles. Women represent 1.2%

percent of the total global seafarer workforce (rising to *circa* 3% in the UK), and thus represent a relatively untapped talent pool for the maritime sector. Barriers to the employment of women in seafaring roles include: the culture of the occupation; lack of knowledge, awareness – and visibility – of women at sea; and slow development of effective policies and strategies to recruit and retain women seafarers.[13] Technology, automation and digitisation of the maritime industry present opportunities both to relocate more roles onshore whilst also for promoting workforce diversity – including the inclusion of women. The practical impact of long periods away from family and social support – as well as issues of job insecurity and risk of injury – are endured by *all* seafarers and will therefore continue to be factors impacting the attractiveness of the sector. However, there are specific issues that disproportionately impact women, such as comfort in using general living, dining, recreation and gym social spaces when in the minority.[14] Breaking the cycle to develop a more inclusive workplace culture for all will require proactive communications from careers services, which emphasise the sector's career opportunities, including world-recognised training, responsibility at early career stage, as well as highly competitive earning potential.

Action to realise a cultural shift in the workplace will promote better seafarer social health, but attention must also focus on improving mental and physical health of seafarers. Societal trends of poor health behaviours (i.e. physical inactivity, poor diet quality, insufficient and poor quality sleep, alcohol consumption and tobacco/nicotine use) contributing to increasing prevalence of non-communicable disease and obesity, are worsening in the UK civilian population.[15] Indeed, overweight and obesity present major global public health concerns,[16] impacting many societies from which the maritime sector recruits its workforce – and continues to represent a significant UK risk.[17] The associated health impacts are well documented in terms of increasing numbers of people living with one or more chronic non-communicable diseases, poorer mental health,[18] reduced quality of life and higher mortality rates.[19]

Seafarers' health protection is a core responsibility of the maritime industry, where cardiovascular diseases, transmittable diseases, mental health, fatigue and stress represent the most widely studied seafarer health issues.[20] Of concern, is the higher prevalence of overweight and obesity amongst seafarers compared with the general population,[21] and this impacts both occupational physical abilities as well as performance of safety-critical tasks at sea. Presently, maritime occupational health in the UK – and fitness to deploy to sea – is overseen by the MCA through a process of (self-report) medical history, medical examination and subsequent certification as 'fit for duty'.[22] This process screens for occupationally safety-critical factors, such as eyesight (including colour blind-ness) and hearing, but also risk of non-communicable disease (e.g. cardiovascular disease, lung disease and diabetes), epilepsy/unexplained loss of consciousness, as well as weight-related health risk. Seafarers with a Body Mass Index over 35 kg.m^{-2} are also required to undertake a physical fitness test to evidence occupational fitness. Living with over-weight and obesity profoundly affects individual health, but also impacts employers, organisational productivity and the wider economy.[23] Interventions to support and promote the (physical and mental) health, wellbeing and performance of the UK's maritime workforce must therefore recognise the complexity of interconnected health problems.[24] Whilst the sector is aware of an urgent need to support seafarer mental health,[25] physical health and wellbeing remain a concern.

This section has identified the people challenges facing the maritime sector, and specifically those employees at sea. Factors of isolation, loneliness, disconnection at sea amidst a connected internet-enabled world, sea-time impacting work-life balance and the ability to enact healthy behaviours, as well as the very real dangers experienced by employees in seafaring roles, reduce the attractiveness of the occupation to new entrants – and hence present risks to growing the workforce to support *Maritime Britain in the 21st Century*. These challenges will affect all seafarers but could be more intensely experienced by those representing minority groups at sea who may experience higher levels of social isolation. The effect of the unique seafarer's occupational environment on individual social, mental and physical health must be recognised. However, in acknowledging that the work setting is complicit in these challenges, and indeed contributing to employee poor health outcomes, this raises the possibility of proactively managing working practices and the setting to improve seafarer health, wellbeing and performance.

In recognising the value of the maritime sector to the national economy, made possible through the high productivity of the sector's workforce, the UK has committed to go beyond the minimum standards in supporting seafarer training, career progression, health and wellbeing. To lead the way in delivering on this intent, the maritime sector needs a coherent People strategy – that can be implemented across both shore-based and sea-facing contexts – to address both immediate and future People challenges.

A workplace Whole System Approach to Maritime Workforce Health Promotion

Approaches to addressing interconnected health problems in western societies – including their militaries – have historically focused upon the symptoms experienced by individuals, rather than root causes at the organisation (employer) level.[26] Adopting a Whole System Approach, recognising both individual and organisational responsibilities, provides a model for tackling complex health problems.[27] To this end, there is learning that could be shared with civilian organisations – and specifically to the maritime domain – from health-performance programmes implemented within the defined context of the Royal Navy (RN). The military context, and especially the RN maritime environment on ships and submarines, presents an occupational setting that is more amenable to strategic management with the aim of supporting workforce health and performance.[28] Indeed, within this hierarchical military environment, the impact of the constrained setting on sailor health behaviours must be acknowledged. Nevertheless, Dorance et al.[29] assert that preventable poor health outcomes would be more effectively targeted by military employers through community-based system approaches, and this could be readily extended to the operational maritime setting of a ship or submarine. Thus, the UK Ministry of Defence developed a holistic strategy to coordinate effective organisation-wide 'whole system' action on physical and mental health.[30]

Operationalising this system thinking, the RN is developing a holistic, pan-organisation, fully integrated, through-career approach to mitigating poor health and promoting sailor performance. Importantly, the RN has embedded civilian and military learning into a programme that is Leadership owned (to ensure prioritisation), managed through the Chain of Command (to ensure coordination and provide health opportunities), but acknowledges the importance of individual sailor knowledge and skills (in building capability) to realise workforce health outcomes. This recognises that positive sailor health *Behaviours* can only occur if: the individual has the *Capability* to engage in the behaviour; the setting (managed by the Leaders through the Chain of Command) presents *Opportunity* that make the behaviour possible and/or prompts the behaviour; and the individual is *Motivated* to undertake the behaviour (i.e. COM-B model).[31] As poor health behaviours tend to cluster,[32] adopting a multi-level, multi-component Whole System Approach, provides a means of tackling complex, interconnected health problems through intervening on multiple determinants.

Why Invest in (Maritime) Workplace Health Promotion?

Embedding an effective, theory-based workplace health promotion intervention onboard RN ships and submarines would realise health and performance outcome benefits to enable individuals to thrive. Organisationally, such Whole System Approach programmes could realise benefits in terms of: increasing staff recruitment and retention; reducing sickness absenteeism; improving presenteeism and productivity; fostering a more satisfied and content workforce; whilst also realising safer working practices.[33] Nevertheless, determining the cost-benefit of such activities has proved difficult to measure. Cost is assigned to things that are easily counted; the direct and indirect impacts of workforce poor health have been difficult to count and hence difficult to assign cost. Moreover, public sector organisations tend to focus upon the number of employees turning up for work today, not always their effectiveness or productivity; their outputs and impact might prove difficult to measure where profit *per se* is not the primary outcome. For example, how might the mitigation of something not happening be measured (i.e. injury or illness), when the workforce is insufficient for the number of jobs to be completed, so the capacity for undertaking additional tasks is reduced? This can result in trade-offs between organisational outputs and individual training and health promotion needs.

Health economics is used to assess the most efficient and effective allocation of finite healthcare resources to maximise (ill-health remediating) benefit. Resource allocation models are based on ameliorating disease burden (i.e. a surviving workforce), not promoting performance (i.e. a thriving workforce). Financial value is determined from the opportunity cost of the poor health (injury and illness) burden. In contrast, health promotion interventions deliver benefit and value through enhancing human performance. But realising this value is time- and context-biased: individuals *value* free-choice (health behaviour) today rather than future ill-health prevention; organisations, especially with stretched workforces, *value* delivery of outputs today rather than future employee health outcomes. Social Return on Investment provides a means of undertaking cost-benefit estimations from complex whole system interventions. Both tangible benefits (e.g. productivity, outputs) and non-tangible benefits (e.g. attractive workplace, reputation) can be determined based on prescribed, conservative cost and value assumptions. Health promotion interventions, which mitigate poor health, are cheaper than future healthcare costs for remediating poor health outcomes.[34] Implementing effective workplace Whole System Approach interventions across the maritime sector, where seafarers are constrained to the ship workplace 24/7 for extended periods, could realise both workforce supply benefits as well as being more cost efficient to the employer.

Both civilian and RN maritime employers have a duty of care to support a healthy and fit workforce, where healthful behaviours are the foundation for occupational health and fitness. Nevertheless, despite recognition of the issues, poor health behaviours remain common and persistent – and employer support *in situ* inconsistent – contributing to workforce issues that impact capacity and capability. Adopting person-centred, context-relevant workplace health promotion interventions, organised through adopting a Whole System Approach, would assist the sector ameliorate some of its more complex workforce issues.

Towards a Workforce Health and Performance Model for Maritime Britain in the 21st Century

The biggest challenges impacting the maritime sector as a whole going forward in the 21st century include: the combined impacts of climate change; the persisting global economic crisis following the COVID pandemic; security risks from hostile states, terrorism and piracy; and cyber risks from threat actors to digital networks.[35] All these risks necessitate a more capable, more agile, more resilient *high-performing workforce* in shore-based and seafaring roles. Conversely, pressures to reduce industry through-life costs are driving technological developments and digitisation to support *lean crewing* models at sea, independent of sector workforce shortages.[36] There is, however, learning that could be adopted from the RN experience to assist in solving complex, maritime sector-wide human resource – capacity, capability and cultural – conundrums.

The seafaring role will continue to present ever greater risk to employees; it is a climatically arduous work environment, which is further deteriorating with climate change, as well as facing ever-present threats from hostile agents. Deploying fewer people into harm's way (lean crewing) by using current, near-term and future technologies (digitisation and automation) could leverage *virtual mass* – in terms of capacity and capability – whilst managing organisational risks. Nevertheless, such risk transfer options provided by technology give rise to more complex marine systems, where these systems could present both cyber vulnerabilities as well as not necessarily reducing the need for people. In this sense, maritime sector people challenges could be regarded as being changed rather than reduced.

Developments in marine systems – supporting all aspects of shipping operations – are requiring a more talented, highly skilled and more present workforce. The maritime sector must therefore compete with other industries that present a more attractive proposition to potential employees, whose career needs and wants are very different to those of a generation ago. A maritime workforce model simplistically and exclusively focussing upon greater technology, to both transfer risk and improve efficiency, will introduce new risks in terms of cyber vulnerabilities, as well as more general risks of degraded adaptability and resilience – where people *per se* can be an organisation's most agile, adaptable, and inherently robust *asset*.

Action towards climate sustainability

Due to the reliance of shipping on fossil fuels, such as heavy fuel oil and marine gas oil, the maritime sector is a significant contributor to global greenhouse gas production.[37] Urgent action is therefore needed to reduce emissions and ensure the sector plays its part in securing a more sustainable future. Climate change *per se*, giving rise to more extreme environmental conditions and weather fluctuations, impacts workforce health[38] and performance. As well as specific and direct harm due to more erratic and dangerous weather and sea states, there are also general, public health threats, including climatic impacts of extreme temperatures and altered infectious disease trends.

The maritime sector is tackling its environmental and sustainability challenges through modernising working practices at both macro- and micro-levels with the intent of improving gross efficiencies. Both shore- and sea-activities are benefitting from the collection and strategic use of big data, coupled with machine learning and operational analysis techniques, to optimise shipping movements. Shore-based activities are being addressed through Composite Index Creation for port regions. Multi-uses of the sea initiatives are cohering understanding on sea-facing activities. The ability to quantitatively assess the environmental impact of port activities in real time, through Composite Index Creation, is vital for timely intervention on climatic impacts – such as pollution.[39]

Development of the maritime economy has resulted in an increasingly crowded ocean space. As well as shipping activities, other interested parties comprise: coastal and maritime tourism – including the cruise ship industry; fisheries, aquaculture and blue biotechnology industries;

inshore and offshore renewable energy production; maritime infrastructure – such as pipelines and cables; as well as oil, gas, sand and mineral extraction activities. Strategically combining competing claims for space, especially where such claims appear mutually exclusive, is achievable and can provide more sustainable and mutually beneficial outcomes.[40] Nevertheless, air pollution compliance challenges in shipping emissions, as well as controls to protect the marine geology amidst natural resource extraction, highlight a need for advanced data analytics; overcoming timely data handling challenges in large-scale environmental impact data sets remains a priority.[41] Successfully addressing environ-mental challenges will require: global strategies and maritime spatial planning; access to (big) data and (machine learning) data analytics from remote and accurate surveillance systems; as well as sectoral education and incentives to attract the right people, trained in the required knowledge, and the skills to uphold sector-wide sustainability regulations.[42]

Action towards economic sustainability

The maritime domain can be viewed as a sociotechnical system, emphasising the inherent interaction between humans, technology, and organisations onboard and between ships (at sea within the marine environment) and shore (including the littoral environs).[43] The collaboration between humans and autonomous systems in the maritime domain is an adaptive team characteristic, impacted by human and situational demands, presenting challenges in terms of the allocation of responsibility,[44] but also presenting opportunities. Whilst digitisation and automation can expedite decision-making, there will be an enduring requirement for people to exercise judgement – especially where there is ethical complexity and/or ambiguity.

The use of maritime Unmanned Autonomous Vehicles (UAV) or drones – operating surface, subsurface or aerially over water – can mitigate health and safety risks to people as well as provide economic benefits.[45] Such craft can effectively replace humans for tasks including: vessel hull and remote infrastructure inspections (e.g. offshore cable, pipeline or wind turbine); area mapping and surveying; humanitarian search and rescue; real-time strategic surveillance; and the rapid transportation of high-value (with respect to time and/or cost) small-scale inventory. The use of UAV in the maritime domain depends on cross-sectoral investment in open-ocean digital architecture. Such networks offer multi-use and technology transfer collaboration opportunities,[46] as well as bridging the digital divide to support seafarer isolation and mental health. However, the necessary national (between industries) and international (between nations) partnering also presents risks and vulnerabilities.

The RN is working with industry and academia, as well as international collaborations across NATO and Five Eyes communities, to explore '... *the power of technology to make the world a safer place.*'[47] Partial solutions to address many repetitive or hazardous maritime tasks and/or tasks that can be performed at reach (e.g. surveying or surveillance), reducing costs and/or risk, can be realised from UAV. However, current technologies do not support all necessary maritime work (e.g. the carrying out of all repair and maintenance aspects following remote inspection); many situations still require human access and skilled remediation work to be undertaken *in situ*. The integration of AI, autonomy and UAV in maritime operations has the potential to enhance navigation safety and reduce maritime accidents. Human error can be reduced through sociotechnical interaction, drawing on methods such as the Functional Resonance Analysis Method (FRAM) to analyse how functions and/or activities might best be undertaken.[48] Nevertheless, accelerated adoption of digital technologies again requires accelerated (people) education and training in these technologies.[49]

Automation and lean crewing are viewed by many as a means of reducing the required workforce, and hence reducing labour costs and/or addressing capacity constraints. While lean crewing may involve fewer people in specific locations, it does not necessarily equate to reducing the total number of 'crew' members; the intent is to reduce the numbers of people in high-threat environments.[50] The focus of lean crewing is to optimise the skills and roles of existing crew, requiring greater crew agility, rather than simply reducing numbers *per se*.[51] Indeed, whilst lean practices can lead to lower job autonomy, they also improve job content for most employees, indicating a complex relationship between indepen-dence and crew size.[52] Additionally, the impact of neuro-technology on maritime and port security – as well as growing concerns of maritime piracy, armed robbery, terrorism, and disruptive tech-nologies – underscore the need for enhanced security measures, which in turn place ever increasing pressures on human resources.[53]

The RN, and the maritime sector more generally, are amidst a time of profound transformation, driven by both technological advancements as well as economic necessity. Integrating digitisation, AI and process automation can reduce required personnel numbers and the physical work demands on seafarers – especially for repetitive tasks. However, system development, implementation and maintenance require a workforce with specialised knowledge and skills. Recruiting individuals proficient in science, technology, engineering, and mathematics is therefore paramount, but competition for attracting and retaining such talent is high. As well as being adaptable, lifelong learners to keep pace with technological advancements, these individuals must be more alert and vigilant than ever before; the greatest strengths of advanced marine systems can also be their greatest vulnerability as global cyber threats escalate. Building a diverse and inclusive workforce is essential for maximising access to such talent and fostering innovation. The RN is taking action to address systemic gender and ethnic disparities through: targeted recruitment from underrepresented groups to harness '… *diversity of thought, skill and talent*';[54] and modernisation of the training pipeline to build and promote a stronger, more inclusive and more resilient workforce.[55]

Towards a Workforce Health and Performance Model

> "*The UK's* [People] *vision for 2050 is a diverse and rewarded workforce with a focus on good maritime welfare that will set a global benchmark for the sector*".
>
> Department of Transport. (2019). Maritime 2050; Navigating the Future.

Given the people-focussed strategic intent for a future maritime workforce, what will be required for Britain to, indeed, '… *go beyond the minimum standards in supporting seafarer training, career progression, health and wellbeing*' in addressing immediate and future people challenges? As discussed, the occupational setting for seafarers has a direct impact upon both physical and mental health. Technology could be utilised to improve sea connectivity, for organisational sustainability and economic benefit, but also to support the physical and mental health of the maritime workforce. Addressing the digital divide between shore- and sea-based workers can also provide solutions to support health and performance interventions, whilst delivering the autonomous and AI capabilities required for a modernised maritime sector. Nevertheless, it must be acknowledged that such a future of maritime autonomy raises cybersecurity, trust, and seafarers' situational awareness as critical considerations.

Highly automated vessels present sector opportunities, but (potentially) smaller (leaner) crews raises new human factors challenges and risks. Seafarer responsibilities and workload need careful man-agement (i.e. reducing the workload through autonomy could reduce situational awareness, but if the workload is too high this could increase stress and human error). Successful implementation of maritime automation systems can only be achieved by understanding the complex interactions between people, tasks, vessels and systems.

The implications of AI and autonomy in naval operations extend to psychological and physical well-being of personnel. The role of *grit* (i.e. courage and determination despite difficulties), as an individual trait impacting organisational performance, is being studied in the context of personnel selection and development for AI-enabled naval operations.[56] Additionally, the need for greater integration of organisational training theory into strategies for developing and implementing workplace resilience training has been emphasised. Indeed, the importance of addressing psychological resilience in the context of AI-enabled naval operations has been highlighted.[57]

Looking forward to a future 21st century maritime workforce, more working adults are reporting long-term health conditions across the UK, which will continue to increase beyond 2030.[58] More people will be out of the workforce on ill-health grounds, but there will also be more people in work with work-limiting health conditions. There are gender (wo-men), ethnicity and age (older) trends to current and projected employee work-limiting condition prevalence. It should be urgently noted that these prevalence trends of work-limiting conditions (i.e. poor mental health, musculoskeletal health and cardiovascular health) are increasing fastest among younger workers and those entering the workforce. As such, to break these patterns of poor national health – and specifically poor health in work – all employers must develop trans-formational ways to support employees to remain '… *well in work.*' Adopting person-centred, context-relevant workplace health promotion interventions, organised as a Leader-owned, management delivered Whole System Approach, could assist the sector ameliorate some of its workforce capability and capacity challenges. This would pave the way to ensuring a secure and prosperous maritime Britain in the 21st Century, and beyond.

1. Centre for Economic and Business Research (Cebr). (2022). State of the Maritime Nation 2019 Report – Maritime UK. (From: https://www.maritimeuk.org/media-centre/publications/state-maritime-nation-report-2022/; Accessed 20 Dec 2023).

2. Matsuzaki K. (2016). The main global economic and social challenges from trade union point of view. Workshop on Maritime Clusters and Global Challenges 50th Anniversary of the OECD Working Party on Shipbuilding. (From: https://www.oecd.org/sti/ind/Session%201_d%20-%20Kan%20Matsuzaki%20-%20Web.pdf; Accessed 20 Dec 2023).

3. Department of Transport. (2019). Maritime 2050; Navigating the Future. (From: https://assets.publishing.service.gov.uk/media/5e6a248786650c7272f4c59d/Maritime_2050_Report.pdf; Accessed 20 Dec 2023).

4. Ward D. (2016). How can the marine industry counteract its aging workforce? (From: https://www.maritimeprofessional.com/news/marine-industry-counteract-aging-workforce-294834; Accessed 20 Dec 2023).

5. Bilir N.A., Scheit L., Dirksen-Fishcer M., Terschuren C., Herold R., Harth V., Oldenburg M. (2023). Accidents, diseases and health complaints among seafarers on German-flagged container ships. *BMC Public Health*. 23: 963.

6. Department for Transport. (2023). Seafarers in the UK Shipping Industry – 2022 (Revised). (From: https://www.gov.uk/government/statistics/seafarers-in-the-uk-shipping-industry-2022/seafarers-in-the-uk-shipping-industry-2022#contents; Accessed 20 Dec 2023).

7. International Chamber of Shipping. (2021). Seafarer Workforce Report. (From: https://www.ics-shipping.org/publication/seafarer-workforce-report-2021-edition/; Accessed 20 Dec 2023).

8. Maritime and Coastguard Agency. (2014). Support for maritime training (SMarT). (From: https://www.gov.uk/guidance/support-for-maritime-training-smart; Accessed 20 Dec 2023).

9. Fraser Nash. (2017). Support for Maritime Training Scheme Review. FNC 51444/44997. (From: https://assets.publishing.service.gov.uk/media/5a81dfc1ed915d74e6234948/support-for-maritime-training-review.pdf; Accessed 20 Dec 2023).

10. Oxford Economics. (2016). Value for money assessment of the Support for Maritime Training Scheme. (From: https://assets.publishing.service.gov.uk/media/5a821babe5274a2e87dc12ec/support-for-maritime-training-review-annex-a.pdf; Accessed 20 Dec 2023).

11. Department of Transport. (2018). Written statement to Parliament; Support for maritime training. (From: https://www.gov.uk/government/speeches/support-for-maritime-training; Accessed 20 Dec 2023).

12. Office for National Statistics. (2023). Data Set: EMP 13; Employment by industry. (From: https://www.ons.gov.uk/employmentandlabourmarket/peopleinwork/employmentandemployeetypes/datasets/employmentbyindustryemp13; Accessed 20 Dec 2023).

13. Kitada M. (2021). Women seafarers: An analysis of barriers to their employment. In: Gekara V.O., Sampson H. (Eds.). The World of the Seafarer; Qualitative Accounts of Working in the Global Shipping Industry. Springer: Cham, Switzerland, pp. 64-76.

14. The Mission to Seafarers. (2022). Women Seafarers Report 2022; Beyond the 2% - Women Seafarers and their Lives at Sea: Reflecting on Our Call to Care (From: https://www.missiontoseafarers.org/wp-content/uploads/The-Mission-to-Seafarers-Women-Seafarers-Report-2022.pdf; Accessed 20 Dec 2023).

15. Everest G., Marshall L., Fraser C., Briggs A. (2022). Addressing the leading risk factors for ill health. A review of Government policies tackling smoking, poor diet, physical inactivity and harmful alcohol use in England. London, UK, The Health Foundation.

16. Organisation for Economic Cooperation and Development (OECD) (2019). The Heavy Burden of Obesity: The Economics of Prevention. OECD Health Policy Studies, OECD Publishing; Paris, France. (From: https://doi.org/10.1787/67450d67-en; Accessed 20 Dec 2023).

17. UK Parliament (2023). Obesity Statistics. (From: https://commonslibrary.parliament.uk/research-briefings/sn03336/#:~:text=Adult%20obesity%20in%20England,is%20classified%20as%20'overweight'; Accessed 20 Dec 2023).

18. Roberts RE et al. (2003). Prospective Association Between Obesity and Depression: Evidence from the Alameda County Study. Int J Obes Relat Metab Disord; 27: 514-521; & Penedo F.J., Dahn J.R. (2005). Exercise and wellbeing: A review of mental and physical health benefits associated with physical activity. Curr Opin Psychiatry. 18(2): 189-193.

19. Flegal K et al. (2007). Cause-specific excess deaths associated with underweight, overweight, and obesity. JAMA; 298(17): 2028-37.

20. Li X., Zhou Y., Yuen K.F. (2022). (2022). A systematic review on seafarer health: Conditions, antecedents and interventions. Transport Policy. 122: 11-25; & Sampson H., Ellis N. (2019). Seafarers' mental health and wellbeing. Institute of Occupational Safety and Health Research Report. (From: https://orca.cardiff.ac.uk/id/eprint/127214/1/seafarers-mental-health-wellbeing-full-report.pdf; Accessed 20 Dec 2023).

21. Nittari G., Tomassoni D., Di Canio M., Traini E., Pirillo I., Minciacchi A., Amenta F. (2019). Overweight among seafarers working on board merchant ships. BMC Public Health. 19: 45. https://doi.org/10.1186/s12889-018-6377-6.

22. Maritime and Coastguard Agency. (2023). Seafarers medical certification guidance. (From: https://www.gov.uk/guidance/seafarers-medical-certification-guidance#what-is-a-seafarer; Accessed 20 Dec 2023).

23. Fallowfield J.L., Carins J. (2023). A work-based whole system approach to improving diet behaviours; realising and measuring the health benefits. In preparation.

24. Public Health England. (2019). Whole systems approach to obesity A guide to support local approaches to promoting a healthy weight. (From: https://assets.publishing.service.gov.uk/media/5d396e7140f0b604de59fde9/Whole_systems_approach_to_obesity_guide.pdf; Accessed 20 Dec 2023).

25. Maritime and Coastguard Agency. (2022). MCA launches digital Wellbeing at Sea Tool to support seafarer health and wellbeing. (From: https://www.gov.uk/government/news/mca-launches-digital-wellbeing-at-sea-tool-to-support-seafarer-health-and-wellbeing; Accessed 20 Dec 2023).

26. Teyhen DS, Robbins D, Ryan BA. (2018). Promoting and Sustaining Positive Personal Health Behaviors – Putting the Person First. Military Medicine: 183(suppl_3):213–9. Available from: https://academic.oup.com/milmed/article/183/suppl_3/213/5194604.

27. Public Health England. (2019). Whole systems approach to obesity A guide to support local approaches to promoting a healthy weight. (From: https://assets.publishing.service.gov.uk/media/5d396e7140f0b604de59fde9/Whole_systems_approach_to_obesity_guide.pdf; Accessed 20 Dec 2023).

28. Shaw A. (2019). Applying a whole systems approach to improve the health behaviours of Royal Naval personnel. PhD Thesis, University of Southampton, UK.

29. Dorrance K. A., et al. (2018). Toward a national conversation on health: disruptive intervention and the transformation from health care to health. Military Medicine 183(suppl 3): 193-197.

30. Ministry of Defence (2022). Defence People Health and Wellbeing Strategy 2022-2027. (From: https://modgovuk.sharepoint.com/sites/intranet/SitePages/hwb-strategy-2022-2027.aspx; Accessed 20 Dec 2023).

31. Michie S., et al. (2011). The behaviour change wheel: a new method for characterising and designing behaviour change interventions. *Implementation Science* 6: 42.

32. Aspy CB, Mold JW, Thompson DM, et al (2008) Integrating Screening and Interventions for Unhealthy Behaviors into Primary Care Practices. *American Journal of Preventive Medicine* 35:S373–S380. https://doi.org/10.1016/j.amepre.2008.08.015.

33. Hassard J., Wang D., Cox T., Muylaert K., Namysł A., Kazenas A., Flaspöler E. (2012). Motivation for employers to carry out workplace health promotion. European Agency for Safety and Health at Work Report. ISBN: 978-92-9191-999-4 (From: https://osha.europa.eu/sites/default/files/motivation-employers.pdf; Accessed 20 Dec 2023).

34. Kimsey L., Hoburg A., Olaiya S., Jones K.D., Richard P. (2018). A systems approach to person-centric health economics. *Military Medicine*. 183 (11/12): 233-238.

35. United Nations Conference on Trade and Development. (2023). Review of Maritime Transport; Report. (From: https://unctad.org/publication/review-maritime-transport-2023#:~:text=Maritime%20trade%20is%20expected%20to, resilient%20future%20for%20maritime%20transport.; Accessed 20 Dec 2023).

36. Chilcott J., Kennedy N. (2018). Enabling lean manning through automation. Conference: International Ship Control Systems Symposium. 02-04 Oct. Strathclyde, Glasgow, UK.

37. Department of Transport. (2019). Reducing the maritime sector's contribution to air pollution and climate change: Maritime emission reduction options. (From: https://assets.publishing.service.gov.uk/media/5d25f15ce5274a586197f093/maritime-emission-reduction-options.pdf; Accessed: 20 Dec 2023).

38. McMichael A.J., Lindgren E. (2011). Climate change: present and future risks to health, and necessary responses (Review). *Journal of Internal Medicine.* 270: 401–413.

39. Miloševic T., Pilicic S., Široka M., Úbeda I.L., Pellicer A.B., Garcia R.V., Salvador C.E.P., Garnier C., Tserga E., Traven L. (2023). The Port Environmental Index: A Quantitative IoT-Based Tool for Assessing the Environmental Performance of Ports. *Journal of Marine Science and Engineering.* 11: 1969. https://doi.org/10.3390/jmse11101969.

40. Bocci M., Sangiuliano S.J., Sarretta A., Ansong J.O., Buchanan B., Kafas A., et al. (2019). Multi-use of the sea: A wide array of opportunities from site-specific cases across Europe. *PLoS ONE.* 14(4): e0215010. https://doi.org/10.1371/journal.pone.0215010.

41. Bui, K. and Perera, L. (2019). The compliance challenges in emissions control regulations to reduce air pollution from shipping.. https://doi.org/10.1109/oceanse.2019.8867420.

42. Przedrzymirska J., Zaucha J., Calado H., Lukic I., Bocci M., Ramieri E., Varona M.C., Barbanti A., Depellegrin D., de Sousa Vergílio M. et al. (2021). Multi-Use of the Sea as a Sustainable Development Instrument in Five EU Sea Basins. *Sustainability.* 13, 8159. https://doi.org/10.3390/su13158159.

43. Vries, L. (2017). Work as done? understanding the practice of sociotechnical work in the maritime domain. Journal of Cognitive Engineering and Decision Making, 11(3), 270-295. https://doi.org/10.1177/1555343417707664.

44. Ellwart, T. and Schauffel, N. (2023). Human-autonomy teaming in ship inspection: psychological perspectives on the collaboration between humans and self-governing systems., 343-362. https://doi.org/10.1007/978-3-031-25296-9_18.

45. Frederiksen M.H., Knudsen M.P. (2018). Drones for offshore and maritime missions: Opportunities and barriers. Centre for Integrated Innovation Management; Innovation Fund of Denmark. (From: https://industriensfond.dk/wp-content/uploads/uniflip/1104464.pdf; Accessed 20 Dec 2023).

46. Patterson, R., O'Donnell, E., Udyawer, V., Brassington, G., Groom, R., & Campbell, H. (2022). Uncrewed surface vessel technological diffusion depends on cross-sectoral investment in open-ocean archetypes: a systematic review of usv applications and drivers. *Frontiers in Marine Science*, 8. https://doi.org/10.3389/fmars.2021.736984.

47. Royal Navy. (2023). Unmanned Warrior. (From: https://www.royalnavy.mod.uk/news-and-latest-activity/operations/united-kingdom/unmanned-warrior ; Accessed 20 Dec 2023).

48. Dominguez-Péry, C., Vuddaraju, L., Corbett-Etchevers, I., & Tassabehji, R. (2021). Reducing maritime accidents in ships by tackling human error: a bibliometric review and research agenda. *Journal of Shipping and Trade*, 6(1). https://doi.org/10.1186/s41072-021-00098-y.

49. Kim, T., Sharma, A., Bustgaard, M., Gyldensten, W., Nymoen, O., Tusher, H., ... & Nazir, S. (2021). The continuum of simulator-based maritime training and education. *Wmu Journal of Maritime Affairs*, 20(2), 135-150. https://doi.org/10.1007/s13437-021-00242-2.

50. Rigby, J. and Savage, I. (2022). Highly autonomous warship technology: bridging the gap to autonomy. Autonomous Ships 2022. https://doi.org/10.3940/rina.as.2022.07.

51. Parker, S. K. (2003). Longitudinal effects of lean production on employee outcomes and the mediating role of work characteristics. *Journal of Applied Psychology*, 88(4), 620-634. https://doi.org/10.1037/0021-9010.88.4.620.

52. Hasle, P., Bojesen, A., Jensen, P., & Bramming, P. (2012). Lean and the working environment: a review of the literature. *International Journal of Operations & Production Management*, 32(7), 829-849. https://doi.org/10.1108/01443571211250103.

53. Ibrahim, A. (2022). The impact of neurotechnology on maritime port security—hypothetical port. *Journal of Transportation Security*, 15(3-4), 119-139. https://doi.org/10.1007/s12198-022-00253-x.

54. Royal Navy. (2023). Opportunities for All. (From: https://www.royalnavy.mod.uk/organisation/our-people/opportunities-for-all; Accessed 20 Dec 2023).

55. Capita. (2023). Capita-led Team Fisher completes final milestone of Royal Navy modernisation contract. (From: https://www.capita.com/news/capita-led-team-fisher-completes-final-milestone-royal-navy-modernisation-contract; Accessed 20 Dec 2023).

56. Lee, J. (2022). The role of grit in organizational performance during a pandemic. *Frontiers in Psychology*, 13. https://doi.org/10.3389/fpsyg.2022.929517.

57. Crane, M., Falon, S., Kho, M., Moss, A., & Adler, A. (2022). Developing resilience in first responders: strategies for enhancing psychoeducational service delivery.. *Psychological Services*, 19(Suppl 2), 17-27. https://doi.org/10.1037/ser0000439.

58. Atwell S., Vriend M., Rocks C., Finch D., Farrington-Douglas J. (2023). What we know about the UK's working-age health challenge. The Health Foundation Report. (From: https://www.health.org.uk/publications/long-reads/what-we-know-about-the-uk-s-working-age-health-challenge?utm_campaign=14222586_Commission%20for%20Healthier%20Working%20Lives%20launch%20%20Nov%2023%20%20WARM&utm_medium=email&utm_source=The%20Health%20Foundation&dm_i=4Y2,8GU7U,4QHAVX,YZB0G,1; Accessed 20 Dec 2023).

From Deep Waters into the Light: Locating Seamen's Women in Naval Social History

Melanie Holihead

Introduction

Twenty years have passed since Nicholas Rodger lamented the existence of 'an enormous void of ignorance' in naval social history.[1] The void in question concerned 'not the minority of women who went to sea, but the wives and mothers who stayed at home, bringing up small children, earning their living as best they might while their menfolk were at sea, enduring years of absence and uncertainty.' These women, Rodger asserted, comprised 'the female half of the naval community as a whole', yet in naval history they were, and to an extent still are, almost entirely absent.

This chapter both considers that absence and sets out recent findings which reveal the women's relationship with and perceived status within the civilian community. Drawing upon original nineteenth-century source data on family background and marital age, it proposes an 'other-ness' distinguishing the naval community of the past from its civilian neighbours. Regretting the absence of naval women's voices in the historical record, and mindful of technological advances affecting the connectedness of ship and shore, it argues for preservation of ephemeral twenty-first century source material – material which future maritime historians may use when bringing to light the lives, experiences and social conditions of present-day naval women.

Invisible Women

The decades that followed Rodger's observation were not without product, for there were worthy attempts to recognise and fill (if only in part) that 'void of ignorance' in naval social history. For example, Margarette Lincoln's *Naval Wives and Mistresses* provided insight into the lives of naval officers' wives, and a glimpse of the social conditions experienced by lower-deck men's spouses.[2] The time-span of Cheryl

Fury's two-volume *Social History of English Seamen* was broader, her focus being on seamen rather than officers.[3] Alongside these, however, were works which focused on so-called 'female tars' (an eye-catching but misleading term), and/or the unrepresentative minority of women who for a variety of reasons, and in a variety of capacities, went to sea. Popular though they were, when it came to the shoreside community these other works contributed little breadth or weight, one going so far as to declare, without evidence, that naval women often resorted to prostitution during their husbands' absence, and asserting, again without evidence, that many a prostitute became a naval wife – slurs which, if applied to other groups in society, would be regarded as pejorative and discriminatory.

That there existed such a void in history; that few historians have been moved even to try to fill the void; and that others, on the basis of scant archival research or cited sources, were permitted by their publishers to dismiss seamen's women as prostitutes, speaks volumes. Naval history was 'not interested in the vast majority of sweethearts and wives, mothers, daughters, sisters, cousins and aunts who made up what we might call the female half of the naval community, whose lives were shaped by the absence of their menfolk in the Navy, but who did not go to sea.'[4] It wasn't as if the women were absent from the record: they were simply ignored, passed over or derided. True, there were approving nods toward their providing support for generations of seamen. Less acknowledged were the qualities required to deliver that support: the women's resilience, self-determination, resourcefulness, independence and agency. Meanwhile, the actuality of their everyday lives, their living conditions, and what nowadays would be called their coping mechanisms, were almost completely ignored.

The Naval Welfare State

The very phrase 'seamen's women' is problematical. It reduces identifiable individuals to relative status, as extensions of their menfolk, worthy of attention only in their connection with the Navy. As an alternative, 'naval women' is useful but ambiguous, applicable to serving personnel and dependants alike. 'Seamen's women' implies relativity, yet as absolutes in their own right these women had individuality and identity. As absolutes, and in their relationship with both Navy and community, they merit recognition.

Their options and legal entitlements were limited by the political and cultural climate of the day, but collectively they had heft enough to affect naval policy, manpower and performance. Their heft revealed itself by proxy, via seamen's responses to the widespread suffering of the naval community on shore. The origins of this suffering lay in the inadequacy and irregularity of seamen's pay, and the absence of a mechanism for men at sea to maintain a trickle of income to their loved ones. When (as many did) naval dependants suffered poverty to the extent of facing destitution, mature and experienced men were prepared to abandon sea service in favour of better and more regularly-paid employment on land. By the early eighteenth century the Navy was forced to admit that if it were not to continue to lose its most valuable men, it must act.

To reduce the impact of prolonged breadwinner absence upon naval families (and by extension upon the Navy itself), one of the largest government bodies of the day was in 1728 moved to create a remittance system, the means by which seamen's dependants could receive financial support in their men's absence at sea.[5] In commerce and industry, entrepreneurs such as Cadbury and Salt would in due course provide facilities intended to enable their workforce to live healthy, virtuous and godly lives, thereby improving manufacturing output, upholding proprietors' Quaker principles, and maintaining profits. In setting up the remittance system, however, the Admiralty did not act out of religious conviction, altruism, the profit motive or humanitarian concern, but out of hard-nosed pragmatism a belief that seamen would be less inclined to abandon sea service if they knew their families had a regular source of income during ships' absence on commission.[6] Its motives were entirely self-serving. The women were simply part of an equation, a means to an end.

This recognition of a mutual dependence and moral obligation linking Navy and naval dependant contrasted sharply with the relationship between the British army and its dependants. Whereas the eighteenth-century sailor could use remittances to get money into the hands of his dependants at home, his soldier peer could not. There would, belatedly, be some provision for soldiers to remit money during the Crimean War, but fragile mechanisms and maladministration would mean some wives never received the sums sent them.[7] Indeed, from 1837 the law explicitly exempted soldiers from any obligation to maintain their dependants, and well into the mid-1860s, when Dickens inveighed against soldiers' wives being left 'without the smallest provision'; neither from army authorities nor parish might the soldier's wife be assured of assistance.[8] Though aware of distress experienced by soldiers' wives left behind when regiments were sent overseas, the army continued to reject proposals to advance wives part of their husbands' pay upon separation, arguing that this would require a change of book-keeping procedures.[9] Meanwhile, outwith the military, the whaling industry had its own, limited means of supporting whalers' wives. In the paternalistic culture of eighteenth-century Nantucket, a whaler's wife in need might be provided with goods or money by shipowners, but only in accordance with her husband's perceived creditworthiness, and as advances charged upon his earnings.[10] As for the merchant service, the Dutch East India Company had since the seventeenth century operated a support system through which 'money letters' allowed annual transfers of a portion of seamen's wages to families at home. British merchant seamen's families enjoyed no such benefit, nineteenth-century shipowners exploiting the image of feckless bachelor Jack to justify their denying the sober, responsible, married merchant seaman the means to support his family on shore.[11] Amid such cynicism, indifference and political caution, in establishing a remittance scheme benefitting the naval community the Royal Navy was breaking new ground.

Logistical difficulties, irregular pay, attorneys' charges and legal formality made the inaugural scheme and its successor less well-used than expected.[12] Stark ascribes this to the system's being intentionally complicated, its setting-up arrangements beyond the wit of most seamen.[13] A more plausible explanation lies in its only applying to seagoing men, and benefitting only wives; for most deep-sea sailors were young single men, and married men were not common at sea.[14] From remittances' shaky start in 1728 there nevertheless evolved a more effective and popular allotment system. By 1858 there were more than seventeen thousand allotments in force across the United Kingdom, supporting many tens of thousands of dependants in port towns, inland cities, remote islands and rural communities, two-thirds of recipients being located in Portsmouth, Devonport, Chatham and Sheerness.[15] Trusted and valued by men and dependants alike, the Royal Navy's allotment system survived into the 1980s when electronic banking rendered it redundant; even then, within the naval community, its passing was lamented.[16]

The Navy's investment in the allotment, and men's usage of it, are proof of its importance; yet beyond Rodger's description of remittances' inception, historians have given only brief nods to either system.[17] This is ironic, for just as allotment payments kept the wolf from many a naval woman's door, so allotment records enable naval women's history to be traced, reconstructed, and recognised. In ignoring the allotment system, naval historians have ignored its beneficiaries, 'the female half of the naval community as a whole'.[18]

Naval Wives: Caricature and Reality

Only recently digitised, Royal Navy ships' allotment registers capture a community of naval women (mothers, sisters, 'trustee' foster-carers of seamen's motherless children or orphaned under-age siblings, but primarily wives) whose homes lay anywhere from Cape Cornwall to Cape Wrath.[19] What they had in common was kinship with, and financial dependence on, a lower-deck Royal Navy seaman. Preserved as series ADM 27 in the National Archives at Kew, ships' allotment registers for 1795-1852 contain the names and addresses of thousands upon thousands of naval dependants, together with wives' dates and places of marriage, and the ages and places of baptism of children entrusted to allottee-foster carers.[20] These data allow the historian to trace seamen's dependants via civil and parish registers, to locate them within national and local censuses, and search for them in contemporary newspaper reportage. Correlation makes it possible to create genograms showing multi-generational naval service; to construct microhistories of named individuals; to map locations of dependants whose seamen had ship, rate or trade in common; to establish patterns of nuptiality, geographical mobility, occupation, household structure, longevity and cause of death; and to discern differences between naval and civilian communities. These broad and close-focus findings can also be set against aspects of seamen's lives, as revealed via ships' muster and description books, surgeons' logs and journals, and (from the mid-nineteenth century onward) individuals' service records.[21]

If 'it is the business of the historian to plunge into the deep waters of the past and to bring up vanished lives', it is both baffling and shameful that it has taken until the twenty-first century for naval historians to give seamen's women the attention they have deserved.[22] Contributing to this neglect may be a popular and longstanding misconception that 'we know about seamen's women'. We have, after all, seen them in cartoons and caricatures, etchings and paintings, heard them sung about in shanties and ballads. They appear as two polarised personæ: on the one hand as faithful Polly-on-the-Shore, on the other as port-town prostitute, the 'Pompey Brute' of popular literature.[23] We find the former, our sepia-tinted Faithful Polly, standing alone on a rocky outcrop, windswept jetty or cliff edge, waving a limp kerchief toward her husband's departing ship, or in a wretched garret, watching her small son play with his model boat, or collapsing in a surfeit of emotion at her returning husband's feet. The obverse of this wholesome image, the 'Pompey Brute', is depicted as a flinty-eyed, full-bosomed, poxed, mercenary, promiscuous creature,

'...[a] fighting ornament of the fair sex...of more than Amazonian stature, having a crimson countenance ... warlike features ... a tumid nose, scarred and battered brows ... blackened eyes ... a pair of brawny arms ... the Portsmouth Poll.'[24] In this guise she appears with bosom bared, tankard in fist, among a roistering group of pub drinkers. She sits wantonly astride Jack's knee, filches coin from his trouser pocket while he lies in post-coital slumber; or (per Rowlandson's sexually explicit caricature), *in flagrante* with Jack in an upper room heaving with coital couples, she cheerfully waves farewell through a brothel's open window as her previous punter's ship puts to sea.[25] Being morally acceptable, the 'Faithful Polly' image appealed to that part of the market which, as the nineteenth-century wore on and the naval Bluejacket distinguished himself as the nation's hero of Crimea, encouraged the wearing of sailor-collars by women unrelated to serving seamen, and sailor-suits by the offspring of shoemakers and pork butchers alike. As nudge-and-wink porn, however, the 'port-town whore' image appealed to quite another (and, we may surmise, more profitable) commercial interest. Later, warning of the dangers of venereal disease, it would be exploited to promote implementation of the Contagious Diseases Acts in garrison and port towns.[26]

What neither image recognised was what lay between these polarities. The unexceptional reality of the seaman's woman and her day-to-day life were not the stuff to titillate or sell copy. Like her predecessors of previous centuries and her twenty-first century successors, our mid-Victorian naval wife was an ordinary woman. She looked no different from her civilian peers. She was no better nourished, no more snazzily dressed. She carried no identification card, wore no uniform, badge or cap-tally, and apart from the absence of her spouse, and her everyday language containing terms more often heard on board ship, there was nothing to distinguish her from her civilian neighbours.[27] Her lived experience was, like theirs, the crowded streets and slum courts of port towns. Her accommodation was poorly constructed and often overcrowded. She bought water by the bucketful from communal pumps; paid rent to private landlords and poor rates to the parish; took in lodgers, or was one herself. True, she had her monthly allotment, that service-specific benefit denied to civilians; but thanks to a 'moiety cap' imposed by admiralty regulations, her allotment income was never more than half her seaman's already miserable wage; for some, it was a fraction of a half, mere shillings to last a calendar month. To stretch it out she participated in the 'economy of makeshift' by which poor women – naval, civilian, urban, rural – borrowed, loaned and traded such goods and skills as they possessed.[28] To combat solitude, and because it was economically prudent, she might relinquish her own household to live with her parent(s), with her married sisters, occasionally with fellow naval wives. She might take on poorly paid employment, usually as needlewoman, laundress or char. Sometimes she got drunk, misbehaved, took risks, was arrested. And by process of deduction, we must accept that sometimes she resorted to prostitution in order to survive. But so did her civilian neighbours: the sex trade was not restricted to the naval community alone.

None of this was newsworthy, or enough to mark her out as so very different from those civilian neighbours. Yet the seaman's woman *was* different. For a start, whereas civilian wives had husbands present to help, direct, take decisions, share the burden, protect or comfort them, seamen's wives managed unaided. They took decisions normally the province of husbands. They cared for their families, disciplined their children, managed their households, made ends meet, endured loneliness. They did everything their civilian peers did, but they did it alone. In their ability to 'take the helm' during their men's absence, in their seemingly perverse willingness to marry men whose occupations routinely took them away for most of their married lives, seaman's women singularised themselves. Speaking of her Portsea-resident naval wife ancestors, Light observes, 'These nineteenth-century women had to wear the trousers. Without their men they got on or they went under.'[29]

Their ability to keep themselves from 'going under' was acquired at an early age, as revealed in data extracted from parish marriage registers pertaining to naval and civilian couples who married in Portsea Island in the period January 1850-March 1851. These data revealed social and behavioural patterns differentiating the naval community from its civilian equivalent, an example of which concerns family background. In Fig. 1 we see that among fathers of naval brides the 29.6 per cent proportion of serving or former seamen was almost three times the 10.3 per cent found among fathers of civilians' brides, suggesting that seamen's daughters were three times more likely to marry sailors than were the daughters of the paternal basket makers, brewers, thatchers and grocers of the civilian group. If we include those brides' fathers whose occupations fell within an ambiguous 'possibly ex-RN' category (for example, carpenters, shipwrights, coopers), the difference becomes even more acute, the combined 44.9 per cent of seamen's brides with naval or ex-naval fathers outnumbering 10.3 per cent of equivalent civilian brides by almost four-and-a-half to one.

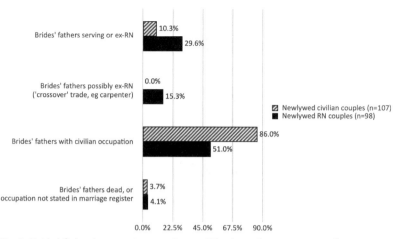

Fig. 1: Brides' fathers' occupations per Portsea Island parish marriage records 1850-51.

These seamen's brides had grown up in households in which it was normal for the breadwinner-paterfamilias to be absent for months, if not years on end; in which mothers were household heads, made the rules, maintained discipline, took decisions. In port town communities this domestic model was replicated in thousands of households, so it is highly likely that the seaman's daughter would mix with the daughters of neighbouring lower-deck seamen. When she visited these children's households she found a woman in charge, bearing the sort of responsibilities her own mother bore, demonstrating the same authority. To the seaman's daughter, this model was the norm, making the notion of a seaman-husband less alien.

It is arguable therefore that in a seaman-suitor's eyes a naval daughter possessed certain advantages, one of which was her being well prepared for life in a naval household. To the civilian suitor the seaman's daughter was a less attractive prospect, as witness the 86 per cent of civilian grooms who chose civilians' daughters as their brides. Civilian grooms were more likely to come from civilian backgrounds: Fig. 2 shows more than 90 per cent were themselves the sons of civilian fathers, hence as children they were unlikely to have experienced prolonged father-absence, or had a mother as household head, decision-maker, disciplinarian. They were more likely to mix in civilian circles, thereby meeting more civilian daughters than naval. Nepotism and/or hopes of occupational advancement via in-laws seem not to have played a part, for only sixteen of our 107 civilian grooms shared the same or similar occupation as their brides' civilian fathers, and then only in humble

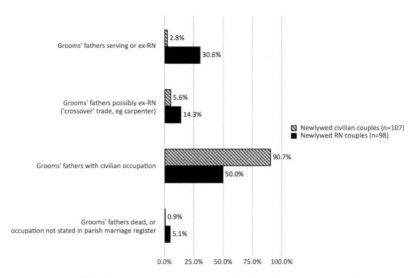

Fig. 2: Grooms' fathers' occupations per Portsea Island parish marriage records, 1850-51.

trades such as labourer, waterman, cordwainer and gardener. Yet here was an undeniable pattern whereby civilian grooms, themselves overwhelmingly the sons of civilian fathers, overwhelmingly chose the daughters of civilians as their brides. Less than ten per cent of civilian grooms married brides from naval backgrounds.

Other than pragmatism, happenstance and social and economic factors, what else could account for this trend? Might the figures suggest that civilian men found the very idea of the naval daughter unattractive, socially suspect? Given contemporary perceptions on womanhood and wifedom, this is not an unreasonable interpretation. The naval daughter's language may have been deemed unwomanly, arcane, too obviously nautical, too salty, too likely to betray her naval origins. She may have been suspected of sharing her menfolk's legendary promiscuity; of sharing, too, her mother's unfeminine self-reliance and resourcefulness, thereby increasing the likelihood of her exhibiting a lack of submissiveness unbecoming the modest mid-Victorian wife, and of expecting a married life offering independence and self-determination. Foreshadowing McKee's mid-twentieth century petty officer's recollection that naval daughters were urged to 'go out and get a sailor' because 'you get your money whether he's there or whether he isn't,' nineteenth-century naval daughters may have been suspected of presuming that half of their (civilian) husbands' wages would be handed over, just as it was in naval circles, for was it not common knowledge that their mothers pocketed their sailor-fathers' 'half-pay'?[30] The association – apocryphal or otherwise – of the sailor's woman with drunkenness and prostitution may also have been a red flag, especially in light of local newspapers' coverage of police court proceedings against sailors' wives.[31] The *Hampshire Telegraph* reported weekly on proceedings in Portsmouth police (magistrates') court.[32] Searches of these reports for references to female defendants' being the wives of butchers, watermen, pensioners, shipwrights, carpenters, smiths, painters, fishermen and bakers in years 1850-9 yielded just two results, yet in the same period the number of defendants referred-to as 'sailor's wife' was more than ten times greater, generating in the reader's mind a connection between 'sailor's wife' and crime. Indeed, the very term 'sailor's wife' was used – and understood – to imply sexual availability, as witness the complainant in an affiliation (paternity) case stating that '… she put a ring on her finger, to pass for a married woman … telling one of the men she was a sailor's wife, as usual, meaning the joke.'[33] The associating of naval daughters with Jack Tar's worst traits was not the only thing likely to discourage the civilian paramour; for in some suitors' minds there may have lurked the unutterable suspicion that a naval daughter would in time find her civilian husband dull, unadventurous, too restrictive, too conventional, too often simply *there*.

Brides' and grooms' nuptial ages, too, differed between naval and civilian communities. Marriage had to be built on material foundations, a centuries-old convention which 'denied marriage to those without material resources, and postponed it for those…able to accumulate them only slowly.'[34] Postponement was common among Victorian working-class couples, a pattern of nuptiality echoed in naval historians' findings. Padfield considers that it would have been impossible for ordinary seamen on a shilling a day or able seamen on 1s 2d to have supported wife and family 'in any conventional sense', arguing that of the 'few' sailors who were married, most were older men, petty officers or warrant officers.[35] Lavery declares that 'only a minority of lower-deck [men] were happily married' (raising not entirely frivolous questions as to whether the majority were unhappily married, or not married, and how relative happiness were measured).[36] Twentieth-century sailors interviewed by McKee agreed that prior to the 1914 introduction of a married man's allowance, (lack of) money was a major disincentive to early marriage, some going so far as to say that one could only be a married sailor despite the Royal Navy, not with its help.[37] A sample of 342 mid-nineteenth-century naval marriages revealed that the mean average age at which

	Mean average age at first marriage (females)	Difference from Portsea Island naval first marriages (females)	Mean average age at first marriage (males)	Difference from Portsea Island naval first marriages (males)
Portsea Island naval first marriages (n=176)	22.5 years		27 years	
England and Wales at mid-century point	24.6 years	+ 2.1 years	25.8 years	- 1.2 years
England & Wales 1800-49	23.4 years	+ 0.9 years	25.3 years	- 1.7 years

Fig.3: mean age at first marriages.

sailors married, as calculated for five-year periods from 1815, varied from 19.5 years in 1815-19 to 28.6 years in 1850-1, a 9.1-year increase over thirty-six years.[38] As to the mean average nuptial age of our 342 naval brides, this showed an upward trend of 7.4 years, from eighteen years in 1815-19 to 25.4 years in 1850-1. These figures, however, relate not to first marriages but to *all* marriages in the sample of 342 unions. With re-marriages of widows and widowers set aside, a net total of 176 first-time unions between never-married naval grooms and their never-married brides revealed (see Fig. 3) that with a mean average age of twenty-seven years, these sailor-grooms were still 1.2 years older at first marriage than the 25.8-year-old average for first-time grooms in England and Wales at the mid-century point, and 1.7 years older than the 25.3-year-old average for first-time grooms marrying in England and Wales in years 1800-49.

This could be read as indicating that sailors' long absences, lack of local social connections and limited courtship opportunities delayed their entry into matrimony. Other social factors affected both naval and civilian communities. For example, parents' reliance on working children's wage contributions, and adult children's sense of filial duty, might keep courting couples waiting years. But with delay came advantage, for by limiting the numbers of children to be supported, and adding an air of middle-class respectability, postponement might improve standards of living.[39] And just as there was a seasonality to country marriages, with workers postponing weddings until after the harvest when extra earnings had accumulated, so some sailors may have steered clear of hasty pre-embarkation unions, deliberately postponing marriage until their ship had returned and paid off. Postponement therefore had purpose, and benefits. It added an air of respectability, and arrears of pay added lump-sum cash to savings; and prolonged separation tested sweethearts' emotional commitment before any legal commitment were made.[40]

So much for seamen-grooms. Different inferences may be drawn about seamen's brides. Though 0.9 to 2.1 years younger at first marriage than those national averages for the 1800-49 period and mid-century point, sailors' sweethearts who had grown up in naval households may have considered themselves ready for life as naval wives. Some may have been wise to the fact that in port towns suffering chronic under-employment they were unlikely to contribute to economic independence via their own earnings.[41] Some, too, may have intuited that, for reasons suggested above, as bridal candidates they possessed relatively low social status locally. In the competitive marriage market of female-heavy port towns, the naval daughter was simply happy to grab the opportunity for wifedom no matter how early in life it presented; and should the perils of sea-service leave her a young widow, and childless, she might still be young enough not only to marry again but to conceive.

Separate Communities, Separate Cultures

The extreme youth of some naval brides, however, raises serious questions. In the sample of 176 first-time naval unions, among twenty-two brides thought to be under sixteen at the altar, twelve- and thirteen-year-olds have been found. These were girls. They would not have begun to menstruate, or finished growing (Laslett notes working-class girls in 1830s Manchester could expect their first period at 15.6 years, Brown finding the average age of menarche in 1845 Birmingham was 15.3 years).[42] Their youth may have protected them from pre- and (for a while) post-marital pregnancy, but few will have been emotionally mature enough to deal with marriage in any other sense than 'playing house', and for many of them marriage meant little more than continuing to live with their parents until sailor-husbands came home from sea. Physical damage due to underage sexual activity was not the only risk they faced. Hard for the most mature naval wife to endure, prolonged husband-absence might strike the child-bride in ways she could not process intellectually or emotionally; and as teenage crushes evaporated, passions waxed and waned, the extremes of mood so often experienced in adolescence might trigger disillusionment and regrets when husband and wife were eventually reunited, if not before.

There were consolations. Couples who married young were more likely to have still-living parents, even grandparents.[43] This had particular significance for young naval brides who were the daughters of seamen, since their still-living mothers were well placed to understand what it was like to have a husband at sea. And not just understand: through her own husband's continuing absence on naval service, or his being deceased, the naval mother might be available to help, even to co-reside during her seaman son-in-law's absence, thus providing her young married daughter with companionship, childcare, understanding born of empirical experience, and on-site advice and support.

Did naval families condone a nuptial latitude eschewed by the rest of the community, and if such a latitude existed, what drove it? Alien to outsiders, was under-age marriage familiar and unremarkable within the naval community? Was it regarded as having practical benefits? Was it a function of parents' indulging their daughters, permitting them to do as they themselves had done?[44]

Beyond such inferences, issues of sailorly solidarity may be proposed. These naval fathers-of-the-bride had for years on end served alongside other seamen, spending more time in their company than with their own wives and daughters on shore. Then as now, the male shipboard community exerted a powerful influence. Men at sea were bound by a common purpose, a shared concern to preserve ship and crew, and by 'neighbourhood norms and customs', peer-group trends powerful enough to shape a breadwinner's notion of the right amount of housekeeping to award his wife.[45] From recognising these bonds it is not too great a leap to the notion of a seaman-father promising to introduce his younger bachelor-shipmate (or, given some bride/groom age-differences, his not-much-younger bachelor-shipmate) to an underage daughter, permitting him to court and in due course marry her. Lavery's declaration that sailors had 'no time for conventional wooing' conveys the challenges faced by young Jack pining for a sweetheart, and by older Jack anxious not to end up an elderly bachelor: how to meet the right sort of girl, obtain an introduction, gain her and her parents' trust, woo and persuade her to marry him, even effect the marriage itself, and all between paying-off and (re-)joining ship.[46] The naval father of a daughter would recognise the challenges facing his unmarried or widower fellows. He might relish the idea of a seaman son-in-law, especially if the suitor were his serving shipmate, or a former messmate with credentials long established, or if suitor's and bride's fathers were 'old ships', all of which connections were identified when couples' family and naval backgrounds were explored.[47]

Feelings, intentions and collaboration being unprovable, the question of why naval parents consented to or connived at daughters' underage marriage must remain just that: a question. Fury's identification of couples' *compatibility* fits with the finding that most of our naval brides were seamen's daughters. In twenty-first century eyes, however, mere familiarity with naval family life is not enough to explain how a child bride might be deemed 'compatible' with a middle-aged husband who would inevitably be absent for years at a time.[48] How could a child bride be expected to set up and run, without spousal support, a marital home? Why marry at all if marriage did not involve the assuming and exercising of adult responsibilities? Why not delay vows until the relationship were established, savings accrued to fund an independent economic unit, until the bride were mature enough to cope with intercourse and domestic management, and old enough to conceive and bear a child? At a time when at national level there was a strong movement toward delaying matrimony, why permit (pre-)pubescent girls to marry?

The finding of under-age brides among our naval newlyweds should not distract from the fact that most seamen's brides were in their twenties upon first marriage. It nevertheless points to a near-tribal adherence to practices rooted in past centuries. That there existed a preparedness to buck a national trend would, in an increasingly conservative society, have been enough to mark naval women as lacking in respectability, as 'other'. When such perceptions are added to popular caricature, ignorance and prejudice, they stretch even further the cultural connection between naval and civilian communities.

These findings emerged from correlation of materials not restricted to the academic researcher with institutional credentials. Ships' allotment registers, census returns, parish and civil registers are generally accessible. From them it has proved possible to piece together an evidence-based picture of naval family life as existed nearly two hundred years ago. But that 'void of ignorance' to which Nicholas Rodger referred is still detectable in terms of which archival resources have been allowed to survive, and which not. For example, as the source from which seamen's women's history best begins, ships' allotment registers come to a sudden end in the mid-nineteenth century. Thereafter they were either superseded by a different form of admiralty record which has neither survived nor been referred-to elsewhere, or (a more likely scenario) they were destroyed by archival weeders who, realising the registers pertained primarily to seamen's [female] relatives, saw no historical value in them. Whatever the explanation, for the period 1852-1982 the Navy's own record of its dependants is lost to history, as is our ability to evaluate from inception to end the impact of a groundbreaking social benefit. Post-1852 allotment records are not the only material lost from the archive.

Missing, too, are the voices of the women themselves, for no journals or collections of letters have survived to reveal their side of the story. A few seamen's letters have been preserved by the National Museum of the Royal Navy, but no wives' correspondence exists to provide the view from the shore.[49]

Implications for Today

Lost to history their voices may be, but naval dependants lived on in their thousands. They live today, not only in port towns, and not only as wives. Their social circumstances have changed, likewise their rights, as women, as voters, as property-owners, employees, citizens, civil partners and wives. Changed, too, are their means of communicating with their loved ones at sea. The twenty-first century naval dependant has access to resources unthought-of by her grandparents' generation, let alone by the mid-Victorian wife. Gone is reliance on handwritten letters, 'bluey' aerogrammes, word-counted telegrams dictated to Portishead radio operators. Communication now is direct, immediate and face-to-face, via cost-free calls on Facetime or Messenger, encrypted WhatsApp messages, postings on social media, and the chat rooms of dedicated, service-inaugurated websites. In terms of immediacy and accessibility, of the ability of serving personnel to support dependants on shore, and *vice versa*, the gains are immense.

What is lost, however, is the physical record of the present-day, the documentary evidence setting out, for exploration by future historians, the relationships between Navy and naval community, and between naval and civilian communities. Lost, too, is the physical record of what twenty-first century naval women – at sea and on shore – both think and feel about these relationships, and their place within them. Sure, these women will, like their foremothers, be locatable in parish and civil registers, naval service records, census records (that is, unless the government decides to scrap the 2031 census, relying instead on 'a network of disparate public sector sources of data).[50] But how will naval women's voices be heard in a hundred years' time if we do not preserve written evidence of what they experienced, how they lived, the challenges they faced, and the strategies they employed in order to meet those challenges head-on? If we in the twenty-first century do not value and preserve evidence of naval women's experience, how will future historians be able to plunge into the deep waters of the twenty-first century past, to bring present-day naval women into the light?

Winner of the 2013 Sir Julian Corbett Prize for Modern Naval History, and the 2018-19 Doctoral Prize awarded by the British Commission for Maritime History, Melanie Holihead completed her DPhil at the University of Oxford. Her *Naval Seamen's Women in Nineteenth-Century Britain* is due for publication by Boydell and Brewer in 2024.

Archival Sources

Kew, National Archives (TNA), Admiralty and Predecessors: Office of the Director General of the Medical Department of the Navy and Predecessors: Medical Journals, ADM 101, 1785-1963

——, Admiralty: Miscellanea: History of the Allotment System in the Navy ('Pitcairn Report'), ADM 7/719, 1858

——, Admiralty: Royal Navy Continuous Service Engagement Books, ADM 139, 1853-72

——, Admiralty: Ships' Musters (Series III), ADM 38, 1793-1878

——, Navy Board, and Admiralty, Accountant General's Department: Registers of Allotments and Allotment Declarations, ADM 27, 1792-1852

Official documents and publications

Contagious Diseases Prevention Act, 27 & 28 Vict., c. 85 (1864)

Mutiny Act, 7 Will. IV and 1 Vict., c. 7 (1837)

Navy Act, 1 Geo. II, st. 2, c. 14 (1727)

Navy Act, 31 Geo. II, c.10 (1758)

House of Commons Debate, Ministry of Defence: Royal Navy Ratings (Allotments), 13, cc311-2W (23 Nov. 1981)

House of Commons Paper no. 295, Navy: 'Return of the Number of Seamen, and Petty Officers of the Royal Navy and Marines, who allot a Portion of their Pay for the Support of their Families and Others; and showing the Place of Residence of such Persons', XXXIX, 13 (1857-8)

Secondary Sources

Hampshire Telegraph, and *Sussex Chronicle* (Portsmouth: publisher unknown, 1799-1961)

August, Andrew, *Poor Women's Lives: Gender, Work, and Poverty in Late-Victorian London* (London: Fairleigh Dickinson University Press, 1999)

Brown, P.E., 'The Age at Menarche', *Journal of Epidemiology and Community Health*, 20 (1966), 9-14

Burton, Valerie, 'The Myth of Bachelor Jack: masculinity, patriarchy and seafaring labour', in Colin D. Howell and Richard J. Twomey (eds), *Jack Tar in History: essays in the history of maritime life and labour* (Fredericton, N.B.: Acadiensis Press, 1991).

Carew, Anthony, *The Lower Deck of the Royal Navy 1900-1939: the Invergordon Mutiny in Perspective* (Manchester: Manchester University Press, 1981).

Crafts, N.F.R., 'Average Age at First Marriage for Women in Mid-Nineteenth-Century England and Wales: a cross-section study', *Population Studies*, 21:1 (1978), 21-25

Dickens, Charles, 'The Girls They Leave Behind Them', *All the Year Round*, 16 July 1864, 544-6

Fury, Cheryl A., 'Seamen's Wives and Widows', in Cheryl A. Fury (ed.), *The Social History of English Seamen, 1485-1649* (London: Boydell, 2012), pp. 253-76

—— (ed.), *The Social History of English Seamen, 1485-1649* (Woodbridge: Boydell Press, 2012)

—— (ed.), *The Social History of English Seamen, 1650-1815* (Woodbridge: Boydell Press, 2017)

Gates, W.G., *History of Portsmouth* (Portsmouth, 1900)

Houlbrooke, Ralph A., *The English Family, 1450-1700* (London: Longman, 1984)

Humphries, Jane, Childhood and Child Labour in the British Industrial Revolution (Cambridge: Cambridge University Press, 2010)

Jolly, Rick and Tugg Willson, *Jackspeak: a guide to British naval slang and usage* (Torpoint: Palamando, 2000)

Kent, David, 'Gone for a Soldier?: family breakdown and the demography of desertion in a London parish, 1750-1791', *Local Population Studies*, 45 (1990), 27-41

Laslett, Peter, *The World We Have Lost: further explored* (London: Routledge, 2000)

Lavery, Brian, *Able Seamen: the lower deck of the Royal Navy from 1850 to the present day* (London: Conway, 2011).

Light, Alison, *Common People: the history of an English family* (London: Fig Tree, Penguin Group, 2014).

Lincoln, Margarette, *Naval Wives and Mistresses* (Stroud: History, 2011).

McKee, Christopher, *Sober Men and True: sailor lives in the Royal Navy, 1900-1945* (London: Harvard University Press, 2002).

McNay, Kirsty, Jane Humphries, and Stephan Klasen, 'Excess Female Mortality in Nineteenth-Century England and Wales', *Social Science History*, 29:4 (2005), 649-81.

Norling, Lisa, *Captain Ahab had a Wife: New England women & the whalefishery, 1720-1870* (London: University of North Carolina Press, 2000).

Outhwaite, R.B., 'Age at Marriage in England from the Late Seventeenth to the Nineteenth Century', *Transactions of the Royal Historical Society*, 23 (1973), 55-70.

Padfield, Peter, *Rule Britannia: the Victorian and Edwardian Navy* (London: Pimlico, 2002).

Perkin, Joan, Women and Marriage in Nineteenth-century England (London: Routledge, 1989).

Rodger, N.A.M., *The Command of the Ocean: a naval history of Britain, 1649-1815* (London: Allen Lane in association with the National Maritime Museum, 2004).

——, 'Dames at Sea: Female Tars by Stark, Suzanne J. (author)', *Times Literary Supplement*: 4879 (1996), 34.

——, *The Wooden World: an anatomy of the Georgian Navy* (Annapolis, Md.: Naval Institute Press, 1986).

Ross, Ellen, *Love and Toil: motherhood in outcast London, 1870-1918* (Oxford: Oxford University Press, 1993).

Ruggles, Steven, 'Reconsidering the Northwest European Family System: Living Arrangements of the Aged in Comparative Historical Perspective', *Population and Development Review*, 35:2 (2009), 249-73.

Skelley, Alan Ramsay, *The Victorian Army at Home: the recruitment and terms and conditions of the British Regular, 1859-1899* (London: Croom Helm, 1977).

Stark, Suzanne J., *Female Tars: women aboard ship in the age of sail* (London: Constable, 1996).

Thompson, F.M.L., The Rise of Respectable Society: a social history of Victorian Britain, 1830-1900 (London: Fontana, 1988).

Tomkins, Alannah and Steven King, *The Poor in England, 1700-1850: an economy of makeshifts* (Manchester: Manchester University Press, 2003) Trustram, Myna, *Women of the Regiment: marriage and the Victorian army* (Cambridge: Cambridge University Press, 1984).

van der Heijden, Manon and Danielle ven den Heuvel, 'Sailors' Families and the Urban Institutional Framework in Early Modern Holland', *The History of the Family*, 12:4 (2007), 296-309.

Venning, Annabel, *Following the Drum: the lives of army wives and daughters, past and present* (London: Headline, 2005).

Woods, Robert, *The Demography of Victorian England and Wales* (Cambridge: Cambridge University Press, 2000).

Wrigley, E.A. and R.S. Schofield, *The Population History of England, 1541-1871: a reconstruction* (Cambridge: Cambridge University Press, 1989).

Unpublished theses

Reibe, Melissa, 'Public Perceptions of Sailors' Wives in Eighteenth-Century England' (unpublished MA thesis, University of Missouri-Kansas City, 2011).

Walton, Oliver, 'Social History of the Royal Navy, c.1856–1900: corporation and community' (unpublished PhD thesis, University of Exeter, 2004)

Web-based sources

Addley, Esther, 'Out for the Count: has Britain already conducted its last census?' 2023) <https://www.theguardian.com/uk-news/2023/nov/03/out-for-the-count-has-britain-already-conducted-its-last-census> [accessed 3 Nov. 2023].

Pappalardo, Bruno, 'A Lot to be Excited About - Admiralty Allotment Registers' (The National Archives, 2019) <https://blog.nationalarchives.gov.uk/lot-excited-admiralty-allotment-registers/> [accessed 13 Jun. 2023].

Rodger, N.A.M., '"I want to be an Admiral"', *London Review of Books*: 15 (2020), <https://www.lrb.co.uk/the-paper/v42/n15/n.a.m.-rodger/i-want-to-be-an-admiral> [accessed 10 Apr. 2023].

Rowlandson, Thomas, 'Goodbye' (Wikimedia Commons, 2005) <https://commons.wikimedia.org/wiki/File:Rowlandson_-_Goodbye.jpg> [accessed 17 Jul. 2023].

1. N.A.M. Rodger, *The Command of the Ocean: a naval history of Britain, 1649-1815* (London, 2004), p. 407.

2. Margarette Lincoln, *Naval Wives and Mistresses* (Stroud, 2011).

3. Cheryl A. Fury (ed.), *The Social History of English Seamen, 1485-1649* (Woodbridge, 2012); Cheryl A. Fury (ed.), *The Social History of English Seamen, 1650-1815* (Woodbridge, 2017).

4. N.A.M. Rodger, 'Dames at Sea: Female Tars by Stark, Suzanne J. (author)', *Times Literary Supplement,* 4879 (1996), 34.

5. *Navy Act,* 1 Geo. II, st. 2, c. 14 (1727); Kew, National Archives (TNA), Admiralty: Miscellanea: History of the Allotment System in the Navy ('Pitcairn Report'), ADM 7/719 (1858).

6. N.A.M. Rodger, *The Wooden World: an anatomy of the Georgian Navy* (Annapolis, Md., 1986), pp. 131-2, 134-5; Melissa Reibe, 'Public Perceptions of Sailors' Wives in Eighteenth-Century England' (University of Missouri: Kansas City, unpublished MA thesis, 2011), p. 30.

7. Myna Trustram, *Women of the Regiment: marriage and the Victorian army* (Cambridge, 1984), p. 56; Jane Humphries, *Childhood and Child Labour in the British Industrial Revolution* (Cambridge, 2010), p. 369.

8. Trustram, *Women of the Regiment,* p. 50; Annabel Venning, *Following the Drum: the lives of army wives and daughters, past and present* (London, 2005), p. 35; *Mutiny Act,* 7 Will. IV and 1 Vict., c. 7 (1837), s. 3; Charles Dickens, 'The Girls They Leave Behind Them', *All the Year Round,* 16 July 1864, 544-6via <http://www.djo.org.uk/all-the-year-round/volume-xi/page-545.html> [accessed 23 May 2017], p. 545.

9. Alan Ramsay Skelley, *The Victorian Army at Home: the recruitment and terms and conditions of the British Regular, 1859-1899* (London, 1977), p. 70, fn. 32, citing Florence Nightingale to Douglas Galton, 21 Sept. 1863, Nightingale MSS 45761.

10. Lisa Norling, *Captain Ahab had a Wife: New England women & the whalefishery, 1720-1870* (London, 2000), p. 133.

11. Manon van der Heijden and Danielle ven den Heuvel, 'Sailors' Families and the Urban Institutional Framework in Early Modern Holland', *The History of the Family,* 12, 4 (2007), 296-309, p. 301; Valerie Burton, 'The Myth of Bachelor Jack: masculinity, patriarchy and seafaring labour', in Colin D. Howell and Richard J. Twomey (eds), *Jack Tar in History: essays in the history of maritime life and labour* (Fredericton, N.B., 1991), 179-98, pp. 184-6.

12. *Navy Act,* 31 Geo. II, c.10 (1758); Rodger, *Command of the Ocean,* p. 317.

13. Suzanne J. Stark, *Female Tars: women aboard ship in the age of sail* (London, 1996), p. 23.

14. Rodger, *Wooden World,* pp. 132, 134-5; *Navy Act 1758,* 31 Geo. II, c. 10.

15. Pitcairn, *Report*, p. 33; Oliver Walton, 'Social History of the Royal Navy, c.1856–1900: corporation and community' (University of Exeter, unpublished PhD thesis, 2004), pp. 88-91; House of Commons Paper no. 295, Navy: 'Return of the Number of Seamen, and Petty Officers of the Royal Navy and Marines, who allot a Portion of their Pay for the Support of their Families and Others; and showing the Place of Residence of such Persons', XXXIX, 13, 1857-8, pp. 13-15. 'Portsmouth' includes all of Portsea Island, 'Devonport' the city of Plymouth.

16. House of Commons Debate, Ministry of Defence: Royal Navy Ratings (Allotments), 13, cc311-2W, 23 Nov. 1981.

17. Rodger, *Wooden World*, pp. 131-2, 134-5.

18. Rodger, *Command of the Ocean*, p. 407. It is notable that of a sample of 2300 allotments declared in the period 1850-52, only 41 (1.8 per cent) named male recipients.

19. Bruno Pappalardo, 'A Lot to be Excited About - Admiralty Allotment Registers' (The National Archives, 2019) <https://blog.nationalarchives.gov.uk/lot-excited-admiralty-allotment-registers/> [accessed 13 Jun. 2023].

20. Kew, National Archives (TNA), Navy Board, and Admiralty, Accountant General's Department: Registers of Allotments and Allotment Declarations, ADM 27 (1792-1852).

21. Kew, National Archives (TNA), Admiralty: Ships' Musters (Series III), ADM 38 (1793-1878); Kew, National Archives (TNA), Admiralty and Predecessors: Office of the Director General of the Medical Department of the Navy and Predecessors: Medical Journals, ADM 101 (1785-1963); Kew, National Archives (TNA), Admiralty: Royal Navy Continuous Service Engagement Books, ADM 139 (1853-72).

22. N.A.M. Rodger, '"I want to be an Admiral"', *London Review of Books*: 15 (2020), <https://www.lrb.co.uk/the-paper/v42/n15/n.a.m.-rodger/i-want-to-be-an-admiral> [accessed 10 Apr. 2023].

23. See for example Patrick O'Brian, *Post Captain* (1972), HMS *Surprise* (1973), *Desolation Island* (1978), *The Fortune of War* (1979), *Clarissa Oaks* (1992), *The Commodore* (1995).

24. G. Pinkard, quoted in W.G. Gates, *History of Portsmouth* (Portsmouth, 1900), pp. 487-8.

25. Thomas Rowlandson, 'Goodbye' c.1790-1810 (Wikimedia Commons, 2005) <https://commons.wikimedia.org/wiki/File:Rowlandson_-_Goodbye.jpg> [accessed 17 Jul. 2023].

26. *Contagious Diseases Prevention Act,* 27 & 28 Vict., c. 85 (1864).

27. For examples of naval language, see Rick Jolly and Tugg Willson, *Jackspeak: a guide to British naval slang and usage* (Torpoint, 2000), *passim*.

28. Olwen Hufton, *The Poor of Eighteenth-century France 1750-1789* (Oxford, 1974), pp. 69-127; Alannah Tomkins and Steven King, *The Poor in England, 1700-1850: an economy of makeshifts* (Manchester, 2003), *passim*.

29. Alison Light, *Common People: the history of an English family* (London, 2014), p. 188.

30. Christopher McKee, *Sober Men and True: sailor lives in the Royal Navy, 1900-1945* (London, 2002), p. 185.

31. The identification of defendants and/or victims as 'sailor's wife' was a journalistic habit not limited to any one newspaper, or to a specific kind of criminal charge. Reporting on three cases of attempted suicide (then a criminal offence), a national newspaper identified one defendant as 'a sailor's wife'. The other two defendants' marital status and husbands' occupations were not mentioned (*Express* (London), 25 Aug. 1852, p. 4 col. D).

32. *Hampshire Telegraph, and Sussex Chronicle* (Portsmouth, 1799-1961), 1850-9.

33. *Hull Packet*, 4 Aug. 1848, p. 6, col. B.

34. Ralph A. Houlbrooke, *The English Family, 1450-1700* (London, 1984), p. 63.

35. Peter Padfield, *Rule Britannia: the Victorian and Edwardian Navy* (London, 2002), p. 24.

36. Brian Lavery, *Able Seamen: the lower deck of the Royal Navy from 1850 to the present day* (London, 2011), p. 86.

37. McKee, *Sober Men and True*, pp. 206-7; Anthony Carew, *The Lower Deck of the Royal Navy 1900-1939: the Invergordon Mutiny in Perspective* (Manchester, 1981), pp. 58-9.

38. The 1850-51 period covers the period Jan. 1850 to Apr. 1851, none of the 342 marriages having taken place beyond that date.

39. Ellen Ross, *Love and Toil: motherhood in outcast London, 1870-1918* (Oxford, 1993), p. 67; Thompson, *Rise of Respectable Society*, pp. 55, 258.

40. David Kent, 'Gone for a Soldier?: family breakdown and the demography of desertion in a London parish, 1750-1791', *Local Population Studies,* 45, (1990), 27-41, p. 39.

41. Kirsty McNay *et al.*, 'Excess Female Mortality in Nineteenth-Century England and Wales', *Social Science History,* 29, 4 (2005), 649-81, *passim*.

42. Peter Laslett, *The World We Have Lost: further explored* (London, 2000), p. 84; Wrigley and Schofield, *Population History*, p. 233 fn. 66; P.E. Brown, 'The Age at Menarche', *Journal of Epidemiology and Community Health,* 20, (1966), 9-14, p. 10.

43. Steven Ruggles, 'Reconsidering the Northwest European Family System: Living Arrangements of the Aged in Comparative Historical Perspective', *Population and Development Review,* 35, 2 (2009), 249-73, p. 253.

44. Numerous examples have been found whereby the parents of child-bride naval daughters had themselves married young.

45. Andrew August, *Poor Women's Lives: Gender, Work, and Poverty in Late-Victorian London* (London, 1999), pp. 124-5.

46. Lavery, *Able Seamen*, p. 87.

47. '"Old ships": Abbreviation for *old shipmate*, someone you have served with before': Jolly and Willson, *Jackspeak*, p. 311.

48. Cheryl A. Fury, 'Seamen's Wives and Widows', in Cheryl A. Fury (ed.), *The Social History of English Seamen, 1485-1649* (London, 2012), 253-76, p. 260.

49. For example, Portsmouth, National Museum of the Royal Navy (NMRN): John Ford, letter to Sarah Evans, NMRN 353/85/17, 18 Jan. 1847; John Ford, letter to Sarah Evans, NMRN 353/85/18, 28 Apr. 1847; John Ford, letter to Sarah Evans, NMRN 353/85/13, 13 Jul. 1845; William Simpson, letter to wife, NMRN 627/86/11, 1 Jun. 1857; William Simpson, letter to wife, NMRN 627/86/9, 19 Dec. 1856.

50. Esther Addley, 'Out for the Count: has Britain already conducted its last census?' The Guardian 2023) <https://www.theguardian.com/uk-news/2023/nov/03/out-for-the-count-has-britain-already-conducted-its-last-census> [accessed 3 Nov. 2023].

Maritime Women: Navigating Uncharted Waters in 21st Century Britain

Monica Kohli

Introduction

Nelson, Captain Kidd, and James Cook are legendary. Sir Francis Drake, Captain Blackbeard are also well known. What they have in common is that they are all men. Historically, the maritime industry has been a male-dominated field. From sailors and captains to shipbuilders, it has always been men who have shaped the course of maritime Britain and they are the ones represented in the industry. In the 21st century the first female to captain a mega cruise ship, a female merchant navy medal awardee, and the female recipient of the IMO Award on exceptional bravery at sea-Captain Kate McCue, Captain Belenda Bennet, and Captain Radhika Menon respectively are increasingly making their mark in the maritime world, challenging stereotypes, and breaking down barriers. However, the stereotype that shipping is a male-centric domain has not changed.

Before we talk about the future, we need to understand our past and the effects of gender discrimination. The reason I am keen to explore this stereotype is because it has had an impact on my life. My father was a Captain in the Merchant Navy. He started sailing when he was 16. The youngest of five boys and a bright student, he failed to get the requisite grades for university and was therefore sent to sea. Though he initially struggled with the rigours of chipping and painting on board, he spent his entire life in the industry. His wife, my mother, joined him on board soon after marriage, and as soon as babies were allowed to leave land, at six months old, I too sailed with them.

I spent the first five years of my life on board merchant navy vessels – bulk carriers – coming ashore only for holidays. I played on the decks, with the young cadets as my nannies and companions, and the hatches and engine room as my playground. The carpenter on board made me a dollhouse to order and the chef cooked my meals, following instructions from my mother.

That was the only reality I knew, and the only house I lived in with any consistency. Shore leave were the breaks from our life at sea. I spent half a decade on the seas, stopping at dozens of countries, watching goods (mostly grain) being loaded and unloaded. The only formal education I had in those years was a few weeks of playschool between family visits when my father was on shore leave. I was five when my first brother was born, and six when my second brother was born. This double arrival prompted my father to get a shore job. He moved the family on land, working for the same company ashore, as many did and still do. At six, having grown up at sea, I didn't know the alphabet or how to count, though I could tell you all about the gangway, the engine room, holds, and bunkers. School was a shock, and I was kept back to be brought up to the standard of other children my age. But I didn't care. I knew I was going to be a sailor when I grew up. My father was my hero. I could envision no other life for myself than that of a seafarer.

However, when I hit my teens and had to choose a career, I ended up choosing … law. All my years growing up I had never seen a single female seafarer, and so, I had internalised that as a woman I could not be one. I don't think this was ever explicitly said to me, but it was reinforced in my every interaction with people in the navy and merchant navy. And I met a lot of them; all my cousins had followed in my father's footsteps to become "shippies". My brother also ended up sailing for an oil major.

I decided that if I couldn't join shipping as a seafarer, I would join the industry from another angle – as a maritime lawyer. I read for a master's in maritime law and thereafter an executive MBA in maritime and now I work in the field of maritime insurance. I work in a Protection and Indemnity Club advising shipowners, traders and charterers on their contracts, disputes, and other legal issues. I love what I do, and I am delighted to be an integral part of the maritime community. I am also President of Women's International Shipping and Trading Association UK (WISTA UK). In this community, I see women around my age – and women younger than me – who went to sea, are at sea, and are planning to be at sea. I wish I had seen them when I was choosing my career.

Since I did not have a role model, which was instrumental in my failure to join the navy, I have made it my mission to ensure women in this career have visibility so that no other young women fail to follow her dreams due to a lack of role models.

History

However, while I aim to give the women of today the visibility they deserve, it is also important to rescue the women of yore from the obscurity of the past. In the late 1800s and early 1900s, England had her heroines in Mary Patten and Grace Horsley Darling. Patten challenged conventional norms by captaining a vessel around Cape Horn while pregnant. Grace Darling is well known for her acts of bravery in rescuing sailors from a shipwreck off the coast of Northumberland. There was also the legendary Chinese pirate Ching Shih, who commanded a vast fleet in the early 19th century. The World Wars saw an influx of women into the maritime workforce as they took on roles traditionally held by men, such as shipbuilders and welders. Although women were officially barred from serving in navies, many served in disguise. They took on roles as sailors and even participated in combat during various naval conflicts, including the Napoleonic Wars and the American Civil War.

Women like Jeanne Baret[1] in the 18th century, who became the first woman to circumnavigate the globe albeit in disguise, and Ida Pfeiffer, a well-known Austrian traveller and travel book author, made significant contributions to maritime exploration and science during the early 19th century.

Women have also played significant roles in maritime exploration and oceanographic science. Notable figures include Sylvia Earle, an oceanographer who has been a pioneer in researching and raising awareness about marine ecosystems. She was named by Time Magazine as its first Hero for the Planet in 1998. However, these are only a handful of names, and the industry has remained predominantly male-oriented, and its only in recent years that we have seen a shift towards greater gender diversity within the sector. Before we look at diversity today, let us see where shipping is currently.

Shipping Today

Shipping as we are all aware, is the engine of global trade, carrying over 90 percent of world trade. It is the lifeblood of the modern world where we are used to mangos out of season and avocadoes in every cafe. Our global lifestyle is dependent on shipping being effective, and for shipping to be effective, suitably qualified seafarers are essential. For maritime trade to be safe, secure, and environmentally sound we need sufficient quality entrants. However, we are seeing a fall in numbers of seafarers. Recent world events that have led to the Houthis targeting specific vessels in the Red Sea, the Ukraine war, piracy, and general disruption have put the spotlight on the dangers seafarers and shipping face. We cannot take safety at sea or seafarers for granted.

Drewry's Manning Annual Review and Forecast for 2023/24 reveals that officer availability deficit is on the rise – a shortage of four percent in the global talent pool, with the shortage expected to go up to nine percent in 2023. This is the highest deficit of seafarers seen by the industry on record and projections indicate this growing deficit is expected to last till at least 2028. The International Chamber of Shipping /BIMCO study prophecies that we will be about 96,000 seafarers short by 2026. International Recruitments need to be a priority, and targeting 50 percent of the population that has been ignored for years could assist in reducing this shortage. We have seen some attempts at introducing this into the conversation when the director general of the Danish Maritime Authority said that he felt that "that diversity is better for safety retention and a variety of factors" (Crew Connect Global Conference in manila, November 2023). Despite all this, the common refrain has not moved from "We have to find out what to do." I believe the discussion should pivot towards "how, where, and what to do", employing diversity toolkits (International Chamber of Shipping provides a diversity Toolkit) to ensure the industry achieves maximum inclusivity with efficiency and effectiveness.

The current facts and figures regarding women seafarers in Maritime Britain are not very encouraging. As of today, women make up a mere two percent of the global maritime workforce. While this figure has been gradually increasing over the past decade, we can all agree, it is nowhere near representative of the population. In the United Kingdom, the representation of women in the maritime industry is slightly higher than the global average, with around four percent of seafarers being female (certified officers). Uncertified officers have a higher representation at about 34 percent and ratings at 27 percent. We are seeing a growth but there is also a glass ceiling.

When I spoke to female seafarers who came ashore, they all spoke about hitting a glass ceiling. They could progress to a certain point after which organisational structures, lack of growth opportunities, lack of mentorship, certain attitudes kept them from having no option but to come ashore.

A single parent mentioned the sense of abandonment she felt when there was no support at all for her through her pregnancy, neither from the company she had sailed with as her contract was over, nor ashore as seafarers were not given benefits on land. She had no option but to look at an alternate career ashore. These examples do not bode well in encouraging women to pursue a career at sea, despite more women from India, Turkey, and the Philippines entering the field and normalising the image of 'female seafarer'.

Traditionally, women are better represented in onshore roles, such as shipping management, maritime law, and port operations. Even this has been a slow growth and it is only now that we are seeing more female partners in shipping law firms, in the higher echelons of powers in marine finance, and in ship broking and insurance. Of course, society is changing and access to education and training opportunities has become more equitable, allowing women to gain the necessary skills and certifications required for seafaring and seafaring adjacent careers. Maritime institutions and academies have implemented initiatives to encourage female enrolment and participation in maritime courses. Women's International Shipping and Trading Association UK (WISTA UK) is leading fundraising for female seafarers together with the Maritime Education Fund, Merchant Navy Training Board, and the Maritime London Officer Cadet Scholarship.

If any woman wishes to pursue a career at sea in the UK and possesses the necessary skills and mindset, access to funding will not be a barrier for her. However, the challenge remains to find these women, to excite them to join the profession, to make seafaring visible and accessible and glamorous. This is where we need to start young and make shipping great again – to children, in schools, and in educational establishments at all ages. I am informed that the percentage of female sea cadets in the UK is over 50% but it doesn't translate into the numbers recruited as yet. As an island nation, shipping should be the first career of choice and we should encourage our brightest and best to join us in the industry.

Progress and Challenges

According to the International Transport Workers Federation's recent collecting Bargaining Agreement, the global supply of seafarers available for service on internationally traded ships is estimated at 1,647,500 and women seafarers comprise only one percent of this figure. After the Covid-19 pandemic it is apparent that the numbers of female seafarers have gone down further.

While there has undoubtedly been progress in increasing the representation of women in maritime careers, significant challenges persist. It is essential to address these challenges to further increase gender diversity in the industry:

Stereotypes about the physical demands of seafaring roles and the perception that they are unsuitable for women still exist. The concept of rough tough sailor men persist and can sometimes manifest in the male cadets not allowing women cadets to do certain jobs in the belief that it is too tough for them. However female officers say that its always possible to do the physical tasks, whether with tools or with teams. One female deck officer I spoke to said that the engine rooms sometimes still may be tough, but for navigating officers it is about managing the resources and getting the work done. And in any event, on the bridge it is all automated, and the deck work is not anywhere near as physically demanding as it used to be. According to her, it is the fatigue which is the issue now for all seafarers, men and women. Hence, there should be no barriers to recruiting women in this field.

After attracting the talent, there is also the need to retain the seafarers. There remains the old-fashioned concern that female cadets will not remain in the industry long-term, as they might be more likely to leave prematurely due to childbearing and caregiving responsibilities. However, as observed in other industries, this concern is not unique to female seafarers; male seafarers also often leave their sea life behind for family or caregiving responsibilities. My father and brother both came ashore once they had families. If the conditions are fair and conducive, seafarers, whether male or female, will continue to work. Through history, the presence of women seafarers on board was considered bad luck. Although one might assume that such thinking has evolved, some shipping companies continue to perpetuate this outdated ideology.

Like many industries, the maritime sector faces a gender pay gap, with women often earning less than their male counterparts. According to the women in Transport Equity Index Report 2024, 58% of organizations surveyed had a gender pay gap of 11% or more compared to the national average of 7.7%. About 54% of organizations surveyed had no formal targets or commitments to increase or maintain gender diversity. Addressing these issues and disparity is essential for achieving gender equity in the industry. Sector wide initiatives are needed for cultivating and empowering women in leadership position such that they are given opportunities to progress in their careers. The scarcity of women in leadership positions within the maritime sector also discourages aspiring female seafarers. Encouraging mentorship and promoting women into leadership roles can help address this issue.

Maritime workplaces, like all workspaces, must foster inclusive and respectful cultures that promote diversity. Combating workplace harassment and discrimination is crucial for retaining women in the industry. We have heard often of bullying on board vessels and women not being given berths at sea on board certain shipping companies because of the harassment culture known to exist on board. This also keeps women away from the career. Rather than address the toxic culture on board the solution has been to exclude women from jobs. These issues are unrelated to women or their capabilities and should really be addressed in isolation to the issue of diversity.

Lack of support during pregnancy and limited routes back to sailing after childbirth has also hindered women's progress in the industry. Access to maternity protection and measures enabling balancing work and family responsibilities would promote gender equality. We have heard of cases where pregnant woman or those returning from parental leave have experienced harassment from coworkers, subordinates, or superiors. To increase the retention of seafarers, some companies have introduced new maternity benefits, including global guaranteed minimum of 18 weeks maternity leave on full pay and a return-to-work program giving women a smoother transition back to work. The Royal Navy has also noticed a change in the women coming back to work after changes in the maternity policy.

If there is maternity protection and measures enabling balancing work and family responsibilities, gender equality at sea will progress. Maternity protection can provide job security and enable all seafarers to have families and remain at work. It is important when re-entering the workforce that seafarers are not degraded from their posts, that they have flexible working arrangements, and have full opportunities for training. The Women in Transport Equity Index report, 2024 recommends that flexible working needs to be developed further by working with women to ensure the working policy reflects women's needs and makes organizations a better workplace for women.

Career Cycle of Women Seafarers

Women stay away from careers in the maritime industry because they face barriers that impact career progression and promotion. For example, women are not promoted aboard vessels due to a bias or gender stereotyping, but this reflects on their ability to apply for roles when they come ashore too; lack of seafaring command then carries over into roles ashore requiring command are unavailable to them, too. These barriers are normally related to the perception of women's capacities rather than any actual lack thereof and are created by management structures and institutions that actively prevent women from choosing maritime as a career.

Since seafaring has traditionally been a male dominated industry, there is also a male culture attached to it. This has led women seafarers to use strategies such as gender identity management to handle and sometimes avoid confrontation on ships in the past. There are numerous historical instances of women dressing as men and hiding their gender to sail. Even today, women tend to adopt behaviour, clothing, lifestyle, and hairstyle associated with the masculine identity.

Women report that they have to work harder to prove themselves or seek acceptance and be seen as capable of performing their job. Each woman represents all women. The burden to be representative can put additional pressure on women. Workplace training and awareness-raising activities challenge gender stereotypes and transform workplace cultures. In male-dominated industries like maritime, training and awareness are crucial components of promoting inclusion and changing workplace culture. Negative biases can be addressed by gender sensitisation, inspiring equal treatment of seafarers during education and training. If there are decent working conditions and mechanisms to enable career development women will consider maritime as a career path and will seek it.

We also see gender-based occupational segregation when looking at companies that hire women. Thus, women end up in hospitality and catering roles. In the cruise industry, women are represented in much higher numbers. Awareness of other seafaring roles, and awareness of opportunities is also key in promoting access to other roles for women. Very slowly, we have seen a change of women's representation in the maritime industry at all levels. A few glass ceilings have also been smashed. High-profile female figures in maritime, such as Rear Admiral Jude Terry OBE, the first woman to hold that rank in the Royal Navy. Capt Karen Davis managing Director at Oil Companies International Marine Forum (OCIMF), and the increasing number of Female Merchant Navy Medal Awardees in the UK have demonstrated that women can excel in leadership roles within the sector, inspiring others to follow suit.

As training institutions, Glasgow, Fleetwood, South Shields and Warsash Maritime School are the major entry point for women seafarers-targeting and marketing the programme to women would assist in attracting women to the profession. Also encouraging participation in more programs, offering more cadet berths or apprentice placements to women would help more women join maritime. Cadets in international exchange programmes tend to be more successful, hence, offering the opportunity of international exchange to women should be a priority. Curriculum revision to include student awareness on gender and cultural issues and provide all students with equal opportunities should be mandatory.

Talking to companies recruiting cadets, I am informed that women (and men) join the sea at a young age, normally a year out of school at about 17 years old. Older cadets are also now being encouraged. Unfortunately, the attrition rate remains high for both men and women. There is a perception that women come ashore a little earlier due to families. However, when they are ready to go back to work there are normally few roles available for them. Recent parental policy changes have provided women with options when coming back after having a family and has reduced the attrition rate as some companies will hold positions for women taking parental leave. The other issue is that women are not upskilled or reskilled to get shoreside roles and stay in the industry. We should be Pinpointing key points of attrition – and put in funding at those stages for reskilling. The issue of lack of access to leadership roles on board by women results in an inability to get jobs ashore, too. An increase in women in leadership positions that will provide visible female representation for younger women enabling them to monitor career progression and have role models to emulate.

Despite the challenges, several initiatives and success stories highlight the increasing prominence of women in maritime Britain. Organizations like WISTA have been instrumental in advocating for gender diversity and providing support to women in the industry. They have observer status at IMO and at United Nations Conference on Trade and Development (UNCTAD) and hence, bring the diversity discussion to the international stage. Scholarships and grants aimed at women pursuing maritime education have been introduced to reduce financial barriers and encourage more female students to enrol in relevant courses.

Mentorship programs that pair experienced female maritime professionals with newcomers have proven effective in promoting career growth and confidence among women in the industry. Experienced officers can share skills, knowledge of career development and soft skills, and conversations can happen in a safe space. Reverse mentoring could also assist with getting junior officers to guide senior on the current position on board.

An element of support also helps retain seafarers and control attrition and of course increase networking. The Women Officers Network at Carnival Cruises is developing their own mentorship programme as they are seeing the benefit of an informal network. Carnival Cruise has currently 448 women officers among a total of 6600 officers. At 8% of the workforce, they are much higher than national and international average. A fifth of their cadet intake this year were women - a promising start to the new year and a positive story to end this section on.

Promoting Women in Maritime

In 2021, the IMO together with WISTA International carried out a women in Maritime survey where they undertook a study of maritime companies and IMO-member states maritime authorities. The results of the survey show that 44 percent of respondents had a formal policy in place to promote gender equality. The most radical policy was the use of quotas. 25% of organisations that responded to the survey had taken this measure. Another interesting finding from the survey was about language. It was noted that gender neutral language in job descriptions was very useful to promote women. This was a zero-cost policy that provided effective results. Gender pay equality was vital to bring about gender parity, the report noted.

The survey reiterated that women make up just about two percent of seafarers globally, but it seemed to note signs of improvement in the industry in increasing number of cadets joining. The survey recommended future action by shipowners and seafarers organisations in bringing about gender equality.

- The first goal was widespread dissemination about opportunities for women in the maritime sector. If women are not aware of a role, they cannot apply. They need to know where to go and how to access funding.
- However, once women have been brought onboard, they also need a safe working environment. The survey underlined the importance of an industrywide effort to circulate and communicate guides that addressed bullying and harassment, seafarers' welfare, as well as other negative perceptions of the maritime industry. These actions would enhance broader awareness of the measures being implemented to address the industry's challenges.

- Women should be included from the outset in all discussions, including when policies are being drafted, and in discussions to promote opportunities for female seafarers.
- Role models should be identified early and a mentoring and networking program for women seafarers and other groups vulnerable to discrimination should be set up. WISTA UK provides free membership for female seafarers and could play an important role in providing relevant networks and connections for them.
- There should be training to highlight gender equality and establish policies of zero tolerance on bullying and harassment. This would benefit not just women but everyone on board vessels, and, in fact, any maritime environment. There needs to be heavy lifting within organisations to make companies truly welcoming and equitable for women.
- Seafarers should be given access to independent counselling networks for mental health issues, such as anxiety and depression. Many resources already exist, some of which have been set up by respected charities. However, their existence and availability are not widely known. Owners have the easy option to explore these existing networks for their employees rather than the burden of setting up something new. It is important to note that not all programs benefiting women are exclusively for women; many are gender-neutral and benefit all seafarers.
- Seafarers should also be provided with sufficient recreational facilities, internet connectivity at a reasonable cost, adequate rest time, shore leave, and relevant annual leave to avoid social isolation and enhance physical and mental health.
- Provide safe gender friendly working environments, appropriate PPE, access to sanitary items and hygiene products and discrete disposal mechanisms as well as put in place zero tolerance measures for harassment and bullying, including sexual harassment.
- Ensure pregnancy testing for women seafarers is available in line with conventions.

From the International Chamber of Shipping diversity tracker 2020, where about 240 people were interviewed, only about 50 percent said that their company actively promoted and encouraged diversity and inclusion. Some said their companies had future plans to have a diversity and inclusion policy in place. More than 50 percent of the companies employed female seafarers as junior deck officers – it will be interesting to note and keep track of how many amongst them progress to senior roles in the industry and within the organisation. Engineering was the field with the least gender diversity, and this is not unlike what we see ashore not just in shipping but in all STEM sectors.

Case for Diversity

It is important to understand why we need to look at diversity in the maritime sector now. The simplest reason is that diversity allows access to a wider talent pool. The upcoming shortage of talent and seafarers has already been identified and which is likely to continue till 2028, makes a case for widening the talent pool. To encourage and enable more women to join the sea should be the urgent need for the industry. With diversity comes the ability to gain an insight into the needs and motivations of the wider client and customer base – the more diversity in the industry, the wider the client and customers and the ways that we can service them.

Diversity also reflects societies and demographics accurately. For instance, 50 percent of the population are women and therefore 50 percent of seafarers should also be women. Diversity enables a broader range of talents and experiences, enables creativity and therefore creates profitability in a shorter time scale. There is enough research to show that diversity makes company's more effective, successful, and profitable. However, full diversity and inclusion is not easy to achieve and requires dedicated efforts at making wider long-term plans and preparing the younger generations to grow within the industry. Attraction to the industry is important but retention and growth is what will make the industry truly diverse.

For a diverse workplace it is important to clearly identify what the company wants to achieve. And each company needs to have its own goal, so the diversity initiative needs to be linked to the specific corporate culture and context to be effective. One organisation's diversity and inclusion program may not be the solution for another. After identifying and planning, it is important to design the structure for diversity and thereafter, plan implementation. And it is important to bring along everyone on the journey. Effective diversity will only be possible when everyone is involved is convinced of its necessity and on board with the process. Further a McKinsey report (Diversity wins, McKinsey Report 2020) reported that companies in the top quartile for gender diversity on executive teams were twenty five percent more likely to have above average profitability than companies who didn't, they concluded after surveying 1000 companies in 25 countries that, in particular, the greater the representation, the higher likelihood of out-performance.

Conclusion

As we progress through the 21st century, the presence and contribution of women in the maritime industry is set to become even more pronounced. The data and facts discussed in this article underscore the progress that has been made but also highlight the challenges that need to be addressed. Gender diversity in maritime not only fosters a more inclusive and equitable industry but also brings diverse perspectives and skills to the forefront. It is crucial for Maritime Britain to continue working towards greater gender parity and creating an environment where women are encouraged to pursue, thrive, and lead in maritime careers.

In conclusion, women in maritime are breaking through the waves of tradition and carving their path in a historically male-dominated industry. With continued support, advocacy, and initiatives, the maritime sector in Britain can look forward to a future where gender diversity is the norm rather than the exception, ensuring a more vibrant and dynamic industry for all.

[1.] The French Navy now have a servicewomen's network named Jeanne Baret in honour of her sailing endeavours. They were established in 2019.

"Blueing" Maritime Britain: towards a Transformative Blue Governance Agenda

Sophie Quintin, Tegan Evans, and Pierre Failler

Introduction

Since the start of the 21st century, growing insecurity in many maritime spaces coupled with concerns about the health of the ocean have emphasised the need to enhance ocean governance.

The emergence of these trends has notably spurred a reassessment of policies related to the sea, resulting in the formulation of holistic strategies at the national, regional, and international levels to tackle a broad range of challenges. Making sense of an increasingly complex landscape of intertwined, often disconnected areas of sea-focused policies, complex arenas of activities, and fragmented research agendas is a task as arduous as it is critical. Against this background, this chapter reflects on the 'blue' essence of British socio-economic development as a multifaceted arena of strategies, policies, and activities. In this regard, the adoption in 2022 by the United Kingdom of its second National Strategy for Maritime Security (NSMS)[1] marks a significant evolution by including the protection of the marine environment as a core strategic objective alongside the more traditional concerns of security, rule of law, and economic prosperity.

Thus, drawing insights from the disciplines of International Relations, economics, and geography, this chapter explores the intersection and co-dependence between the maritime security and Blue Economy agendas. It weaves an argument along the 'blue' thread of ocean resilience and health posited as a premise for a secure and prosperous future for Britain. It advocates for the development of a transformative blue governance agenda to balance sea-based economic development with the conservation and responsible use of marine resources. After briefly setting the United Kingdom's "blue" scene (Section 1), the chapter reflects on the nexus between maritime security and maritime economy. Section 2 proceeds to explore maritime security as a multifaceted area of state activity with a focus on the significance of introducing ocean sustainability and resilience in the NSMS. The analysis then examines the UK maritime domain as a space for the generation of sustainable economic development through the concept of Blue Economy (Section 3). Finally, in congruence with the conference's aim of fostering a holistic understanding of Britain's maritime endeavours, the paper calls for a transformative blue governance agenda to reinforce synergies through more creative thinking, transdisciplinary conversations, and research (Section 4).

1. Britain's Blue Treasure

The centrality of the ocean to civilisational development is well established in scholarship, as is Britain's contribution to the great maritime adventure of humanity (Abulafia;[2] Attali;[3] Coutansais;[4] Fernandez-Armesto;[5] Paine[6]). In his cultural history of the sea marine sociologist John Mack[7] explains that the sea has shaped civilizational developments because of the "ways human beings interact because of it, navigate their course across it, live on and around it." Geography and the ocean as the dominant natural environment on Earth therefore matter because as Kaplan[8] reminds us it is the very backdrop of History. Hence British civilizational developments were and will continue to be influenced by the very fact it is an island state on the western end of the European continent surrounded by seas that are integral to its identity and culture (Mackinder cited in Marshall).[9] Over centuries, its peoples have therefore developed a unique and complex relationship with the ocean that explains why the maritime sector has become the lifeblood of its economy and prosperity (NSMS).[10] It is blessed with a vast blue space comprising the UK Marine Area (298 thousand square miles)[11] and the marine zones of the UK Overseas Territories and Crown Dependencies (2.32 million square miles) (NSMS).[12] A strong diverse maritime culture has established itself along its coastlines,[13] driving the growth of a maritime economy now forming the bedrock of its present-day prosperity as discussed more fully in Section 3.

If its vast maritime domain is unquestionably a 'blue treasure' it cannot afford to spoil for future generations, research has uncovered how the global acceleration in its use in the post-Cold War era has brought its health to crisis point. In the context of global geopolitical instability of the last two decades, the unsustainable negative impact of human activity on biodiversity and rising sea-borne security threats has ushered a historic 'revolution in thinking' to address challenges (Bueger & Mallin).[14] Across the world, coastal states and ocean governance architectures have struggled to handle and adjust to a widening range of maritime threats as diverse as plastic pollution, piracy, unsustainable fishing practices, sea migration and competing claims over resource-rich areas to name but a few. Many of these phenomena are not *per se* new but threats to the ocean have intensified to unprecedented levels at a time when blue spaces are expected to be the engine of development worldwide (Jouffray et al).[15] If a healthy ocean is quite simply vital for our climate and our survival on Earth as a species, the pace of industrialisation is degrading its health on an unprecedented scale (Halpern et al).[16] Since the 2010s, the acuteness of the problem has garnered considerable political support to address it with an emphasis on a sustainable integrated approach to development. The adoption in 2015 by the United Nations of the Sustainable Development Goals (DDGs) with SDG#14 (Life below water) focusing on the ocean is a case in point (UNDPSG).[17] The treaty on Biodiversity Beyond Nation-al Jurisdiction (BBNJ)[18] supported by Britain and adopted by the General Assembly in August 2023, is the latest illustration of the international community's drive to increase the protection of the ocean and enshrine its protection into the Law of the Sea.[19]

In this era of 'blue acceleration' defined as a "race among diverse and often competing interests for ocean food, material, and space" (Jouffray et al),[20] Britain's blue spaces are also facing multiple security threats and environmental challenges. In the last decade, ocean advocates have consistently argued that, for all the discourse of international leadership on environmental protection and high standards in its regulatory framework, the UK has fallen behind other European states in protecting its waters. The House of Lords report[21] highlights 'unacceptable' levels of pollution from treated and untreated sewage releases *inter alia* warning that the regulatory bodies have lost public confidence. Microplastic pollution is another area of concern with research showing its impact on our climate and marine life (Ford et al).[22] As underlined by leading experts, it is now high time to "turn off the plastic tap" with an international treaty (UNEP).[23] No coastal state whose prosperity depends on the ocean for trade and resources, least of all an industrialised island state like Britain, can afford to ignore the impact of damaging human activity on its maritime domain and on the health of its people. Research has underlined the urgency and complexity of the task ahead, advocating a holistic approach to ocean governance. Indeed, as a natural environment, British seas need to be better protected and its resources (living and non-living) exploited sustainably, they must also be secured to ensure that its sea-dependent economy continues to sustain prosperity in a more uncertain international security context.

The Paradigm of Maritime Security: Reflection on the UK National Strategy for Maritime Security

The recent discovery of a stone age wooden structure on the northern shores of the Isle of Wight is the oldest archaeological evidence of shipbuilding on the British Isles[24] (BBC News).[25] Indeed, from the moment primitive crafts were built by coastal dwellers, the sea became a 'strategic entity' of human interaction, both cooperative and competitive (Holmes).[26] The maritime dimension of security and the central role played by the Royal Navy in shaping British and world history have been amply studied (Wilson;[27] Redford & Grove[28]). In this regard, the seminal work of Mahan (1890) on the geostrategic essence of the ocean, with his theorisation of the relationship between naval power and economic prosperity, has lost neither its strength nor relevance in the 21st century.[29] Indeed, against a background of 'blue acceleration' and a rise in maritime insecurity in many areas, the sea has risen in salience in international security policy agendas rekindling interest in maritime scholarship (Germond).[30] In International Relations, buzzwords tend to be transient, waxing and waning in discourse over time. However, the sharp increase in the frequency of inter-state conflicts in the 2020s (Davies et al),[31] with many of them affecting security at sea, ensures that maritime security as an issue-area remains well entrenched in the international security agenda.[32]

The piracy crisis in the Indian Ocean off the coast of Somalia (2007-2017) triggered a rethink in the framing of debates on security at sea beyond the traditional 'hard' security approach focusing on the state (Bueger & Mallin).[33] Though ubiquitous in public and academic discourse, the question of its nature is still remarkably open-ended. The seminal matrix (see Fig. 1) designed by Bueger[34] remains a good visualisation of the expansion of the concept beyond traditional security, with the categorisation of research topics and policy initiatives under four dimensions (human security, national security, economic development, and maritime environment). It illustrates the multifaceted, flexible nature of the concept and security practice of international relations. Looking beyond the definitional fog, two points can be made. First, as an umbrella term 'maritime security' has gradually subsumed a wide range of maritime challenges and areas of academic inquiry (Tangredi;[35]

Maritime Security Matrix

MARINE ENVIRONMENT   ECONOMIC DEVELOPMENT

MARINE SAFETY   BLUE ECONOMY

Accidents   Pollution   Smuggling

Terrorist   Climate   **MARITIME**   Piracy   IUU Fishing
Acts   Change   **SECURITY**

Arms   Inter-state   Human
Proliferation   Disputes   Trafficking

SEAPOWER   RESILIENCE

NATIONAL SECURITY   HUMAN SECURITY

Fig 1: Maritime security matrix from Bueger (2014, p.161) illustrating the key dimensions and relationships of maritime security and marine issues.

Bueger;[36] Bueger & Edmunds;[37] Till;[38] Otto[39]). For the purpose of this paper, they are categorised as 'hard' and 'soft' security concerns. Secondly, reflecting on two decades of responses to insecurity it can be argued that the conceptual fuzziness continues to instrumental in mustering collaborative initiatives. These have ranged from international security projection operations, capacity-building programmes, and the establishment of maritime security architecture where none existed before as was notably the case for West and East Africa (Ali;[40] Bueger, Edmunds & McCabe).[41] The imperative of adjusting to changing security environments[42] has also prompted a worldwide flurry of strategy-making and, in the global north, a rethink of existing architectures.

Britain is a case in point. As a major maritime power, it has a long tradition of strategic adjustments to changing maritime security contexts actioned with the introduction of new defence reviews and reforms to its security architecture (Grove cited in Bueger et al).[43] In this regard, the 2010s marked a turning point with the adoption of its first strategy using the 'maritime security' paradigm in 2014.[44] The 2022 revision is a comprehensive 116-page document that illustrates the shift towards holistic thinking. Its inclusive understanding of maritime security[45] combined with an integrated approach to problem-solving is reflected in the enunciation of the strategic objectives: 1) Protecting our homeland, 2) Responding to threats, 3) Ensuring prosperity, 4) Championing our values and finally 5) Supporting a secure, resilient ocean. To operationalise this evolution in thinking, the Joint Maritime Security Centre (JMSC) was established in 2019 to better coordinate operations at sea.[46] In their analysis, Bueger et al[47] highlight three significant innovations the 2022 NSMS. First, the significance of the collegiate approach to the drafting process to ensure alignment with the interests and visions of stakeholders (public sector, academia, and civil society) is underlined.[48] Secondly, the new framework offers a chance to operationalise the comprehensive approach thus integrating defence, diplomacy, and development as advanced in the broader 2022 'Integrated Review'[49] (Bueger et al).[47] Finally, the revised strategy has embedded marine environmental considerations as a core strategic objective.

Security, as Gray[50] stresses, is central to the "high business of the state," and an imperative to ensure its survival. The NSMS does what a strategy should do, which it is to set clear objectives with a plan of action prioritising the protection of the Realm (1&2), its maritime economy, and reaffirming the government support for the Law of the Sea (LOSC) norms that underpin the sea-based world order. It also highlights that as a multifaceted arena of state activity, implementing maritime security requires the involvement of a wide range of institutions. However, the Royal Navy fundamentally remains the linchpin of the country's security and prosperity which ultimately depend on its capacity to defend the principles of free trade, freedom of navigation and the international liberal order to which it has contributed so much as a major sea power (NSMS).[51] With its many case studies and consolidated approach, this strategic refresh not only underlines the interconnected nature of the ocean, but also the geostrategic essence of maritime security. As highlighted in section 1, the increase in the use of maritime spaces has not only caused political tension, but now threatens the health of ocean upon which lives are so dependent. This brings us to the introduction of the ocean as an object to be secured and an endangered 'blue treasure' to be protected within a maritime security framework (Objective 5).

For coastal states maritime security is the "cadre of activities – legislative, executive, judicial, military, and police actions – designed to respond to a collective need for order and protection from internal and external threats" (Klein).[52] These have traditionally included responses to illicit activities (fisheries, customs, and marine pollution) (See Fig. 1) with naval forces playing important roles in policing maritime spaces. By setting support to an "ocean that is effectively governed, clean, healthy, safe, productive, and biologically diverse" (NSMS),[53] the new strategy goes further in its conceptualisation of maritime security and conception of the ocean as an inter-related transnational security complex. Indeed, it now includes the imperative of supporting a "'resilient ocean', meaning one in which biodiversity loss is reversed and the sustainability of any economic exploitation of ocean resources ensured" (Bueger et al).[54] Embedding ocean sustainability in maritime security debates is crucial because healthy oceans ultimately contribute to political stability. The strategic refresh highlights that the implementation of sustainable practices in the maritime sector helps preserve (or restore) marine ecosystems to ensure an equilibrium between biodiversity and the preservation of the livelihoods of coastal communities. Addressing issues like overfishing, pollution, and climate change not only protects the environment but also enhances maritime security by fostering economic stability and reducing conflicts over scarce marine resources. In our era of blue acceleration, it is therefore critical that marine environmental concerns and the objective of ocean resilience and health become integral to maritime security conversations, strategies and practice.

To conclude, the symbiotic relationship between sea power, economic development and the law of the sea is well established, and its dynamics are the engine of the liberal sea-based economic order (Tangredi;[55] Krasna;[56] Booth[57]). As the latest strategic adjustment to a constantly evolving inter-national context, the new NSMS seeks to strengthen the self-reinforcing cycle that has promoted continuous economic growth and enabled globalisation with the ability to undertake oceanic voyages (Till;[58] Klein[59]). It has advanced the principle of an integrated approach to maritime security as a multifaceted endeavour by broadening the spectrum of issues addressed by including the ocean, which in effect makes sustain-able ocean development integral to UK maritime security interests. Britain's maritime domain is the fifth largest in the world with sovereign territories sprinkled around the globe, which is a challenge in terms of governance. As briefly highlighted in Section 1, Britain's blue treasure is impacted by human activities which makes the progression towards a Blue Economy all the more important to reinforce the synergies between the components of the virtuous circle.

2. The Growth of the Blue Economy Concept: Lessons to be Learned in Centralising Sustainability in Development

As outlined above, maritime security has always been fundamental to the UK maritime economy. The latest iteration of the NSMS[60] does include some consideration of the critical importance of preserving the health of maritime environments, but it does not include broader considerations of sustainable development. Section 2 also outlines the implications of the traditional narrow interpretation of economic activity at sea which omits considerations of sustainability. Sustainable development has been an undeniable catalyst for global policy and development, since the inception of the Brundtland Commission in 1987, where the seminal definition "development that meets the needs of the present without compromising the ability of future generations to meet their own needs" was formulated (WCED).[61] Global policies such as the Sustainable Development Goals have enshrined the importance of sustainable development on a global stage through 17 holistic development goals (Biermann).[62]

Considerations of sustainable development within traditional ocean, maritime and marine sectors is thus urgently required. The evolution of the blue economy in contrast to traditional maritime security conceptualisations evidences this turn to sustainable development, and has since exploded as a concept in the last decade. The blue economy began in response to the growing emphasis on the green economy as part of Rio+20 in 2012 by small island states, advocating for recognition of the centrality of ocean environments to health, culture, and the economy (Silver).[63] Currently, roughly 47 Commonwealth countries are implementing or have undertaken political commitment towards the concept in some form (Voyer, Benzaken and Rambourg),[64] and an 'African blue economy wave' is sweeping the continent with diverse arrangements arising to implement the blue economy (Spamer).[65] Recent ambitions have been globally aligned through the High-Level Ocean Panel for a Sustainable Ocean Economy, a growing coalition of now 18 countries which aims to "advance a more prosperous and resilient future for people and the planet" in 2020 (High Level Ocean Panel).[66] Significant private sector interest has also facilitated movement with the concept, with significant support from actors such as The Economist, World Bank and the OECD (OECD).[67]

In contrast to the maritime economy, the blue economy concept has reinvigorated and re-centralised our fundamental reliance on 'blue' environments for survival through the lens of economic development but emphasises the importance of sustainable development. Despite this widespread attention and implementation, the concept remains difficult to define, with definitions often reflecting national priorities. In general, the blue economy can be defined as the sustainable use of ocean resources for economic growth, improved livelihoods and jobs, and ocean eco-system health. Thus, the concept balances sustainable economic growth against ocean conservation and societal resilience and equity at its core. Competing and conflicting definitions hinder true progress towards global sustainability, however, with significant risk for 'blue-washing' or the deceptive overstating of the sustainability of interventions in ocean spaces (Voyer).[68]

The lack of definition is most prevalent when deciding which sectors are included in a blue economy approach, with notable uncertainty surrounding whether extractive industries such as deep-sea mining can be considered part of a sustainable blue economy. For example, a report by UNEP's Sustainable Blue Finance Initiative[69] (2022) proposed that there was no way in which deep-sea mining could be consistent with the core values of a sustainable blue economy. In 2023, however, India launched an exploratory deep-sea mining project (valued at around €460 million) to advance the Indian blue economy (Landrin).[70] Extractive industries and hydrocarbons represent a critical area in which diverging interests of the sustainable blue economy must be reconciled: conservation of vulnerable deep-sea environments against the economic gains of rare materials (Mallin and Barbesgaard).[71] Historically, maritime security has been included as an implicit sector within the wider collection of traditional ocean industries, but a significant opportunity exists to identify synergies between the blue economy and maritime security more formally, as will be discussed in the following section.

The blue economy is not a panacea to the sustainable development of ocean environments, and several challenges must be considered when advocating for a blue economy. There is concern that the blue economy may facilitate a 'business as usual' approach to economic growth and fail to achieve sustainable development through the prioritisation of environ-mental and social health. Bennett et al[72] argues that over time the term has been diluted from the reassertion of sustainable development to instead "encapsulate international interest in the growth of ocean based economic development", and risks side-lining equity and conservation in the process. Additionally, the blue economy risks re-entrenching existing power dynamics and private ownership of ocean resources. Virdin et al[73] identified 100 transnational corporations account for 60% of total ocean revenue, emphasising the risk of blue acceleration and 'ocean grabbing' through private actors. The blue economy should not privatise the ocean – it should embody holistic sustainable development that prioritises equitable decision making.

The economic imperative for a blue economy approach in the UK is obvious. As an island nation with a strong maritime history, the blue economy paradigm could naturally align with sustainable development initiatives (as outlined above in Section 2, 'Britain's blue treasure'). Kontovas et al[74] characterise the UK's blue economy as encompassing coastal tourism, marine non-living resources (mainly oil and gas), port activities, shipbuilding and repair and maritime transport, which contributed around €2 billion to UK national gross value added in 2017. However, uptake of the concept within the UK is slow. The UK officially joined the High-Level Ocean Panel in 2022 following the Lisbon Ocean Conference, adding around 7 million km^2 of maritime territory to the collective ambitions of ocean health, wealth, knowledge, equity and finance (Ocean Panel).[75] Beyond this, little progress in charting a vision towards the blue economy has been made with the exception of Scotland. Scotland released a Blue Economy Vision in 2022, which outlines long term ambitions that span environmental, social and economic priorities, and identifies the next steps for blue economy realisation (Marine Scotland).[76]

Section 3 has highlighted that with its inclusion of ocean sustainability as a core objective alongside other more traditional security concerns, the new NSMS is charting a course in the right direction. This holistic approach to security represents an opportunity for linking those paradigms together and integrating them in terms of policy making and implementation. The UK therefore needs to learn from the blue economy approach to embed the core principles of sustainable development across maritime sectors. As discussed above, the UK has a rich maritime heritage, primarily focusing on maritime security. The question therefore arises, how does the UK begin to move from a maritime security emphasis to adopting the sustainable development blue economy focus? The relationship between maritime security and the blue economy is implicit at best (Potgieter)[77] and the foundational role of maritime security in blue economy planning is largely omitted. Limited exploration of the synergies and conflicts between the two concepts has been undertaken in academic literature, with the exception of Voyer et al,[78] Potgieter[76] and Bueger.[79] At present, two key perspectives exist discretely in the literature: maritime security as an enabler of the blue economy; and maritime security as a sector in the blue economy.

Maritime security plays the foundational role of establishing secure and safe navigable waterways that allow for offshore development, trade, and activities. The clearest example of this is the role of maritime security in the prevention of crimes such as piracy, terrorism, and smuggling, which present several challenges to maritime trade as discussed above in Section 2. As Menzel[80] details, the threat of piracy in the Strait of Malacca and Gulf of Aden in 2005 caused shipping insurance rates to rise and incurred the redirection of trade "massive" costs. Coordinated efforts by a diverse pool of actors in the region, including "a coalition of navies, coastguards, international organisations and private maritime security personnel", have reduced the threat of piracy and allowed trade to continue (Menzel;[79] Bueger and Edmund).[81] Beyond the obvious security imperative, the services encompassed within the broad paradigm of maritime security include human security and capacity for disaster management, to ecosystem management protection and protection against environmental crime such as illegal dumping at sea (Voyer et al).[82] Offshore surveying, provision of oceanographic data and navigational charts are the bedrock of all maritime activities. In the UK, a long-standing maritime heritage of "Trust in God and an Admiralty chart" evidences the extent to which maritime security supports offshore activity (Haslam).[83] Despite these diverse provisioning services, the role of maritime security in supporting the blue economy is often undervalued and implicit in blue economy agendas and strategies globally.

A secondary perspective regards maritime security as a sector of the blue economy, including sectors such as shipbuilding, innovation in surveillance and monitoring, although this exists as a less formal sector (Voyer et al).[81] In 2022, the UK Government pledged an investment of £4 billion into the UK shipbuilding sector, a sector which contributed £2.8 million in 2020 (National Shipbuilding Office).[84] Reimagining this growth as part of the blue economy agenda would prioritise environmental and social demands alongside economic considerations. In short, maritime security and the blue economy should be regarded as two sides of the same coin, despite limited discussion of the intersections between the two. As Voyer et al[81] summarises, the two are mutually codependent. Beyond whether or not maritime security is considered an enabler or discrete sector of the blue economy, creating holistic and integrated ways of managing and 'blueing' maritime sectors represents an urgent change in UK maritime governance.

3. Setting A New Course For Transformative Blue Governance

This chapter has sought to highlight that the objective of ensuring continued blue prosperity for the United Kingdom in the 21st century cannot be done at the expense of the health of the ocean upon which it relies. The complexities of putting in place a policy and implementation framework that guarantees success in the attainment of the five objectives of the NSMS necessitates interdisciplinary conversations and multi-disciplinary collaborations to put into action the much-preached holistic approach. This research has outlined a need for change in the UK: to encapsulate the importance of sustainable development in maritime security, as learned from the blue economy approach. These changes can be realised through a broader transformation to a blue governance approach, to ensure that the diverse facets of marine, maritime, and ocean governance systems are holistically managed and coordinated (Bueger et al).[85]

Blue governance is a holistic approach that recognises the inter-connectedness and interdependencies of diverse 'blue' sectors. Blue governance as a concept has been pioneered by the African Union through their seminal Blue Governance Framework (AU-IBAR)[86] which has been created to streamline approaches towards the blue economy. As a concept, blue governance advocates for the consideration of all blue sectors, and therefore requires a governance system that "ensure[s] overall consistency, coherence and synergy and develop[s] bridges and lever-age[s] resources between various implementation plans for strategies" (Africa Blue Economy Strategy).[85] In other words, blue governance prioritises integration and holistic governance to achieve sustainable development. Thus, blue governance can be considered as the natural evolution from the current governance approaches that regard these sectors and activities as separate and under-emphasises the importance of sustainability. As illustrated by the ocean claims figure below (Fig. 2) the ocean is, after all, a highly interconnected and interdependent environment where impacts and activities do not conform to socially constructed boundaries.

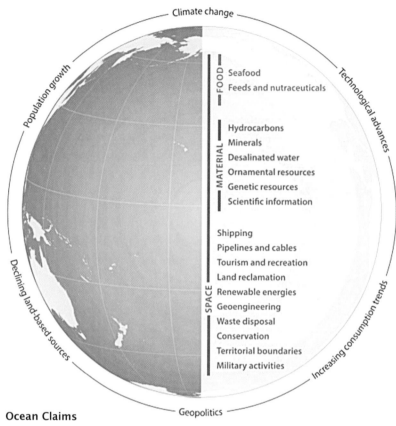

Ocean Claims

The ocean is increasingly regarded as an engine of present and future human needs for food, material, and space. Claims were identified and categorised through an iterative process aimed at understanding oceans uses of direct relevance for ecosystem sustainability, human well-being, and economic growth. Around the globe are some of the key distal drivers shaping this new global ocean context.

Fig 2: Competing claims on ocean environments as illustrated by Jouffray et al.

Thus, blue governance represents a transformative approach to ocean governance, effectively 'blueing' the existing governance by enshrining sustainable development at the core of 'blue' activities (Fig. 3). Blue governance emerges as a way to achieve the simultaneous trans-formations required in UK maritime governance. Transformative chan-ge, while a growing area of academic exploration, remains poorly understood in terms of its practical realisation (Evans et al).[88] While trans-formative theory is diverse, significant practical insight can be obtained from leverage points, which are often used to describe

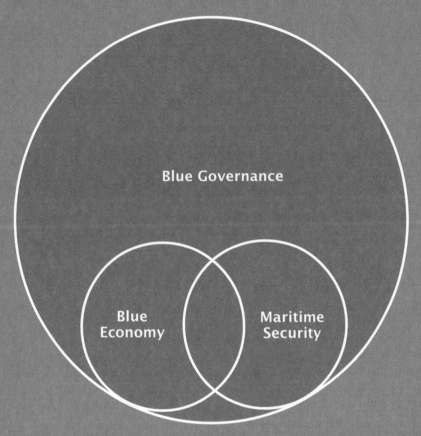

Fig 3: Charting blue governance as a concept. Authors' illustration of the natural overlap between the blue economy and maritime security, and how these can be joined together under blue governance.

transformative pathways in system thinking. Leverage points are defined as places to intervene in a system, where a small shift can have a disproportionate impact across the system, with deeper leverage points allowing for more radical change (Abson et al;[89] Davelaar;[90] Meadows[91]). Using a leverage point approach heuristically at this stage emphasises that transformation should be targeted at the deeper, intangible elements of a system, such as values, paradigms and intent. Moving towards a blue governance approach, while requiring all levels of leverage to be used, represents a shift of the deepest levels towards integrated and coordinated governance of blue environments.

In essence, it is argued that the virtuous maritime cycle which has served Britain to date must be reinforced because, as two spheres of practice, maritime security and maritime economy form an inter-dependent system. In less uncertain times, these two spheres of activities and academic inquiry have tended to exist in parallel and must therefore be reinvigorated. As highlighted above, the blue intellectual revolution has generated a new momentum in bridging intellectual gaps. In our current era of blue acceleration – within an international security context that is fast-changing, unstable and uncertain – the dynamics of the self-reinforcing circle must be reinvigorated and progressed to incorporate new challenges such as the protection of the ocean. In our current era of blue acceleration in the use of the ocean, it is necessary to avoid fragmentation of purpose and increasing synergies in policymaking and implementation between the various components. Hence, our proposal for a virtuous blue circle as a conceptual path to sustainable development incorporating a healthy and resilient ocean (Fig. 4).

Evolving the virtuous circle requires a transformation to blue govern-ance. In the UK, this transformation should prioritise all facets of sustainable development while addressing the persistent problems of maritime and ocean governance (Evans et al).[92] There are multiple places to intervene in a system to create transformative change, but it is largely agreed that addressing 'deep' and often intangible elements of a governance system (such as values, knowledge, culture and commun-ication patterns) is most effective (Davelaar;[93] Abson et al[94]). The next paragraphs outline two possible transformations to be undertaken in pursuit of blue governance in the UK.

To address this deeper change, it is recommended firstly that a trans-disciplinary research agenda be pursued in pursuit of knowledge and policy generation for sustainable development. Transdisciplinary research recognises the inherently holistic and integrated nature of the oceans and brings multiple disciplines and perspectives (including beyond academia) into knowledge creation (Strand et al).[95] The transdisciplinary approach of the authorship team of this chapter (spanning international relations, legal analyses, geography, economics and consultancy experiences from diverse national contexts) begins to highlight the merits of a blue governance approach in the UK. To be truly transdisciplinary, however, this conversation needs to continue beyond traditional conceptual-isations of 'maritime actors.' The NSMS has begun this process through its collegiate generation, but trans-disciplinarity must extend beyond strategy creation.

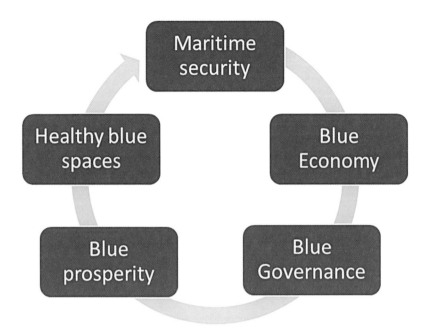

Fig 4: Towards an evolution of the virtuous maritime cycle, incorporating the blue economy, blue governance, blue prosperity and healthy blue spaces.

Building on the imperative of holistic governance for sustainable development, it is well established that marine governance in the UK is complex, with significant capacity for improved coordination and collaboration across the diverse sectors and silos characteristic of marine governance (Boyes and Elliott).[96] In line with the recent advances of the NSMS, and in parallel with the prioritisation of integrated governance as part of a blue approach, it is proposed that a transformational change in UK governance should promote synergy and coordination at a governance level through the creation of a Ministry for the Ocean to coordinate maritime activities. This proposition is not new. Voyer et al[97] identified 13 countries that have created Ministries or governmental Departments to coordinate and shape blue economy implementation. Indeed, movement towards a more coordinated and integrated govern-ance structure for the oceans is slow but progressing. In 2022, an All-Party Parliamentary Group for the Ocean was launched, with the objective of creating a platform for ocean knowledge, research and solutions. In a similar vein, in 2022 the UK House of Lords debated the creation of a Minister for the Oceans. Creating a single Ministry for the

Ocean (or Blue Ministry) would allow for a streamlined and integrated ocean governance hub, which would allow for diverse ocean and maritime activities to be managed in synergy and in accordance with sustainable development.

Conclusion

This chapter has outlined the dependence of the UK on the preservation and protection of its blue treasure, and the need to evolve the concept of maritime security beyond the traditional virtuous circle of maritime development. The Blue Economy offers a way to enshrine sustainable development as part of this evolution. The symbiotic and reinforcing relationship between maritime security and the Blue Economy was also outlined, despite the limited discussion of the interrelationships between the two in the literature. This chapter has sought to contribute to emerging debate by advocating for a 'blueing' of maritime security through a transformation to a 'blue governance' approach. Blue govern-ance represents a way to ensure that the fundamental principles of maritime security and sustainable development are mutually reinforcing. In short, to evolve the virtuous circle of maritime security into the 21st century. This Chapter has outlined two steps forward to formalising and realising a blue governance approach, firstly by fostering trans-disciplinarity, and secondly by creating a Ministry of the Oceans. Underpinning both recommendations is the need to commit to a holistic way of governing ocean resources.

The ocean has been a theatre of competition and collaboration from the beginning of the maritime adventure of humankind. For Britain, better governance in all the aspects of this complex endeavour in the 21st century is an imperative for its survival as a prosperous island-nation. With its strong maritime tradition as a sea power, as a centre of academic excellence, and with the support of grassroot ocean activism, we believe the UK is well placed to move forward the debate and practice towards a more integrated blue governance framework to reinvigorate its virtuous maritime cycle for future generations.

1. National Strategy for Maritime Security, (2022), https://www.gov.uk/government/publications/national-maritime-security-strategy.

2. D. Abulafia, *The Boundless Sea: A Human History of the Oceans,* (Penguin Random House, 2019).

3. J. Attali, *Histoires de la mer,* (Fayard, 2017).

4. C.P. Coutansais, *Une histoire des empires maritimes*, (CNRS 2016).

5. F. Fernandez-Armesto, *Pathfinders. A global history of exploration*, (W.W. Norton & Company, 2006).

6. L. Paine, *The sea and civilization: A Maritime history of the world,* (Atlantic Books, 2013).

7. J. Mack, *The Sea. A Cultural History.* (Reaktion Books, 2011) p. 13.

8. R.Kaplan, *The revenge of geography. What maps tells us about coming conflicts and the battle against fate*, (Random House, 2012) p. 28.

9. T. Marshall, *The power of geography. Ten maps that reveal the future of our world.* (Elliott and Thompson, 2021) p. 151.

10. National Strategy for Maritime Security, (2022) p. 6 https://www.gov.uk/government/publications/national-maritime-security-strategy.

11. The UK Marine Area (UKMA) is 3.5 times the national land territory surface.

12. National Strategy for Maritime Security (2014). p. 17 https://www.gov.uk/government/publications/national-strategy-for-maritime-security.

13. Ordinance Survey estimates the total length of its UK Maritime Area coastline at 31,368km.

14. C. Bueger and F. Mallin, Blue paradigms: understanding the intellectual revolution in global ocean politics, 1719–1739. International Affairs, (2023) 99(4).

15. J.B. Jouffray, R.Blasiak, A.V. Norström, H. Österblom, and M. Nyström, The Blue acceleration: the trajectory of human expansion into the Ocean, One Earth, (2020) 2(1), 43-54 (43). https://www.sciencedirect.com/science/article/pii/S2590332219302751.

16. B.S. Halpern, M. Frazier, J. Afflerbach, J.S. Lowndes, F. Micheli, C. O'Hara, C. Scarborough, & K.A. Selkoe, Recent pace of change in human impact on the world's ocean, Sci. Rep., 9, (2019) 1-8.

17. United Nations Development Programme (2015). https://www.undp.org/sustainable-development-goals/below-water.

18. Biodiversity Beyond National Jurisdiction, (2023). https://treaties.un.org/doc/Treaties/2023/06/20230620%2004-28%20PM/Ch_XXI_10.pdf.

19. Intergovernmental Conference on an international legally binding instrument under the United Nations Convention on the Law of the Sea on the conservation and sustainable use of marine biological diversity of areas beyond national jurisdiction (General Assembly resolution 72/249).

20. J.B. Jouffray, R.Blasiak, A.V. Norström, H. Österblom, and M. Nyström, The Blue acceleration: the trajectory of human expansion into the Ocean, One Earth, (2020) 2(1), 43-54 (43). https://www.sciencedirect.com/science/article/pii/S2590332219302751.

21. House of Lord report, Sewage pollution in England's waters, (2022).

https://lordslibrary.parliament.uk/sewage-pollution-in-englands-waters/.

22. H.V. Ford, N.H. Jones, A.J. Davies, B.J. Godley, J.R. Jambeck, I. Napper, C. Suckling, G.J. Williams, L.C. Woodall, and H.J. Koldewey, The fundamental links between climate change and marine plastic pollution, Science of the Total Environment, (2022).

23. United Nations Environment Programme, Turning off the Tap: How the world can end plastic pollution and create a circular economy, (2023). https://wedocs.unep.org/bitstream/handle/20.500.11822/42277/Plastic_pollution.pdf?sequence=4.

24. The research was conducted by the Maritime Archaeological Trust (2019).

25. BBC News, Wooden Stone Age platform found on seabed off Isle of Wight, (2019). https://www.bbc.co.uk/news/uk-england-hampshire-49405708.

26. R. Holmes, *A brief guide to maritime strategy.* (Naval Institute Press, 2019) p. 4.

27. B. Wilson, *Empire of the Deep: The Rise and Fall of the British Navy.* (W & M, 2014).

28. D. Redford, & P. Grove, *The Royal Navy. A history since the 1900.* (UK: Bloomsbury Publishing, 2019).

29. His seminal work "The Influence of Sea Power upon History: 1660–1783" (1890) positing the interrelationship between prosperity and sea power has continued to resonate today and to influence strategic thinking beyond the confines of Western scholarship and policymaking as for instance in Asia.

30. B. Germond, The geopolitical dimension of maritime security (2015). *Marine Policy*, 54, 137–142.https://doi.org/10.1016/j.marpol.2014.12.013.

31. S. Davies, T. Pettersson, and M. Oberg, Organized violence 1989–2022, and the return of conflict between states. Journal of Peace Research, 60(4), (2023), 691–708.

32. The Ukraine conflict has had a serious impact on maritime traffic and has for example highlighted that the use of sea drone by a small navy can cause considerable damage to a major sea power like Russia.

33. C. Bueger and F. Mallin, *Blue paradigms: understanding the intellectual revolution in global ocean politics.* 1719–1739. (International Affairs, 2023) p. 7.

34. C. Bueger, What is maritime security? *Marine Policy, 52,* (2015) 159-164. https://doi.org/10.1016/j.marpol.2014.12.005.

35. S.J. Tangredi, *Globalization and Maritime Power,* (2002). Institute for National Strategic Studies.

36. C. Bueger, What is maritime security? *Marine Policy, 52,* (2015) 159-164. https://doi.org/10.1016/j.marpol.2014.12.005.

37. C. Bueger, & T. Edmunds, Beyond seablindness: a new agenda for maritime security studies, International Affairs, 93(6), (2017). 1293-1311.

38. G. Till, *Sea power. A guide for the twenty-first century* (3rd edition). (Routledge, 2013).

39. L. Otto, *Global Challenges in Maritime Security*, (Ed.) (Springer, 2020).

40. K-D. Ali, *Maritime Security Cooperation in the Gulf of Guinea: Prospects and Challenges*. (Brill Nijhoff, 2015).

41. C. Bueger, T. Edmunds, & R. McCabe, *Maritime Security, Capacity Building, and the Western Indian Ocean*, (Palgrave Macmillan, 2021) https://doi.org/10.1007/978-3-030-50064-1_1.

42. Amirell (2016) distinguishes four phases of maritime security: Phase 1, the Iberian period of maritime security (c. 1450–1600); Phase 2, the era of the trading companies (c. 1600–1850); Phase 3: the era of Sea Power (c. 1850–1990), and finally, Phase 4, the post-Cold War era (c. 1990–the present).

43. C. Bueger, T. Edmunds, & S. Edwards, Innovation and new strategic choices, The RUSI Journal, 166:4, (2021). 66-75 (66) (67), DOI: 10.1080/03071847.2021.1981777.

44. The first country to adopt such a wider maritime security agenda and problematization was the United States of America. The 9/11 attack prompted the United States to lead in this regard with the launch in 2005 of a new integrated national strategy against a background of maritime insecurity challenges in the era of globalization.

45. The understanding chosen is very broad and is reflected in the statement on what maritime is about, namely "upholding laws, regulations, and norms to deliver a free, fair, and open maritime domain." (NSMS, 2022, p.12).

46. According to the NSMS (2022, p.16), "the JMSC is at the centre of our response to maritime security. It works with stakeholders across government to develop a 'Whole System Response' to maritime security threats".

47. C. Bueger, T. Edmunds, & S. Edwards, Innovation and new strategic choices, The RUSI Journal, 166:4, (2021). 66-75, DOI: 10.1080/03071847.2021.1981777.

48. The drafting of the 25 sections of the UKNSMS involved over 50 specialists from different UK departments and agencies, consultations between agencies and meetings with academic experts, industry, and many other stakeholders (Bueger et al., 2021, p.68).

49. In March 2021, the government launched a key strategic document to steer the UK's security response or 'Integrated Review; 'Global Britain in a Competitive Age: The Integrated Review of Security, Defence, Development and Foreign Policy'.

50. C. Gray, Strategy and Security. *Infinity Journal*, 4(3), 11-15 (2015). https://www.militarystrategymagazine.com/article/strategy-and-security/.

51. National Strategy for Maritime Security (2022) p. 76. https://www.gov.uk/government/publications/national-maritime-security-strategy.

52. N. Klein, *Maritime security and the Law of the Sea*. (Oxford University Press, 2010) p. 2.

53. National Strategy for Maritime Security (2022) p. 13. https://www.gov.uk/government/publications/national-maritime-security-strategy.

54. C. Bueger, T. Edmunds, & S. Edwards, Innovation and new strategic choices, The RUSI Journal, 166:4, (2021). 66-75 (71), DOI: 10.1080/03071847.2021.1981777.

55. S.J. Tangredi, *Globalization and Maritime Power*, Institute for National Strategic Studies, (2002).

56. J. Krasna, *Maritime power and the Law of the Sea. Expeditionary operation in world politics*. (Oxford University Press, 2011).

57. K. Booth, *Law, force and diplomacy at sea*. (George Allen & Unwin, 1985).

58. G. Till, *Sea power. A guide for the twenty-first century*. p.17.

59. N. Klein, *The Oxford Handbook of the Law of the Sea*, Maritime Security. D. Rothwell (Ed.), (Oxford University Press, 2015). pp. 582–603.

60. National Strategy for Maritime Security, (2022). https://www.gov.uk/government/publications/national-maritime-security-strategy.

61. WCED, U. Our common future, (1987).

62. F. Biermann, N. Kanie, & R.E. Kim, 'Global governance by goal-setting: the novel approach of the UN Sustainable Development Goals', Current Opinion in Environmental Sustainability, 26 (2017), 26-31.

63. J.J. Silver, & L.M. Campbell, 'Conservation, development and the blue frontier: the Republic of Seychelles' debt restructuring for marine conservation and climate adaptation program', International Social Science Journal, (2018), 68 (229-230), 241-256.

64. M. Voyer, D. Benzaken, & C. Rambourg, 'Institutionalizing the Blue Economy: an examination of variations and consistencies among Commonwealth countries', Philosophical Transactions of the Royal Society (2022). B, 377(1854), 20210125.

65. J. Spamer, 'Riding the African blue economy wave: a South African perspective'. 4th International Conference on Advanced Logistics and Transport (ICALT) (2015) pp. 59-64.

66. High Level Ocean Panel. 'Transformations for a sustainable ocean economy', (2020). https://oceanpanel.org/wp-content/uploads/2022/06/transformations-sustainable-ocean-economy-eng.pdf.

67. OECD, '*The Ocean Economy in 2030*', (Paris: OECD Publishing, 2016). https://doi.org/10.1787/9789264251724-en.

68. M. Voyer, C. Schofield, K. Azmi, R. Warner, A. McIlgorm, & G. Quirk, 'Maritime security and the Blue Economy: intersections and interdependencies in the Indian Ocean', Journal of the Indian Ocean Region, (2018), 14(1), 28-48.

69. UNEPs Sustainable Blue Finance Initiative (2022), https://www.unepfi.org/blue-finance/.

70. S. Landrin, 'India launches deep-sea mining project to develop "blue economy"', Le Monde, (2023), https://www.lemonde.fr/en/environment/article/2023/01/11/india-launches-deep-sea-mining-project-to-develop-the-blue-economy_6011138_114.html (Accessed: 08 November 2023).

71. F. Mallin, & M. Barbesgaard, 'Awash with contradiction: Capital, ocean space and the logics of the Blue Economy Paradigm', Geoforum, (2020). 113, 121-132.

72. N.J. Bennett, A.M. Cisneros-Montemayor, J. Blythe, J.J. Silver, G. Singh, N. Andrews, A. Calò, P. Christie, A. Di Franco, E.M. Finkbeiner, and S. Gelcich, & U.R. Sumaila, 'Towards a sustainable and equitable blue economy'. Nature Sustainability, 2(11), (2019) 991.

73. J. Virdin, T. Vegh, J.B. Jouffray, R. Blasiak, S. Mason, H. Österblom, & N. Werner, 'The Ocean 100: Transnational corporations in the ocean economy', Science Advances, 7(3) (2021).

74. C. Kontovas, A.A. Bras, C.H. Chang, A. Romano, M.C.P. Poo, J. Wang, & Z. Yang, 'Fostering innovation in the blue economy within the United Kingdom (UK): A stakeholders' perspective', Ocean & Coastal Management, (2022), 224, 106143.

75. Ocean Panel, 'United Kingdom Joins High Level Panel for a Sustainable Ocean Economy' (2022). https://oceanpanel.org/united-kingdom-joins-high-level-panel-for-a-sustainable-ocean-economy/ (Accessed 9 November, 2023).

76. Marine Scotland, 'A Blue Economy Vision for Scotland', (2022). https://www.gov.scot/publications/blue-economy-vision-scotland/.

77. T. Potgieter, 'Oceans economy, blue economy, and security: notes on the South African potential and developments', Journal of the Indian Ocean Region, 14(1) (2018), 49-70.

78. M. Voyer, C. Schofield, K. Azmi, R. Warner, A. McIlgorm, & G. Quirk, 'Maritime security and the Blue Economy: intersections and interdependencies in the Indian Ocean', Journal of the Indian Ocean Region, (2018), 14(1), 28-48.

79. C. Bueger, 'We are all islanders now' – Michel's blue economy kaleidoscope and the missing link to maritime security. (2018).

80. A. Menzel, 'Maritime Security and the Blue Economy', *Routledge Handbook of Maritime Security*, R-L Boşilcă, S. Ferreira, & B.J. Ryan, (Eds.), (Routledge, 2022) p. 268 https://doi.org/10.4324/9781003001324.

81. C. Bueger, & T. Edmunds, Beyond seablindness: a new agenda for maritime security studies, International Affairs, 93(6), (2017) 1293-1311.

82. M. Voyer, C. Schofield, K. Azmi, R. Warner, A. McIlgorm, & G. Quirk, 'Maritime security and the Blue Economy: intersections and interdependencies in the Indian Ocean', Journal of the Indian Ocean Region, (2018), 14(1), 28-48.

83. D.W. Haslam, Changing the Admiralty Chart. The Journal of Navigation, 32(2), (2009) 164-170.

84. National Shipbuilding Office, 'National Shipbuilding Strategy', (2022), https://assets.publishing.service.gov.uk/media/6231b9e2e90e070ed32f18ce/_CP_605___National_Shipbuilding_Strategy_Refresh.pdf. (Accessed 13 November 2023).

85. C. Bueger, & T. Edmunds, Beyond seablindness: a new agenda for maritime security studies. International Affairs, 93(6), (2017). 1293-1311.

86. AU-IBAR, 'Africa Blue Economy Strategy', 2019. https://www.au-ibar.org/sites/default/files/2020-10/sd_20200313_africa_blue_economy_strategy_en.pdf.

87. J.B. Jouffray, R.Blasiak, A.V. Norström, H. Österblom, and M. Nyström, 'The Blue acceleration: the trajectory of human expansion into the Ocean', (One Earth, 2020) 2(1), 43-54 (44) https://www.sciencedirect.com/science/article/pii/S2590332219302751.

88. L.S. Evans, C.C. Hicks, P.J. Cohen, P. Case, M. Prideaux, D.J. Mills, 'Understanding leadership in the environmental sciences', Ecology and Society, 20(1), (2015). art50. https://doi.org/10.5751/ES-07268-200150.

89. D. J. Abson, J. Fischer, J. Leventon, J. Newig, T. Schomerus, U. Vilsmaier, H. von Wehrden, P. Abernethy, C.D. Ives, N.W. Jager & D.J. Lang, Leverage points for sustainability transformation Perspective. Volume 46, pages 30–39, (2017).

90. D. Davelaar, Transformation for sustainability: A deep leverage points approach. Sustainability Science, 16(3), (2021) 727–747. https://doi.org/10.1007/s11625-020-00872-0.

91. D.H. Meadows, *Thinking in systems: A primer*, (Chelsea Green, 2008).

92. L.S. Evans, C.C. Hicks, P.J. Cohen, P. Case, M. Prideaux, D.J. Mills, 'Understanding leadership in the environmental sciences', Ecology and Society, 20(1), (2015). art50. https://doi.org/10.5751/ES-07268-200150.

93. D. Davelaar, Transformation for sustainability: A deep leverage points approach. Sustainability Science, 16(3), (2021) 727–747. https://doi.org/10.1007/s11625-020-00872-0.

94. D. J. Abson, J. Fischer, J. Leventon, J. Newig, T. Schomerus, U. Vilsmaier, H. von Wehrden, P. Abernethy, C.D. Ives, N.W. Jager & D.J. Lang , Leverage points for sustainability transformation Perspective. Volume 46, pages 30–39, (2017).

95. M. Strand, K. Ortega-Cisneros, H.J Niner, M. Wahome, J. Bell, J.C. Currie, & A. Winkler, 'Transdisciplinarity in transformative ocean governance research – reflections of early career researchers', ICES Journal of Marine Science, 79(8), (2022) 2163-2177.

96. S.J. Boyes, & M. Elliott, 'The excessive complexity of national marine governance systems–Has this decreased in England since the introduction of the Marine and Coastal Access Act 2009?', Marine Policy, (2015). 57-65 (63).

97. M. Voyer, D. Benzaken, & C. Rambourg, 'Institutionalizing the Blue Economy: an examination of variations and consistencies among Commonwealth countries', Philosophical Transactions of the Royal Society (2022). B, 377(1854), 20210125.

Industry and Prosperity

British Prosperity and the Royal Navy: A Global Maritime and Underwater Power

Diving Deep: Britain's Critical Submarine Cable Infrastructure

Human-Technology Partnerships

British Prosperity and the Royal Navy: A Global Maritime and Underwater Power

Dr Carl Stephen Patrick Hunter OBE

Introduction

The UK's economic prosperity is and always has been interlinked with its maritime security. 95% UK physical trade is carried on the oceans and 96% all UK global financial transactions, and the internet itself, in the undersea network of cables below them.[1] The map of the undersea cable network (Map 1) follows remarkably closely to the map of the global shipping and trading routes (Map 2), showing the UK as the geographical centre of global trade and finance. This reliance of national and global security on the sea is secured by the ability of the Royal Navy (RN) to control and protect those undersea networks and shipping routes through its sustained ability to project and sustain surface naval effect above, and strategic submarine effect under, the oceans around the world.

This places the RN at the heart of UK prosperity, both on and under the oceans. It should, and does, focus its efforts on the global regions, shipping lanes, undersea cable routes, and maritime choke points that carry and channel the greatest concentration of global trade, where adversarial disruption and contestation are highest. Global prosperity is a UK national interest and exists more in the maritime than the continental domain. For example, 30-40% of all global trade, valued at 3.5 trillion USD annually, passes through the Strait of Malacca. This chokepoint also channels 80% of China's oil and gas and 90% of all Japan's.[2] What happens in the Strait, therefore, impacts the entire globe, and its closure to or restriction of allied-bound shipping would be a significant blow to UK interests.

The UK's export strategy aims to achieve £1 trillion worth of exports by 2030, and currently half of its exports in value terms are goods, versus services.[5] Its recent trade successes include new agreements with Australia and New Zealand and joining the Comprehensive and Progressive

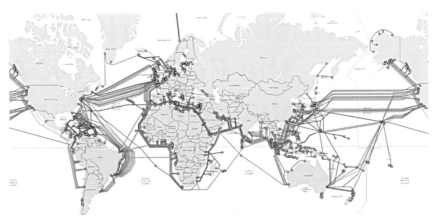

Map 1: The World's Undersea Cable Network.[3]

Map 2: The World's Shipping Routes, UCL Energy Institute.[4]

Agreement for Trans-Pacific Partnership, which represents 15% of global GDP.[6] The UK is forging new defence industrial partnerships too. AUKUS will produce generation-after-next capabilities for Australia, the UK, and the US in the underwater battlespace, and support a new level of UK and allied submarine activity in the Indo-Pacific. The Hiroshima Accords signed with Japan – alongside the Global Combat Air Programme (GCAP) to build a sixth-generation stealth combat aircraft and the UK-Japan Reciprocal Access Agreement – facilitate reciprocal access and cooperation between the Self-Defence Forces of Japan and the UK's Armed Forces.

Expanding the UK's trade and defence material flows with Indo-Pacific countries underlines the indivisibility of maritime security in the Indo-Pacific with the UK's economic interests and its role in upholding freedom of navigation. This, if violated, could put trade and commercial shipping at risk, leading to higher costs for all, as is demonstrated by the Houthis' attacks on commercial shipping in the Red Sea. The UK's Indo-Pacific "tilt" is today a systemic and constant one within its global goals, supported by a panoply of agreements in the region ranging from AUKUS, GCAP, CPTPP Accession, and ASEAN Dialogue Partner status, to the UK-Japan Hiroshima and UK-South Korea Downing Street Accords. These exist alongside other agreements with the US and Europe like UK leadership of the Joint Expeditionary Force, the UK-US New Atlantic Charter 2021, the Atlantic Declaration 2023, the UK-EU Trade and Cooperation Agreement, and the Windsor Framework. As a result of these, the UK today looks with equal strategic and trade opportunity to the US, Europe, and Asia. Using Britain's defence assets and diplomacy in the public sector domain to enable trade and finance in the private sector, surface and underwater deployments and facilities, supported by these agreements, facilitates the very freedom needed to trade successfully.

These mutually supporting relationships are key to British prosperity in a highly contested world. The Integrated Review (IR) and the Integrated Review Refresh (IRR) balanced the interests of the UK in the Euro-Atlantic with those in the Indo-Pacific, in what can be called a 'horizontal geostrategic plane'; what happens in one theatre affects the other, just as what happens in the Baltic Sea affects the Black Sea, in what one might call the "vertical geostrategic plane."[7] Thus, UK interests in the Euro-Atlantic and Indo-Pacific are indivisible. British prosperity dep-ends on success in both regions, above, and under, the oceans.

This chapter begins by identifying the vitality of the RN's success in the maritime theatre to national prosperity. The Strait of Malacca, as a chokepoint for the most vital artery of global trade which is located in an increasingly contested region, is a core example of where the RN must succeed in securing open oceans. With a particular focus on the increasingly crucial dominance of the underwater battlespace, the RN's current position and future is laid out as it relates to this area of strategic vitality. Then, as a prime example of 'futureproofing' the RN, AUKUS is examined as a case study of a new model of collaboration between UK Science, UK Defence, and UK Industry, alongside initiatives set forth by science and industry. It is this renegotiation of military-industrial-scientific collaboration which will be foundational to the RN's success in its duty to safeguard British and global prosperity, focusing its strategic efforts where the highest concentrations of trade interests and adversarial actions are present, to defend the rules-based international order by protecting the former and deterring the latter.

Leveraging Prosperity and Strategic Advantage from the Ocean

Strengthened trade and financial relationships are the prerequisites of global prosperity, but prosperity depends on stability and security. Because the UK is an archipelago and a global maritime, trading and investment power, it is natural for it to look to the oceans, where around 70% of the world's population live within 200 kilometres of a coastline.[8]

For this reason, the RN is fundamental to the UK's trading, financial, scientific, and technological success. In the Autumn of 2023, both of Britain's aircraft carriers were at sea – one leading a multinational capability in the North Atlantic – while Littoral Response Group (South) deployed to the Eastern Mediterranean.[9] Building on the deployment of Carrier Strike Group 2023, the deployment of a new Carrier Strike Group 25 will demonstrate British maritime leadership from the Euro-Atlantic to the Indo-Pacific. It will help cement the new agreements with Australia, New Zealand, Japan and CPTPP itself, in trade and finance, whilst bringing regional stability and security in defence and diplomacy.

In 1904, Adml Jackie Fisher said: "Five keys lock up the world … Singapore, The Cape, Alexandria, Gibraltar, Dover".[10] Today, one would add the Panama Canal, the Strait of Hormuz, and others, but the basic truth remains the same (see Map 1). Possession of bases and facilities near maritime choke points can be catalysed as a strategic advantage; they act as portals between the world's oceans, and it is in the interests of a maritime power to secure free and open oceans upon which global trade flows. Given the existence of these chokepoints as much in the underwater as the surface domain, it is a pivotal reason why the RN's Submarine Service has a primary focus on the Russian submarine fleet in the Euro-Atlantic and the Chinese submarine fleet in the Indo-Pacific. The inclusion within AUKUS of a rotational submarine presence based in Australia at HMAS Stirling indicates increasing concern about the Chinese threat. The presence of this threat in the underwater as well as the surface domain is also why the RN as a whole has a focus on the undersea domain, where the RN's Submarine Service and its technological capabilities make the United Kingdom a global underwater power.[11]

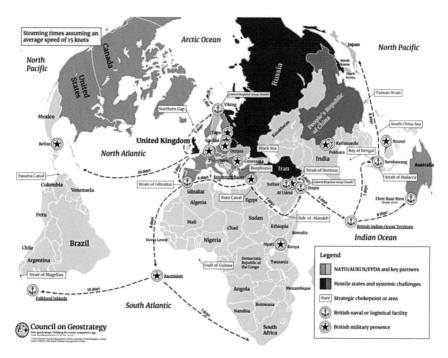

Map 3: The RN's Global Reach by James Rogers, Council on Strategy: British power is derived from the disproportionate effect the RN brings to bear, by its strategic maritime mobility on and under the oceans.

More than 100 years have passed since Adml Fisher's comments and it is important to acknowledge that the UK still has influence over several of these chokepoints: the English Channel, the Strait of Gibraltar, the Suez Canal (from the Sovereign Base Areas on the island of Cyprus) and the Strait of Malacca, via the RN's logistics facility in Singapore. The UK also exerts influence over the Strait of Magellan from the Falkland Islands.

Trade Flows, British "Ocean Literacy" and Maritime Choke Points

As an archipelagic, outward-focussed nation, British policy can be surprisingly "sea-blind". The UK should seek to achieve a state of comprehensive "ocean literacy" and communicate to the nation that the RN is a non-negotiable safeguard of its economic prosperity and national security, noting that global commerce occurs above and undersea. The 'Art of Admiralty', as a product of the UK's 500-year maritime legacy, is

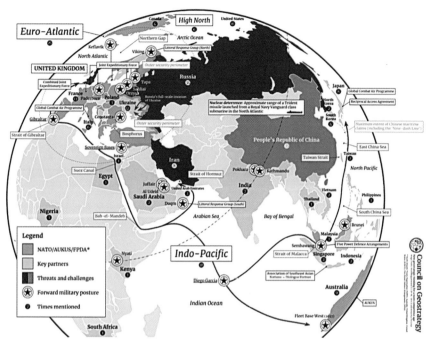

Map 4: The 'Refresh' of the Integrated Review by James Rogers, Council on Geostrategy. In March 2023 the UK Government published the 'Integrated Review Refresh: Responding to a more contested and volatile world'.[12] This map visualises the geography of British power described in the Integrated Review Refresh.

predicated on comprehensive ocean literacy, and may have seen a decline since the dissolution of the very Admiralty which generated it in 1964. One example of the RN embracing ocean literacy and acting to uphold national prosperity in the underwater domain is the RN's expansion of its capabilities to protect Critical Undersea Infrastructure by commissioning its new Multi-Role Ocean Surveillance Ship (MROSS), RFA *Proteus*.[13]

Similarly, the RN must adapt and recalibrate its focus to protecting where the free flow of this trade is most at risk and contested. Greater priority must be given to the Strait of Malacca, and if necessary, resources diverted from its efforts in the Strait of Hormuz or Gibraltar Strait.[14] The US Secretary of the Navy emphasised this in January 2024, saying that "renewed British engagement in this vital region could not come at a more pivotal time, as our shared vision for a free and open Indo-Pacific with other like-minded nations is being challenged".[15] AUKUS enables the Royal Navy to regenerate in a nuclear-powered fleet the global capabilities of its Submarine Service, lost when it transferred its conventional submarine squadrons to the Royal Canadian and Royal Australian Navies. This comes from recognition of the same strategic indivisibility between the Euro-Atlantic and Indo-Pacific that Canada already has, by geographical virtue of its Atlantic and Pacific coasts and the consequent disposition of its Fleets in Halifax, Nova Scotia and Vancouver Island, British Columbia.

Global stability and security are the prerequisites of global prosperity (the latter being a UK national interest), and this finances collective security, constituting a 'Prosperity Continuum'. The 'Prosperity Continuum' states that the UK domestic prosperity is dependent on the preconditions of domestic stability and security, which finance the UK's collective security, in turn enabling the conditions of global stability and global security which are the prerequisites of global prosperity. This is why global prosperity is a UK national interest. Whilst the UK is conversant with this, its implication that the majority effort should be applied to the geostrategic confluence of global trade and adversarial contestation in today's recurring era of state competition must be considered a strategic imperative.[16] The Chinese assertion of its self-declared nine dash line in the South China Sea is the one of the greatest threats to maritime trade present today. Whilst the RN and UK Defence understandably focuses on multi-domain integration for the successful application of military effort at war, it might also apply this highly refined capability at the largest confluence between global prosperity and contestation first, at the point of "global trade's fulcrum", in the region of the Strait of Malacca.

The consequence of the IR's "Indo-Pacific tilt" was to balance Euro-Atlantic and Indo-Pacific efforts based on the idea that, in the global maritime domain, both regions are mutually supporting and therefore indivisible in relative terms of importance.[17] By accepting that the UK's primary global effort is maritime, identifying and safeguarding the principal concentrations of economic interests should be the focus of the UK's capabilities. The expansion of China's submarine fleets and increasingly ambitious territorial claims in the South China Sea threatens the Strait of Malacca.[18] Concern with this key chokepoint is not just an exercise of self-interest. The majority of China's and Japan's energy imports pass through the Strait of Malacca.[19] At its narrowest point it is only 1.7nm wide. Control of the Strait of Malacca therefore heavily influences the South China Sea strategically, just as adversary underwater actions in the Arctic today materially affects those in the Atlantic. The ability to exert near-total economic control over the straits would provide the capability to neutralise China while supporting key allies like Japan.

The RN's Chinese and Russian Submarine Threat in the Indo-Pacific

> Today one can metaphorically walk across the Strait of Malacca itself upon the conning towers of the combined submarine fleets if moored alongside there, so densely equipped with them are the nations in Asia that have them. – Carl Stephen Patrick Hunter OBE

The People's Liberation Army Navy Submarine Force (PLANSF) operates a fleet of 62-75 nuclear and conventional submarines split between three fleets – The North Sea Fleet, the East Sea Fleet, and the South Sea Fleet. Combined with the 25-27 submarines of the Russian Pacific Fleet, this totals to a conservative calculation of 87 potentially hostile submarines operating in the Pacific region. When considered as a potential threat to vital regional shipping lanes, and the integral importance of that maritime trade to British economic vitality, submarines emerge as of crucial importance to guaranteeing British interests, both regionally and globally. The construction of 20 SSNs for the RN and Royal Australian Navy (RAN) through the AUKUS agreement will add both mass and new capabilities to the existing fleets, with enhanced interoperability with the US Navy Submarine Force, to create an allied, one-submarine force capable of countering the increasing Chinese underwater battlespace.

Most of this number of potentially hostile submarines is made up of diesel-electric attack submarines in addition to the 11 SSBNs in the

Submarine Class	PLANSF	Russian Navy Pacific Fleet	Total
SSBN	6	5	11
SSN/SSGNs	6 (+3 in reserve)	10	16
SS/SSKs	50 (+10 in reserve)	10–12	60–62
Total	**62 (75 including reserves)**	**25–27**	**87–89 (100–102 including reserves)**

Table 1: Chinese and Russian Submarine Strengths in the Far East by Jack Goldsack, Centre for Underwater Acoustic Analysis, 2023.

region, and another 16-19 SSNs. The scale of this threat, both numerically and qualitatively, to British interests is therefore considerable – and whilst it is wholly recognised that the RN is "allied by design", Chinese submarine capabilities are expanding; with an additional 10 SSNs/SSBNs either planned or under construction by the PLANSF, this threat will only continue to grow. [20] It is therefore a vital consideration for British strategy that this threat must be credibly deterred by a significant British and allied underwater capability in the region, given its intense geostrategic importance, hence the AUKUS agreement. Alongside meeting these new threats to regional security with the necessary capabilities to deter them, the RN must also continue in its duty to the nation in providing the UK's nuclear deterrent and its ability to maintain operational advantage in the global underwater battlespace. Both of these missions place the RN's nuclear submarines as integral to the UK's National Security and the UK's global future, not only to deter aggression, but to strategically contain the Chinese maritime threat to its home waters.

Submarines and the Underwater Trade Domain

A cursory look at the map of the world's shipping routes and undersea network of cables shows that the submarine and underwater technologies of the United Kingdom as a global underwater power are as indispensable to the RN under the seas, as UK Carrier Strike is above it. Dominance in the underwater domain maintains global stability and security in a world where state-on-state competition is resurgent, a point which is becoming increasingly recognised by the UK's allies within NATO.

> But with modern technology and modern Russian submarines, the North American security bubble is not what it used to be. And with China, it is not if, but when, China is operating in both the Atlantic and the Arctic.[21] – Rear Admiral Parchell, RCN.

Vice Admiral Daniel Dwyer, USN, and Commander of the US 2nd Fleet, says:

> *As we see the emergence of the Russian Submarine Force back in the Atlantic … Presence matters. If we are not there, we cede the area to someone else, where they can dictate the rules. That may be counter to the rules-based international order. We need to demonstrate we can*

operate in any environment, any time of day … With China's growing bond with Russia, there is greater concern about Chinese intentions.[22]

Though the Admiral was speaking of the Atlantic and Arctic, it is no different in the Indo-Pacific.

Nuclear submarines have provided the platform for the UK's independent nuclear deterrent and underwater global power for over 50 years, deterring the most extreme threats to its national security and way of life, helping to guarantee the UK's security and that of its allies. The 'Silent Service' was advanced, developed and supported by UK Scientists at the Admiralty Research Laboratories (ARL) during the Cold War, and from those at Defence, Science and Technology Laboratory (DSTL) and the private sector since. Whilst this strategic sovereign capability was developed and delivered during the Cold War era, the UK still faces credible threats from existing and emerging nuclear-armed states as well as state-sponsored nuclear terrorism. The fundamental purpose of the nuclear deterrent is to preserve peace, prevent coercion, and deter aggression. Since 1969, the Continuous-at-Sea-Deterrent (CASD) has provided a minimum, credible, independent nuclear deterrent, assigned to the defence of NATO and considered essential to guarantee the safety and security of the UK and its allies.

Successive Governments recognise the relevance of the UK maintaining a nuclear deterrent, not only for today but also for the immediate future, and believe that the submarine remains the optimal means to deliver the deterrent. This is illustrated by the commitment to a once-in-two-generations programme to modernise the UK's nuclear forces. The 4 existing Vanguard Class submarines will be replaced with 4 Dreadnought Class, with the first entering service in the early 2030's.[23] This significant investment in the future security of both the UK and its allies demonstrates that the UK's nuclear commitment remains undiminished, strengthening the UK's relationship with the United States. The UK continues use its Special Relationship to work closely with the US to ensure warheads remain compatible with the Trident Strategic Weapon System, with cooperation underpinned by constant amendments to both the 1958 Mutual Defence Agreement and the 1963 Polaris Sales Agreement.

The protection and maintenance of CASD is only possible by ensuring that the supporting capabilities remain credible to maintain Operational Advantage, one such capability being the attack submarine (SSN). Since their introduction in 1901, RN submarines have been at the forefront of underwater warfare. In 1960 the RN launched its first nuclear-powered submarine, HMS *Dreadnought*. Before that, the Navy experimented with HMS *Excalibur* and HMS *Explorer*, High-test Peroxide (HTP) and very high-speed conventional submarines. Between 1967 and 1969, the RN commissioned all 4 of its Resolution Class Polaris-equipped SSBNs, placing CASD at the heart of UK National security ever since, and replacing them with the Trident-equipped Vanguard Class commissioned from 1993-99. The rest of the Submarine Service transitioned to an all-nuclear SSN attack submarine fleet in 1994, which offer the necessary capabilities to help maintain the UK's global, underwater dominance.

Today, the RN's Astute Class SSNs combine qualities of stealth, endurance, reach, speed, autonomy, flexibility, and strike.[24] These characteristics give nuclear-powered submarines unparalleled freedom of worldwide operations, including underneath ice in the Arctic, in support of national, NATO, and coalition operations, and a vital capability to gain and maintain Sea Control. Their anti-submarine warfare, anti-surface warfare, intelligence-gathering, surveillance, target acquisition, reconnaissance (ISTAR), special forces, and long-range precision TLAM strike systems capabilities make them a pivotal, strategic capability of UK Defence. The importance placed on this potent capability is clear with the announcement of the AUKUS agreement. This will see the introduction of a common SSN design into the RN and RAN in the late 2030s featuring the cutting-edge of UK, US, and Australian technology. Uniquely, this will break new ground; SSN-AUKUS will be the first international project in the history of nuclear submarine construction to build to a common design.[25]

SSN deployments, like the undersea network of cables themselves, are unseen. The 1982 Falklands War demonstrated the strategic implications of their deployment on adversarial planning and capabilities, and today they are even more powerful in their ability to neutralise threats in the underwater domain. It is a key duty of the RN, in collaboration with the government, to ensure that its submarine capabilities are capable of deterring aggression from adversaries in sensitive regions, especially the Indo-Pacific. AUKUS, and its tripartite foundation, is a representation of the RN's recognition of this duty and commitment to fulfilling it, by adding a submarine permanent presence to its current permanent presence in the Indo-Pacific, established by the 5-year deployments of HMS *Tamar* and HMS *Spey*. This Indo-Pacific permanent presence was described by the RN in 2024 as 'just as relevant' as deterring the Russian threat in the Euro-Atlantic, since the Navy's role in maritime operations is 'fundamental to protecting the nation and helping it prosper.'[26]

The UK's Equal Global Opportunity in the USA, Europe, and Asia

In the future, the Indo-Pacific will be 'the crucible for many of the most pressing global challenges.'[27] The UK Government has announced its intention to become the 'European partner with the broadest and most integrated presence in the Indo-Pacific'. In March 2023, the Government published the IRR to reflect Russia's invasion of Ukraine and other geostrategic developments.[28] This Refresh highlighted the vitality of undersea cables and pipelines, following on from the destruction of the Nord Stream 2 pipeline and sabotage to cables in the Baltic Sea. It also reaffirmed commitment to the Indo-Pacific, warning that tensions in the region are increasing and 'conflict there could have global consequences greater than the conflict in Ukraine', indicating the need for an RN SSN presence in the Indo Pacific.[29] The Government also referenced plans to develop a new network of Atlantic-Pacific partnerships, of which AUKUS is one. Alongside this, in July 2023, the Ministry of Defence responded with the refreshed Defence Command Paper 2023 (DCP23), reflecting the defence aspects of the IRR.[30] The MOD articulated the need to shift from a platform-centric to technology-centric mindset. Har-nessing new and emerging technologies is central to this shift, and the MOD identified AUKUS pillar 2 projects as capabilities that will 'help us to maintain our technological and military edge in an increasingly contested and unstable strategic environment.'[31]

Building, testing, and deploying a naval vessel to warfighting capability can take 10 years. In a world where new adversaries can emerge in short periods of time, the capacity of UK Defence to think to the future is therefore vital. Simultaneously, the global seascape is changing; the opening of the Northwest Passage, and possibly a Northeast Passage too could drastically reshape the flow of global shipping, and with it the operational requirements of the RN. In the modern rules-based international order, freedom of navigation is integral to facilitating maritime trade, and this is a particularly important consideration in emerging regions of interest. New bases, vessels, and alliances will need to be created to continue the RN's mission in supporting British, and indeed global, security – building on the success of the RN's new bases in Bahrain and Duqm, Oman. This is a principal component of the UK's commitment to stabilizing and securing the Persian Gulf alongside the

Gulf Co-operation Council (GCC) States and of its overall strategic effect in the Indo-Pacific.

> The vast size of the Pacific Ocean for instance presents its own challenges for naval forces. Covering more than 60 million square miles or 30 percent of the Earth's surface, the Pacific Ocean is larger than the landmass of all the continents combined. – US National Oceanic and Atmospheric Administration[32]

Today, the UK's global underwater power status is exemplified through its AUKUS Agreement with Australia and the United States in the Indo-Pacific, just as much as its P3 Maritime underwater power is with the United States and France in the Euro-Atlantic, by the Trilateral Submarine Agreement, an aim of which is to co-ordinate anti-submarine warfare (ASW) operations and achieve a standardised approach to them.[33] This is vital in an era when submarine and underwater operations in the Atlantic and Arctic evolve and become a unitary operating space with extensive Russian and looming Chinese submarine operations to contest their stability. As with the RN's adoption of new permanent presence in the Indo-Pacific, its existing permanent presence in the Atlantic is being enhanced by this agreement to counter the threat to it.[34]

In UK National Security terms, this would also cement the RN's and its Submarine Service's place at the "Crown Jewels of Government" level, alongside Five Eyes, the Special Relationship, CASD, and NATO. In other words, the RN itself would join CASD at that level, securing both its and the nation's future. This would guarantee the RN's prominence by its "strategic Art of Admiralty gift" to global stability, security, and prosperity. In doing so, it would help to successfully deter a future maritime war with China and Russia in the Indo-Pacific, Russian naval threats (particularly in the underwater domain in the Atlantic and Arctic) and maintain stability in the wider Middle East. The 2023 deployment of Type 45 Destroyer HMS *Diamond* to the Red Sea 'to bolster international efforts to maintain maritime security' demonstrated this enduring global role of the RN and its place in alliance partnerships.[35]

A key question for the RN now, however, is whether it can provide continuous maritime security and carrier strike capabilities globally and develop its wider, nascent, permanent presence. This is particularly pressing within the increasingly contested Indo-Pacific, where the highest strategic threat to the rules-based international order exists, in addition to its standing and emergency commitments. Over the last 20 years, the increase in the scale of both the submarine and surface fleets in the region is significant. China alone is on course to having a 550-ship fleet by 2030, the majority of these being 'modern multi-role platforms featuring advanced anti-ship, anti-air, and anti-submarine weapons and sensors.'[36] To maintain its position – which has been achieved through decades of diplomacy, negotiation, and sacrifice – the UK must ensure that it can stand up to such aggressive expansion, and AUKUS is a model of the commitments the UK will be required to make to do that.

Opportunities for UK Science in and beyond AUKUS Pillar 2 Advanced Technologies

AUKUS is a landmark security and defence partnership to support a free and open Indo-Pacific by strengthening regional and global security through the development and manufacture of a world-leading nuclear-powered submarines and the generation of advanced technologies split into 8 categories. GCAP is a similar trilateral relationship - between the UK, Japan, and Italy – to develop and manufacture a world-leading 6th generation aircraft.[37] The implications of GCAP for the RN could be dramatic with the prospect of a marinised fighter variant providing a 6th generation carrier strike capability.

AUKUS is a case of the recognition of the necessary interconnectivity between science, defence, and industry, and the opportunities this brings to all three allied partners. Two of these partners are already global underwater powers in the UK and US, and AUKUS will generate a third in Australia. Pillar 1 will manufacture the next generation SSN AUKUS for the RN and RAN through collaboration with the US; this will be the first nuclear submarine in history to be built for two navies.[38] AUKUS Pillar 2 relates to advanced technologies across 8 areas. Research into technologies such as AI, quantum, underwater, and hypersonic/counter-hypersonic technologies, will establish the 'products' of AUKUS as 'generation-after-next ones.'[39] Many of these may have dramatic civil scientific applications in time at a scale that may eclipse the stated policy ambition to reach 2.4% of GDP investment in research and development by 2027.[40]

AUKUS is therefore a tripartite endeavour to succeed at home and overseas, to generate economic and scientific hope in the former, and to meet the UK's "Global Force for Good" ambition in the latter as the AUKUS nations aim to deliver credible SSN deterrents and advanced technologies. It represents an opportunity to define the UK's core capabilities and values in a reformed, public service-led approach to the

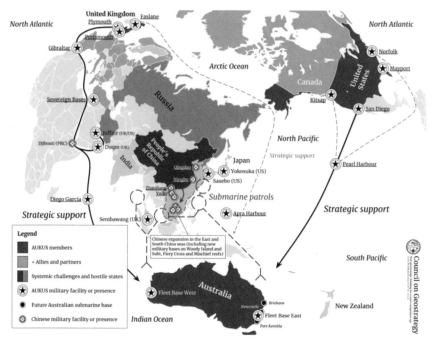

Map 5: A map of AUKUS, by James Rogers, Council on Geostrategy, showing the unique security partnership in the Indo-Pacific between the United Kingdom, the United States, and Australia.

UK Defence, UK Science and UK Industry relationship, achieved by a national, shared public-private sector understanding. Moreover, the commitment of the UK Government of £4 billion in the design and prototyping phase, with an expected total outlay in the hundreds of billions, represents a recognition that the UK is a maritime nation which is bound to the sea.

AUKUS (and GCAP) offer the UK university sector significant scientific and technological opportunities. Particularly with AUKUS Pillar 2, the future civil "spin-off" benefits potential in quantum technology and AI are vast. As potentially the most strategic tripartite agreement since 1945, it is an opportunity for the UK university sector to involve themselves in ensuring the success of such a significant programme, and in the process benefitting from the significant funding opportunities AUKUS will bring. Opportunities for collaborators represent no less than a joining of UK economic and strategic goals, with UK Defence serving as the unifying factor. The opportunity to reform the UK

Defence-Science-Industry relationship now exists in a "new alliance", as referenced in the DCP23, though it will take a complex effort from all three to create new relationships and discourses that will underpin the most efficient and fruitful collaboration.[41]

Reforming the UK Defence, UK Science and UK Industry Relationship

The UK has a wealth of talent and capability across Defence, science, and industry; it is second only to the USA in Nobel Prizes for science, having educated more Nobel Prize winners in one Cambridge College than entire peer nations.[42] The UK has 4 of the world's top 10 universities.[43] The scientific and industrial opportunities of AUKUS and GCAP are at a level not seen in decades. Two leading British industrial sectors, maritime and aerospace, are contained within these programmes, both of which are partnered with Indo-Pacific nations. The Indo-Pacific therefore contains not only both the UK's greatest trade interests and adversarial threats, but also the scientific relationships supporting its most important future defence programmes.

Looking beyond their defence implications, the opportunities for civil scientific progress may well exceed that of Horizon, the EU's funding programme for research and innovation. But to cohere these for strategic advantage, a new relationship between UK Defence, science and industry will have to be created. This would be one in which the same funding and prosperity would be available but moving away from a relationship based on exquisitely specified platforms that unintentionally risk manufacturing obsolescence, to a more visionary relationship which generates constantly updating platforms instead. This comes with the integrated ability to operate across the underwater, surface, air, land, cyber and space domains.

Although UK science contains some of the world's most brilliant minds, there have been times when areas of UK research have deliberately avoided sustaining Defence. This has been predicated on a natural distaste for war. However, in today's contested and competitive global environment there is tremendous opportunity for UK science to see that their desire for peace is a shared one with Defence, and that industry can bind both together with this shared pursuit.

The IR, the IR Refresh and AUKUS could be as important to the future rules-based international order as the post-war settlement created by the UK and USA from 1945. At that time, one US Navy Captain engineered what became nuclear propulsion at sea in the US Navy

Submarine Service and US Civil Atomic Energy on land: VAdml Hyman Rickover.[44] He achieved this and much more by understanding that most people within the defence "Primes" act out of self-interest rather than public service. By establishing a team of dynamic, forward-looking US Naval Officers to work alongside industry and scientific colleagues who shared the same foresight, VAdml Rickover revolutionised both naval warfare and energy generation. There are significant parallels between this and what the UK is doing today with AUKUS. VAdml Rickover said that:

> A wise man who stands firm is a statesman, and a foolish man who stands firm is a catastrophe ... Human experience shows that people, not organisations or management systems, get things done.[45]

Some would rightly contend the latter to some degree and propose that balance between each is best. The "Rickover effect", however, was to identify those people who understood that industry had to not only meet US DoD specifications but to create a level of performance not previously required. It had a purpose to absorb those special few to create a core alongside the specially selected USN Officers, whilst working in civil sector alignment with the US Department of Energy. That ultimately inspired hundreds of thousands of USN-DoD-Industry personnel across the USA to create the nuclear propulsion standards within AUKUS today and that Adml Houston has inherited from VAdml Rickover as Director, Naval Nuclear Propulsion Program. The subsequent UK-USA agreement in 1958 created the conditions for the submarine nuclear propulsion records that both navies have established since that moment.

UK Defence innovation may be at the same point today as that which VAdml Rickover found in the USA in 1945, with an opportunity to create peerless innovation that lasts the next 75 years. What the UK can achieve is the 'science superpower' ambition set out in IR 2021.[46] When one recognises the interdependent and mutually supportive nature of Defence, science, and industry, the requirement for all three to operate in alignment is clear. The UK cannot expect to contend with adversarial superpowers if it does not have the corresponding scientific and industrial capabilities to support Defence. There is concern within UK Defence that the current relationships are not working, seeing the relationship as transactional with industry and often remote from science. All three must reform in today's contested and competitive world to generate a strategic advantage.

The DCP23 sets out a clear vision for a "New Alliance" with industry, which must now be properly pursued.[47] In practical terms, this will require a new industrial profile, with renegotiated relationships between the defence Primes and lower-tier suppliers. Alongside this would be a new willingness on the part of industry to invest in research and development, to support a system which provides a problem-finding capability, rather than just solutions to specific problems. Delivery speed is a key consideration within the capability of defence, and specifically the RN, to adapt to changing strategic demands; the 10-year timeline of warship development should not continue to grow. This model therefore calls for a completely reorganised and new, integrated relationship between UK Defence, UK Science, and UK Industry.

A New Post-Integrated Review Era of Public Service-led UK Science

Recognising the need for a step-change in the relationship between Defence, science, and industry to deliver scientific and technological advantage for the UK's Defence, the Durham Institute of Research, Development, and Invention (DIRDI) was created at Durham University. DIRDI aims to cohere science (through Durham University), industry (in the form of relationships with industry, specifically in the North-East), and Defence, through the establishment of the Centre for Underwater Acoustic Analysis (CUAA), in an agreement with the RN as a 'gift to the nation'. This public service-led model aims to produce a scientific mass supporting UK Defence at a level which has not been seen since 1945.

> We believe that a new way of undertaking successful British science is possible, freed from the constraints of conventional funding, by UK Industry and UK Academia working with HM Government in a "whole of nation" spirit, underpinned by the nobility of public service. Designed to energise brilliant young minds, in a 20-year shared, national endeavour to succeed and flourish by finding, for senior academic leadership levels, the very reason why they came into science at all. If we unlock the hopes of our senior Professors of science, and engineering, and match those to the dreams of our young Scientists, a very bright future is possible for our United Kingdom in our globally contested and competitive world. – DIRDI's vision, Carl Stephen Patrick Hunter OBE[48]

The aim of the CUAA is to support the RN's Submarine Service, to do whatever research it can to ensure that every submarine that is 'sent out, comes safely home', is more effective when on patrol, and to enhance the RN's strategic role. Underpinning all this is a realisation that science and industry should assume a responsibility to support UK Defence, since prosperity is predicated on the national and global security which UK Defence provides. This realisation seeks to bind together public and private sector ambition, and through recognition of shared interests comes mutual support. In turn, this mutual support can be expanded to generate "economic hope" and support the "levelling up" agenda. This promotes and supports the growth of the whole-of-nation endeavour in public service-led science.

Credibility Matters

At this time of strategic threat, success hangs in the balance. It will be defined at sea. Of the top economies by 2050, none are landlocked. The oceans are the world's 'superhighway.'[49] If the UK accepts this, then the RN needs to configure its maritime strategy on a scale that enables the fulfilment of it.[50] The UK is an island, maritime, strategic, and global nation. The RN and the Art of Admiralty define the UK and enable all four. As Winston Churchill observed:

> "We are with Europe, but not of it. We are linked but not
> combined. We are interested and associated but not absorbed," and,
> "If Britain must choose between Europe and the open sea, she must
> always choose the open sea".[51]

The UK cannot forget the 'Defence-Diplomacy-Development Trinity' which generates national and global security.[52] Developing these as core national capabilities, alongside Trade, Finance, Science, and Culture as private-sector capabilities, will allow the UK to define itself globally. When aligned, the UK realises its 'global force for good' aims in a complex world that has never needed UK distinguishing values more, and which relies on a rules-based order and free trade. This system has lifted 1.5 billion people out of poverty in 30 years and is threatened by some of the UK's more powerful competitor countries with their 'one foot in, one foot out' approach to it.[53]

As a global nation, Britain relies on the 'Prosperity Continuum' to succeed.[54] Prosperity generates national stability and security and which, when combined with UK values overseas, helps deliver greater collective security and global security as its consequence. Security on and under the oceans is a prerequisite for any other pursuits in the maritime domain. As the Secretary of State for International Trade put it, 'All trade is strategic. It is also economic. It is also social.'[55] By securing the oceans with its surface capabilities such as Carrier Strike, and its undersea SSN capabilities alongside CASD, the RN is at the heart of all three.

This is the UK's Maritime Century

But how does the UK now define itself? The UK is a Permanent Member of the UN Security Council. British Defence has the 2nd largest military budget in NATO and is one of the 2 priority nations within the Five Eye intelligence-sharing powers.[56] The UK is at the heart of the 53 nations of the Commonwealth. It is a G5 economic power, occupying the position of the 2nd largest economy in Europe; some predictions see the UK as the largest within 20 years' time.[57] London is at the world's global financial heart. With the 4 SSBN submarines of CASD, the 5th generation strike capabilities of the 2 *Queen Elizabeth* Class aircraft carriers, and the amphibious warfare capabilities of the 2 littoral response groups, the UK is one of only 5 navies with substantive carrier strike, submarine, and amphibious capabilities. Outside the USA, the UK is the only state which can regularly and independently project and sustain naval power, via the replenishment vessels of the Royal Fleet Auxiliary. The RN is a globally capable navy, able to operate and sustain around the world, with a balanced fleet of warfighting, maritime security, and the support assets necessary to provide full spectrum of political choice.

The RN is at the heart of British prosperity. Government and the British public expect much of the RN's senior leadership team. But, as in any organisation, there is a mutual, national responsibility to support the RN's efforts: whether in industry or science, which should see their roles as implicit to RN success; or to wider UK Trade and UK Finance, whose very existence and economic hope depend on the RN's success. By guaranteeing open oceans, free trade, and freedom of navigation, the RN is the foundation on which national success lies. The new collaborative approach to research and development, initiated by UK Defence with AUKUS and being expanded by UK Science and UK Industry, will be instrumental to supporting this effort; no part of the UK Defence-UK Science-UK Industry relationship could exist without the other. The vitality of the UK economy is utterly dependent on trade, which is almost entirely conducted by sea. The RN operates ships in a state of "persistent presence" from the Atlantic, to the Gulf and the Indo-Pacific, to protect the confluences of global trade and adversarial threats to stability. Since the greatest threat exists in the Indo-Pacific, where the UK has numerous vital trade and strategic interests, the RN must expand its permanent presence to be equivalent to its Euro-Atlantic presence in its ability to safeguard national interests. The Royal Navy is the exceptional strategic fulcrum upon which UK and allied interests, to maintain global stability, security, and prosperity, depend.

Global Prosperity is principally a maritime phenomenon, on and under the oceans. It is a UK national interest and provided by the RN and, to Admiral Rickover's point, its people, and its senior leadership. It is enabled by the RN and its allies generating its pre-conditions of global stability and global security, in the post-Integrated Review "horizonal geostrategic plane" of the Euro-Atlantic and Indo-Pacific, and at the confluences of its greatest concentrations of global trade and adversarial contestation. AUKUS prevents the prospect of China's global disruption to the rules-based international system, by generating a future allied "one-submarine-force" underwater capability to neutralise the PLAN's future 550-ship fleet in the Indo-Pacific, and Russia's submarine force in the Euro-Atlantic. It can operate in disaggregation, or by aggregation and concentration of allied underwater dominance. Because the Royal Navy operates CASD, 5th generation UK carrier and littoral strike and top tier SSN capabilities, future proofed by AUKUS, the United Kingdom is a global maritime and underwater power, and the enabler of British prosperity.

Acknowledgements

I wish to acknowledge the kind assistance of Mrs Chloe Barker, Mr Daniel Dobrowolski, Ms Luciana Garstang and Mr Jack Goldsack.

1. Figures published by Maritime UK https://www.maritimeuk.org/about/about-us/#:
~:text=Supporting%20over%201%20million%20jobs,
over%20%C2%A3500bn%20per%20year [accessed 30 January 2024].

2. Sean Paterson, 'Dire Straits: Malacca, Singapore and the Future of the Global Economy', Asia Scotland Institute, 2023 <https://asiascot.com/op-eds/straits-of-malacca> [accessed 11 December 2023]. 'The Strait of Malacca's Global Supply Chain Implications', Institute for Supply Management, 21 November 2023. https://www.ismworld.org/supply-management-news-and-reports/news-publications/inside-supply-management-magazine/blog/2023/2023-11/the-strait-of-malaccas-global-supply-chain-implications/#:~:text=The%20volume%20of%20trade%20that,
navigates%20through%20its%20waters%20annually [accessed 30 January 2024].

3. https://arstechnica.com/information-technology/2016/05/how-the-internet-works-submarine-cables-data-centres-last-mile/2/ [accessed 29 January 2024].

4. Map of commercial shipping routes by University College London's Energy Institute, 2016. UCL Energy Institute https://www.shipmap.org/ [accessed 29 January 2024].

5. Department for International Trade, Made in the UK, Sold to the World (UK Government, November 2021), p. 5 https://assets.publishing.service.gov.uk/media/6194be15e90e070449d49cd2/made-in-the-uk-sold-to-the-world.pdf; Department for Business and Trade, 'UK Trade in Numbers ', GOV.UK (UK Government, 2023) https://www.gov.uk/government/statistics/uk-trade-in-numbers/uk-trade-in-numbers-web-version [accessed 8 December 2023].

6. Zachary Torrey, 'TPP 2.0: The Deal Without the US', The Diplomat, 3 February 2018 https://thediplomat.com/2018/02/tpp-2-0-the-deal-without-the-us/ [accessed 30 January 2024].

7. Ministry of Defence, 'Defence Command Paper 2023: Defence's Response to a More Contested and Volatile World', GOV.UK, 2023 <https://www.gov.uk/government/publications/defence-command-paper-2023-defences-response-to-a-more-contested-and-volatile-world> [accessed 10 December 2023].

8. Celia McMichael and others, 'A Review of Estimating Population Exposure to Sea-Level Rise and the Relevance for Migration', Environmental Research Letters, 15.12 (2020), 123005 (p. 12) <https://doi.org/10.1088/1748-9326/abb398>.

9. 'HMS Queen Elizabeth's Autumn Deployment Ramps up with Intensive Flying Operations', Royal Navy, 2023 <https://www.royalnavy.mod.uk/news-and-latest-activity/news/2023/october/18/231018-qnlz-flight-deck-operations>; 'Royal Navy Destroyer Deployed to the Gulf on Maritime Security Mission', Royal Navy, 2023 <https://www.royalnavy.mod.uk/news-and-latest-activity/news/2023/november/29/231129-diamond-heads-for-the-gulf>.

10. Luke Gibbon, 'What's the Context? 15 February 1942: The Fall of Singapore ', Gov. Uk, 2017 <https://history.blog.gov.uk/2017/02/15/whats-the-context-15-february-1942-the-fall-of-singapore/> [accessed 9 December 2023].

11. Ministry of Defence News Story, 'Royal Navy task force to deploy with JEF partners to defend undersea cables', 20 November 2023 https://www.gov.uk/government/news/royal-navy-task-force-to-deploy-with-jef-partners-to-defend-undersea-cables [accessed 16 November 2023].

12. Ministry of Defence, 'Defence Command Paper 2023: Defence's Response to a More Contested and Volatile World', GOV.UK, 2023 <https://www.gov.uk/government/publications/defence-command-paper-2023-defences-response-to-a-more-contested-and-volatile-world> [accessed 10 December 2023].

13. Ministry of Defence Press Release, 'New Royal Navy Surveillance Ship to protect the UK's critical underwater infrastructure', 24 March 2021 https://www.gov.uk/government/news/new-royal-navy-surveillance-ship-to-protect-the-uks-critical-underwater-infrastructure [accessed 10 December 2023].

14. Sean Paterson, 'Dire Straits: Malacca, Singapore and the Future of the Global Economy', Asia Scotland Institute, 2023 <https://asiascot.com/op-eds/straits-of-malacca> [accessed 11 December 2023].

15. Speech by USSECNAV Carlos Del Toro to the Royal United Services Institute, 25 January 2024. https://rusi.org/members-event-recordings/recording-us-secretary-navy-addressing-challenges-rules-based-maritime-order-red-sea [accessed 26 January 2024].

16. Department for International Trade, 'Embracing the Ocean: A Board of Trade Paper ', GOV.UK, 2022 <https://www.gov.uk/government/publications/board-of-trade-report-maritime/embracing-the-ocean-a-board-of-trade-paper-web-version> [accessed 8 December 2023].

17. Cabinet Office, 'Global Britain in a Competitive Age: The Integrated Review of Security, Defence, Development and Foreign Policy', 2021 <https://www.gov.uk/government/publications/global-britain-in-a-competitive-age-the-integrated-review-of-security-defence-development-and-foreign-policy> [accessed 10 December 2023].

18. 'Geoeconomic Crossroads', Interview with Kaewkamol Pitakdumrongkit, The National Bureau of Asian Research, 5 October 2023. https://www.nbr.org/publication/geoeconomic-crossroads-the-strait-of-malaccas-impact-on-regional-trade/ [accessed 10 December 2023].

19. Sean Paterson, 'Dire Straits: Malacca, Singapore and the Future of the Global Economy', Asia Scotland Institute, 2023 <https://asiascot.com/op-eds/straits-of-malacca> [accessed 11 December 2023].

20. Ministry of Defence, 'Defence Capability Framework', July 2022. https://assets. publishing.service.gov.uk/media/62d7d1668fa8f50c0a8a4029/MOD_Defence_ Capability_Framework_Accessible_Jul22.pdf [accessed 10 December 2023].

21. Rear Adml Parchell RCN, Janes Defence Weekly 13 Dec 2023 Issue, p. 23.

22. Vice Adml Daniel Dwyer, USN, Commander of the US 2nd Fleet, Janes Defence Weekly 13 Dec 2023 Issue, p. 25.

23. Claire Mills, 'Replacing the UK's Nuclear Deterrent: Progress of the Dreadnought Class', House of Commons Library, 2023 <https://commonslibrary.parliament.uk/ research-briefings/cbp-8010/>.

24. 'Astute Class', Royal Navy <https://www.royalnavy.mod.uk/equipment/submarine/ astute-class>.

25. 10 Downing Street, 'Fact Sheet: Trilateral Australia-UK-US Partnership on Nuclear-Powered Submarines', GOV.UK <https://www.gov.uk/government/publications/joint-leaders-statement-on-aukus-13-march-2023/fact-sheet-trilateral-australia-uk-us-partnership-on-nuclear-powered-submarines> [accessed 11 December 2023].

26. 'Royal Marine beats submariners to take charge of Navy's global operations', The Telegraph, 31 January 2024 https://www.telegraph.co.uk/news/2024/01/31/royal-marine-in-charge-royal-navy-global-operations/ [accessed 31 January 2024].

27. Cabinet Office, 'Global Britain in a Competitive Age: The Integrated Review of Security, Defence, Development and Foreign Policy', 2021 <https://www.gov.uk/ government/publications/global-britain-in-a-competitive-age-the-integrated-review-of-security-defence-development-and-foreign-policy> [accessed 10 December 2023].

28. Cabinet Office, 'Integrated Review Refresh 2023: Responding to a more contested and volatile world', 2023 https://www.gov.uk/government/publications/integrated-review-refresh-2023-responding-to-a-more-contested-and-volatile-world [accessed 10 December 2023].

29. Cabinet Office, 'Integrated Review Refresh 2023: Responding to a more contested and volatile world', 2023 https://www.gov.uk/government/publications/integrated-review-refresh-2023-responding-to-a-more-contested-and-volatile-world [accessed 10 December 2023].

30. Ministry of Defence, 'Defence Command Paper 2023: Defence's response to a more contested and volatile world', 2023 https://www.gov.uk/government/publications/ defence-command-paper-2023-defences-response-to-a-more-contested-and-volatile-world [accessed 10 December 2023].

31. Ministry of Defence, 'Defence Command Paper 2023: Defence's response to a more contested and volatile world', 2023 https://www.gov.uk/government/publications/defence-command-paper-2023-defences-response-to-a-more-contested-and-volatile-world [accessed 10 December 2023].

32. National Oceanic and Atmospheric Administration US Department of Commerce, 'How Big Is the Pacific Ocean?: Ocean Exploration Facts: NOAA Office of Ocean Exploration and Research' <https://oceanexplorer.noaa.gov/facts/pacific-size.html#:~:text=The%20Pacific%20Ocean%20is%20the,4%2C000%20meters%20(13%2C000%20feet).> [accessed 9 December 2023].

33. US Central Command News, 'UK, France and US Sign Trilateral Submarine Agreement' https://www.centcom.mil/MEDIA/NEWS-ARTICLES/News-Article-View/Article/1202609/uk-france-and-us-sign-trilateral-submarine-agreement/ [accessed 16 December 2023].

34. Ministry of Defence, 'Defence's response to a more contested and volatile world', July 2023 https://assets.publishing.service.gov.uk/media/64b55dd30ea2cb000d15e3fe/Defence_Command_Paper_2023_Defence_s_response_to_a_more_contested_and_volatile_world.pdf [accessed 16 December 2023].

35. Statement by the Defence Secretary, reported by Emily Atkinson for the BBC, 'HMS Diamond: British warship shoots down suspected attack drone in Red Sea', 17 December 2023 https://www.bbc.co.uk/news/uk-67738032 [accessed 17 December 2023].

36. Pentagon's report to Congress, Military and Security Developments Involving the People's Republic of China. 29 November 2022. P. 72. https://s3.documentcloud.org/documents/23321290/2022-military-and-security-developments-involving-the-peoples-republic-of-china.pdf [accessed 10 December 2023].

37. Ministry of Defence and 10 Downing Street, 'PM Announces New International Coalition to Develop the next Generation of Combat Aircraft', GOV.UK <https://www.gov.uk/government/news/pm-announces-new-international-coalition-to-develop-the-next-generation-of-combat-aircraft> [accessed 11 December 2023].

38. 10 Downing Street, 'Fact Sheet: Trilateral Australia-UK-US Partnership on Nuclear-Powered Submarines', GOV.UK <https://www.gov.uk/government/publications/joint-leaders-statement-on-aukus-13-march-2023/fact-sheet-trilateral-australia-uk-us-partnership-on-nuclear-powered-submarines> [accessed 11 December 2023].

39. Fact Sheet: Implementation of the Australia-United Kingdom-United States Partnership (AUKUS), 5 April 2022. https://www.gov.uk/government/publications/implementation-of-the-australia-united-kingdom-united-states-partnership-aukus-fact-sheet/fact-sheet-implementation-of-the-australia-united-kingdom-united-states-partnership-aukus [accessed 10 December 2023].

40. Department for Business, Energy & Industrial Strategy, 'Industrial Strategy: building a Britain fit for the future', November 2017 https://www.gov.uk/government/publications/industrial-strategy-building-a-britain-fit-for-the-future [accessed 31 January 2024].

41. Ministry of Defence, 'Defence's response to a more contested and volatile world', July 2023 https://assets.publishing.service.gov.uk/media/64b55dd30ea2cb000d15e3fe/Defence_Command_Paper_2023_Defence_s_response_to_a_more_contested_and_volatile_world.pdf [accessed 16 December 2023].

42. 'UK Universities Top Destination for Nobel Winners', British Council, 2015 <https://www.britishcouncil.org/contact/press/uk-universities-top-destination-nobel-winners#:~:text=The%20University%20of%20Cambridge%20again, of%20Manchester%2C%20who%20taught%20seven.>.

43. Figures published by QS World University Rankings 2024 https://www.topuniversities.com/world-university-rankings.

44. 'Navy to Commission Submarine Hyman G. Rickover', U.S. Department of Defense <https://www.defense.gov/News/Releases/Release/Article/3556738/navy-to-commission-submarine-hyman-g-rickover/https%3A%2F%2Fwww.defense.gov%2FNews%2FReleases%2FRelease%2FArticle%2F3556738%2Fnavy-to-commission-submarine-hyman-g-rickover%2F> [accessed 11 December 2023].

45. Quoted in Theodore Rockwell, The Rickover Effect (iUniverse, 2002).

46. Cabinet Office, 'Global Britain in a Competitive Age. The Integrated Review of Security, Defence, Development and Foreign Policy', 2021 <https://www.gov.uk/government/publications/global-britain-in-a-competitive-age-the-integrated-review-of-security-defence-development-and-foreign-policy> [accessed 10 December 2023].

47. Ministry of Defence, 'Defence Command Paper 2023: Defence's Response to a More Contested and Volatile World', GOV.UK, 2023 <https://www.gov.uk/government/publications/defence-command-paper-2023-defences-response-to-a-more-contested-and-volatile-world> [accessed 10 December 2023].

48. DIRDI's Vision. Available at: https://dirdi.org/about-us/.

49. C. Parry, Super Highway: Sea Power in the 21st Century, (Elliott and Thompson, 2014).

50. C. Parry, Super Highway: Sea Power in the 21st Century, (Elliott and Thompson, 2014).

51. W. Churchill, Saturday Evening Post, 15 February 1930.

52. Speech by Dr Carl Hunter to the Conservative Foreign and Commonwealth Council, 18 September 2018. https://www.brugesgroup.com/blog/speech-by-the-bruges-group-s-dr-carl-hunter-to-the-conservative-foreign-commonwealth-council [accessed 10 December 2023].

53. *Ibid.*

54. Ibid.

55. 'The Trade Dividend', Speech delivered by Secretary of State for International Trade Dr Liam Fox to the Inaugural Trade Dinner at Mansion House, 17 October 2018. Available at: https://www.gov.uk/government/speeches/the-trade-dividend.

56. 'Infographic: Where NATO Defense Expenditure Stands in 2022', Statista Daily Data, 2022 <https://www.statista.com/chart/14636/defense-expenditures-of-nato-countries> [accessed 11 December 2023]. 'Member Countries', Commonwealth <https://thecommonwealth.org/our-member-countries> [accessed 10 December 2023]; 'EU Country Profiles ', European Union <https://european-union.europa.eu/principles-countries-history/country-profiles_en> [accessed 10 December 2023].

57. The Centre for Economics and Business Research, Cebr's World Economic League Table, 2013, p. 5.

Diving Deep: Britain's Critical Submarine Cable Infrastructure

Matthew T.E. Bowden, Glenn A. Lipsham and
Devon A. Johnson

Introduction

As a maritime nation, Britain's reliance on the sea as a strategic enabler and resource is well documented through history and within the chapters of this book. Less well understood or known is the nation's role in the development of the global submarine cable infrastructure upon which the United Kingdom, and indeed the rest of the world, are inherently reliant.

Around the globe, at the bottom of lakes, seas, and oceans, lies a vast and intricate network of submarine cables performing two essential functions: the transfer of data; and power transmission. Telecommunications cables are the central nervous system of the internet, connecting land masses by carrying the contemporary world's most valuable commodity – data. Fibre-optic cables are the pathways through which we communicate with one another across the world through email and social media, as well as how we connect to the internet via our mobile devices, televisions, computers, and gaming consoles. They facilitate the global economy, processing millions of financial transactions a minute, thereby serving as the backbone of both domestic and international trade and commerce. Yet, the public remains largely unaware of the fact that satellites and mobile networks are *not* the prominent transmission paths, and that the nebulous 'cloud' is made possible by the physical infrastructure of the submarine cable system. It is only when there is a disruption to service – for example, the 2022 fault on a cable connecting the British mainland to Shetland Island or the Taiwan earthquake of 2006 resulting in a multiplicity of severed submarine cables – that it becomes evident just how quickly our interconnected society is crippled without data. This is particularly impactful when it results in an inability to conduct commercial transactions in a society where cash cannot adequately compensate.

Garnering even less attention, but equally as critical, are the submarine power cables. In concert with much of the world, Britain is transitioning toward a net zero future, and power cables are a crucial component to achieving this objective. The utilisation of renewable energy resources for electricity generation is growing, especially offshore where wind, wave and tidal energy are being harnessed. For power to be transferred from the generation sites to the points of demand, a transmission and distribution network, or grid, is required. Power cables form these vital connections. For example, each offshore wind farm has cables running from the turbine towers to the offshore substation and then to shore. To balance power loads and avoid wasting energy, grid operators work together to coordinate power usage between regions and nations through submarine power cables forming an increasingly linked and interconnected grid. These high-capacity submarine power cables facilitate transmission addressing power demand peaks and troughs, promoting more efficient use of power and enabling far higher renewable uptake than would otherwise be possible.

The aim of this chapter is to address prevailing misconceptions by providing an overview of the two main types of submarine cables as well as the limitations and challenges resulting from Britain's dependence upon the submarine cable system.

Submarine Telecommunications Cables

Since the very first copper wire was laid across the English Channel in 1850, directly connecting two nations, the United Kingdom has been at the forefront of this submarine technology. British inventors and entrepreneurs were instrumental in the development of submarine telegraph cables. The very first transatlantic submarine cable, the Atlantic Telegraph, was laid in 1858,[1] spanning a distance of three-thousand two hundred kilometres, connecting Newfoundland, Canada to Great Britain by way of Valentia Island, Ireland, enabling for the first-time intercontinental communication. Lauded in the papers of the time, this remarkable achievement was a joint venture between British engineer, Charles Bright, and American entrepreneur, Cyrus Field.[2] The Atlantic Telegraph laid the foundation for today's critical global network of digital highways linking the most remote regions on earth to the data centres and services that enable internet access. Itself a British-led innovation, the internet continues to evolve, and submarine cables have played a pivotal role in changing cultures, in effect shrinking the globe by increasing the rapidity and spread of information and reshaping the nature and method of conducting business. These advances in comm-unication have changed how entities influence stakeholders on an almost hourly if not minute-by-minute basis. Whilst the access points to this global architecture are varied, including satellite phones, mobile devices, cars, refrigerators, and all types of computers, ultimately each still rely on the network of submarine cables to connect data centres thereby enabling the diffusion of modern civilization's data and communications.

The evolution of the submarine telecommunication cable was relatively gradual by today's standards, taking a little over a century for the morse code reliant telegraph to be replaced by the telephone line. As a medium, submarine telegraph and latterly coaxial cables grew in capacity until reaching a zenith of four thousand simultaneous calls at once on Trans-Atlantic Telephone Cable 7 (TAT-7), one of the last coaxial cables operating between the United Kingdom and the United States before it was taken out of service in 1994. Since the technology's inception, British companies have played a crucial role in the develop-ment of these international and intercontinental submarine networks. The *Eastern Telegraph Company*, later known as *Cable & Wireless*, was founded in 1852 and became one of the largest submarine telegraph operators globally. It played a significant part in expanding the network and connecting Britain with various parts of the world. Even today, many of those employed in the submarine cable sector can trace their or their company's roots back to *Cable & Wireless*.

Across the submarine sector, British manufacturers developed ex-pertise in cable design, construction, handling equipment and laying techniques. Modern installation systems use the same fundamental principles and whilst the makeup of a submarine data cable has changed materially, the model has hardly diverged from early designs. Today's data cables consist of a central core of optical fibres surrounded by numerous protective layers from high-strength steel to a polyethylene insulator, with varying degrees of armoured protection to protect from physical threats on the seabed.

The submarine cable system is comprised of two parts: the 'wet plant', the section where the cable travels from beach manhole to beach manhole under an expanse of water; and the 'dry plant', the section which consists of the cable's connection from the beach manhole to the onshore facility or cable landing station.

The actual submarine data cable is made up of several key components determined in the main by the length of the cable, the pro-tection it requires, and the number of points it connects. Depending on its length and thus the attenuation experienced along its transmission path, optical amplification may be required; typically, for cables over 400km in length. A short data cable without amplification is the simplest form of modern submarine cable and has the added benefits of low maintenance and generally a lower risk of failure due to a reduction in complexity both beneath the waves and in the cable landing station. Consequently, it is normally lower in cost with respect to installation, maintenance, and operation. These cables are ideal for connecting sites across short water expanses, such as offshore installations or islands, or when building festoons to connect a chain of landings or sites along a coastline or between islands. For longer data cables, repeaters are required to overcome the attenuation, necessitating a powered cable, which increases the complexity of the submarine system.

When installing submarine data cables, a Branching Unit may be used to deliver connectivity to multiple locations or points-of-presence. These devices utilise optical and wavelength splitters to either take the main optical signal and split it down different cable segments or combine optical signals for onward transmission down the main submarine cable.

Once landed, normally via a beach manhole, the submarine cable connects into a Cable Landing Station. It is here that the submarine cable terminates and connects to the terrestrial backhaul network and ultimately a point-of-presence such as a data centre. The equipment housed in a Cable Landing Station converts signals from the shore transmission network and prepares them for transmission over the submarine cable and back again. This is achieved through multiplexing (and demultiplexing) different wavelengths of light into a single optical fibre to maximise fibre capacity. The landing station equipment also monitors and controls the submarine cable system and provides protection against cable failure by switching to backup cables or alternative networks. Even on a relatively short and less complex submarine cable, the equipment housed in the Cable Landing Station is complex but central to the provision of the resilient, high capacity, low latency services that end users now deem the 'norm'. The complexity of the equipment housed in the cable landing stations increases further for systems over 400km that require power for amplification.

Since the beginning, development across the telecommunications submarine cable sector has been predominantly fuelled by strategic and subsequently socio-economic drivers with national interests and commercial enterprises developing, building and maintaining the global architecture. Incumbent telecommunications providers initially laid, maintained, operated, and owned cable systems. However, there has been a marked shift with large elements of today's systems falling under the domain, albeit not exclusively, of some of the largest companies on the planet. Those responsible for the construction and installation of submarine systems do not normally own the cables, focusing instead on the delivery of the systems. This is representative of the broader trends reshaping cable ownership which have expanded beyond traditional telecommunication network providers in the UK and globally such as *British Telecom, Orange, AT&T*, and *Vodafone* (as well as other national or international organisations with regional interests) to include cloud service providers such as *Microsoft (Azure), Meta, Google (GCP)*, and *Amazon (AWS)*. It is these 'hyperscalers' who are responsible for the uptick in single ownership of systems and a new style of consortia ownership. These companies have their own submarine cable teams but rely on others to advise, develop and build their submarine infrastructure which they then operate. As a result, hyperscalers, also colloquially known as 'Over-the-Tops' (OTTs), have driven the global capacity up significantly since their decision to enter the submarine cable sector as cable owners rather than companies that lease cable capacity – a significant commercial change.

As societies become ever more data reliant and thus dependent upon fibre-optics, the industry continues to expand. The global submarine cable network plays an ever more central role in economic, commercial, military, diplomatic, and personal communications, transactions and exchanges. With that usage comes a strategic dependency that is of importance to both Britain and the rest of the world.

Submarine Power Cables

As well as its influence over the development of the global telecommunications submarine cable network, Britain has also had a significant impact on submarine power cables and interconnectors and, more recently, the nations' offshore grid development. As opposed to their fibre-optic counterparts, aluminium and copper are at the core of these power cables, their high voltage transmission capability enabling power sharing between countries and power distribution between regions.

In the late 19th and early 20th centuries, British engineers and companies such as *Siemens Brothers* and *Johnson & Phillips* participated in the development and installation of submarine power cables, connecting power systems between Britain and neighbouring countries. The close relationship between Britain and France resulted in the two nations pioneering the development of cross-channel power inter-connection, their first endeavour being the 160MW Cross-Channel Cable laid between the United Kingdom and France in 1961. It was replaced in 1986 by the much larger Interconnexion France Angleterre 2000 with a 2GW capacity and a further project, Interconnexion France-Angleterre 2 (IFA 2), was completed in 2020. The original project laid the foundation for subsequent interconnector projects which have evolved into a well-established regional power grid. IFA 2 supports the exchange of clean energy between Britain and France and is capable of exporting 1000MW of power – a quantity equivalent of powering one million homes – and is one of a series of interconnectors, either in operation or construction, that link the United Kingdom with continental Europe, Scandinavia and, perhaps in the future, Africa.

The development of international power sharing continues today with National Grid, partnering with other European Transmission System Operators, building longer and more complex submarine inter-connectors between Belgium, Ireland, Denmark, Germany, Norway, and The Netherlands, as well as further power links with France. This development drive for interconnectors capacitating a market for power sharing is mirrored internationally with projects around the world either going through planning or feasibility studies or in the early stages of construction. More broadly, the use of submarine interconnectors is facilitating energy transition by enabling the increasingly important market for the sale of green energy, reaffirming the status of energy as a commercially strategic resource.

Significantly greater in diameter than their fibre-optic equivalents, submarine power cables are in some ways more fragile, requiring protection and maintenance during both installation and subsequent operation. This is a potential strategic vulnerability. Forming Britain's key links for transference of power both internationally and around the country with the ongoing development and installation of an offshore grid network, these High Voltage Direct Current (HVDC) systems are increasingly designed as a lattice of inter-connected capability with off-shore energy sources such as windfarms envisioned to connect directly into future interconnectors. The remit to operate and maintain them resides with the system owners, and so protection and restoration of these assets is undertaken on a commercial impact basis rather than a strategic one.

As the reliance on submarine power cables increases, so, in turn, does the vulnerability to disruption of the whole electricity system. Grids are designed to lose a certain amount of power (n-1 condition) over a short period without failing. As submarine power cables become larger, and if they are laid in proximity, the failure of multiple systems in close succession may cause a system wide failure. Furthermore, power cables take considerably longer (10 times) to repair than telecommunications cables, meaning a cascade of faults is a more disruptive issue.

Strategic Models: Commercial vs National

When looking through the lens of maritime Britain, what are the implications of this submarine cable infrastructure development now and for the nation's immediate future? There are several threads to be explored, but central to almost all of them is one critical tenet:

> Domestic and global developments of submarine infrastructure in both telecommunications and power have been designed and constructed according to a commercial model.

That is to say that everything from initial feasibility studies, routeing, survey, cable protection mechanisms installed during construction, operation and maintenance, and network/system resilience have been developed or put in place based on commercial interests. A prime example illustrating how the submarine cable system has been shaped by a commercial model is the pictorial of the global telecommunications pathways which show how cable systems predominantly follow the same pathways as shipping routes. Although much of the earth's surface is covered in water, cable networks are laid across a very small percentage of that space. It is no accident that their routeing is along the most travelled sea lanes since the industry's commercial interests in low latency for data cables, and low cost, have led to cables being laid along the shortest routes between commercial and population centres. Whilst this is a generalisation, it holds true for a very high percentage of the world's cable routes, be they telecommunications or power. Given that telecommunications operators building cables to link financial hubs do so competitively, it does not come as a surprise. Furthermore, it explains why many cable landing stations or beach manholes are the termination sites of multiple cables as it maximizes capacity and decreases construction and operational costs, whilst simultaneously making more efficient the cables' connection to the 'backhaul' or shoreside infrastructure. However, having multiple cables travel the same routes and then converge at one point of termination creates chokepoints in the system which are an increasing strategic concern. Examples of submarine cable chokepoints include the Red Sea, the Suez Canal, the Straits of Malacca and Singapore, the Gibraltar Strait, the Panama Canal, the approaches to New York, and similarly Marseille and Lisbon, and, importantly for the United Kingdom, the south-west approaches to the English Channel. The internet and its submarine infrastructure has not developed with maritime security in mind. Coupled with the leading role commercial enterprises have had in the design and installation of submarine infrastructure, from a maritime strategic perspective, the absence of national strategic considerations has left the system rather vulnerable, particularly when it comes to chokepoints.

This is an often-discussed point amongst the submarine cable community. Yet, without incentives to consider alternative paths, cable operators and owners (both telecommunications and power) will route cables according to commercial viability as opposed to prioritising national or strategic resilience. This is especially apparent when acting in the national interest conflicts with commercial reality; the demand for greater capacity and an interest in minimising system installation and maintenance costs influences considerations. Recent discussions have indicated that as the availability of seabed space and deconflicting users of the marine space become more challenging, both on and under the water, concerns regarding seabed congestion and landing station or convertor station siting will be key drivers when considering tele-communications and power cable installation and routeing moving forward.

Whilst cable outages off the Northeast coast of Scotland and in the Baltic Sea have served to highlight to a wider audience the potential vulnerability of submarine cables and pipelines, these instances are unlikely to have an immediate effect on well-established routeing or submarine infrastructure protection mechanisms. In the same timeframe as these instances of disruption, there has been a steady drumbeat of cable outages attributable to the usual triumvirate of cable failure causes, namely: (1) anchor contact; (2) fishing vessel interaction; and (3) seabed movement, either general or caused by a natural disaster. Neither tele-communications nor power cables are immune to these occurrences, though their methods of protection and construction differ which results in contrasting risk profiles. The approach to repairing the different cable systems also varies with the nature of the systems, where they are laid and their commercial importance influencing the cost of repairs and restoration. The type of damage, the kind of cable damaged and whether the cable is insured all then dictate the mechanisms of repair and restoration that the cable owners employ. Given that neither the Public Sector nor the Royal Navy are equipped to repair cable faults, the responsibility falls with the Private Sector according to either the maintenance and repair agreements the system owner has contracted or the bespoke mechanisms they have put in place for restoration of the system post incident. Despite submarine cables being part of the United Kingdom's Critical National Infrastructure (CNI), as of right now, if a cable faults – regardless of whether it was accidental, an act of sabotage or an outright attack – all repairs will be managed by the Private Sector and constrained by typical factors such as mobilisation, repair ship availability and time. As submarine cable infrastructure does not operate under a national strategic model, there are challenges and limitations when it comes to the systems' strategic resilience and security from planning to response coordination.

The Strategic Implications of an Integrated System

Britain is reliant on the submarine cable infrastructure within both its territorial waters and that which extends beyond its Economic Exclusion Zone to International Waters. The UK's commercial, social and strategic engagements, and decision making, combined with its ability to power homes, businesses and national services, depend heavily on this Critical National Infrastructure, a strategic reliance shared with many across the global community. This raises an interesting point regarding the designation of CNI for submarine assets such as cable systems.

For those cables such as the Scotland to Shetland telecommuncations cable or the export power cable that connects UK Offshore Windfarms to shore, the designation of CNI is appropriate. What benefit the designation bestows is a different discussion and one for the relevant government departments to undertake in concert with regulatory authorities and the submarine cable sector. Yet, the designation of CNI is not necessarily sufficient to apply to all submarine cables, be they interconnectors delivering power sharing capability between nations or telecommunications cables connecting countries' data centres. These systems span different countries and are frequently owned by inter-national companies or consortia. As such, they are subject to a different set of challenges regarding their operation, maintenance, and resto-ration. Differing terminology and approaches to regulation, permitting, and consent across international boundaries complicates both the dev-elopment and construction of systems in addition to the maintenance, ongoing survey and restoration, and recovery at end of system life.

Another challenging facet of submarine cables being part of a broader integrated ecosystem is the supply chain. From the storage of spare cable and joints and the securing of new cable, particularly HVDC, to vessel flag status and the nationality of cable ship captains and crew assigned to undertake repairs or maintenance, the supply chain network does not always align with British interests. With the increasing distances and complexities of both interconnectors and telecommunications cables, international considerations are increasingly relevant to 'British' submarine cable systems. For example, the 2Africa Cable lands at some 50 different sites along its diverse routeing from the United Kingdom to Mediterranean France and around Africa. In doing so, the system crosses multiple international sea and land boundaries. It is submarine cables such as these, as well as other submarine infrastructure, which more accurately defined as Critical *International* Infrastructure. Britain's and other nations' reliance on such systems and the inter-dependencies that are inherent in their existence are arguably not fully understood, explored or mitigated at a national strategic level. There remains a reliance wholly on commercial entities for restoration and repair prioritisation. The reality of the extent of this vulnerability and the associated risks remains opaque.

From Britain's perspective, national reliance on submarine cables and the data and power they carry is a strategic maritime dependency that extends into most homes, businesses and government service providers in Britain. The cause of a submarine cable fault does not need to be nefarious to be serious. Something as common as a vessel underway dragging an anchor in the southwest approaches to the English Channel has the potential to disrupt large numbers of important systems. With the maintenance capability available today, a significant fault may take months to recover from. The international nature of the cable systems, their ownership and their stakeholders, coupled with the nature of the maintenance authority approach to restoration, or more *ad hoc* method-ologies such as the complex restoration process for inter-connectors, complicates all outage scenarios. This is particularly relevant to multiple system outages if a fault occurs at a chokepoint. To be clear, the industry perspective of commercial restoration is something that is dealt with routinely throughout the sector. However, in the instance that British strategic interests dictate a divergent set of priorities from that which are being implemented through the commercial response, the levers to address this at home and internationally are intricate to say the least, and ineffective at worst. Factor in the power vs telecommunications restoration prioritisation, and other states having the potential to dictate where repair ships are sent (noting that not all cable repair ships are capable or equipped to repair all the different types of submarine cables), restoration of a 'significant cable outage' becomes a complex scenario to manage and resolve in a timely manner. The repercussions of such a scenario are heightened by an unlikely but not unforeseeable occurrence wherein two submarine cable chokepoints simultaneously suffer outages.

In 2024, the availability of both cable and jointing resources for the telecoms industry are well established and maintained. Available repair vessels are at a commercial level where the operational expenditure is sustainable for the cable owners when considering current cable fault levels. However, in the case of a major event impacting numerous submarine cables at once, current repair vessel resources would be stretched, and cable repairs prioritised accordingly by the owners. Power cable vessels are less numerous than telecommunication cable repair vessels, and repairs take significantly longer. Factoring in challenges in the power cable supply chain, this has the potential to result in significant delays in restoration. Vulnerabilities in the supply chain are not easily rectified as factory manufacturing capacity throughout the world is limited and exacerbated by the increasing global demand for construction. This is particularly apparent for the manufacturing of HVDC power cables, the type used in long distance and high-capacity power systems. European power cable factories are taking orders today for cable delivery 5 years hence and beyond. In response, major submarine interconnector projects around the world are factoring in the establishment of their own cable supply chains to design and manufacture the cable they need, for installation and for maintenance. Without careful oversight, there is potential for a shift in commercial control that will see both power and fibre cable manufacturers flexing commercial muscle to drive through a net lowering of factory acceptance standards or an enforcement of programme and delivery changes that increase risk in cable systems due to the quality and timeliness of delivery of new and repaired systems. For this reason, investment in major interconnectors is starting to include the building of bespoke cable factories to support projects with a demand for thousands of kilometres of HVDC cable. A recent example of this is *SunCable*, a company with a vision to construct an interconnector to share Australian solar power with Singapore. The company is in discussions with global cable manufacturers to jointly develop, construct and operate an advanced high voltage (HV) cable manufacturing facility with the AAPowerLink project from Darwin, Australia, to Singapore as an anchor customer.[3]

The specialist shipping needed to install and repair these complex submarine systems is also increasingly in demand. There has been much sector discussion over the age and availability of the global submarine cable fleet with a significant proportion of the current fleet not capable of HVDC power cable installation or repair. These concerns are being alleviated by a series of decisions by cable installation companies such as *Prysmian Group*,[4] *Orange Marine*,[5] *Nexans*,[6] and *NKT*[7] to procure new cable ships. Yet not all these vessels will be equipped with full scope repair capability for all cable types. Moreover, these ships take time to build and are being procured because the commercial imperatives necessitate their delivery to fulfil existing or future planned submarine cable contracts. They remain privately owned and operated and are not state assets, nor have any British companies thus far partaken in these endeavours, and so they are ultimately unlikely to be immediately responsive to Britain's needs unless they are simultaneously aligned with commercial or other nations' imperatives. This puts the United Kingdom at a strategic dis-advantage both commercially and, potentially, with respect to national security and resiliency.

To further illustrate, in the event of an incident that results in several submarine systems suffering outages, the initial response will be immediate but driven by commercial restoration arrangements that are in place rather than a higher strategic consideration. Noting such an instance could well affect both telecommunications and power cable systems, coordination of restoration priorities and the allocation of resources to fulfil such crisis response activity has significance but limited national strategic input. It should be noted that Britain's commercial partners and international cable owners would be responsive to such a scenario, but that at each end of a cable is oftentimes a different nation with its own strategic considerations. In the event of a catastrophic series of outages in Britain or, in the worst-case scenario, across the world, international politics, strategic and commercial arrangements and prioritisation of asset restoration become very muddled and challenging to resolve. Britain no longer dominates the submarine cable sector in terms of resourcing, be it cable supply or vessel availability, as the country no longer has cable factories manufacturing HVDC cable and only has limited fibre cable output. *Global Marine Systems Limited* are the only British company with true high seas cable maintenance and repair capability. Having sold off their HVDC interests, they deal only with telecommunications fibre cable. *Xlinks* is a prospective British cable owner taking a similar approach to *SunCable* and is considering both the building of a factory in Hunterston and the commissioning of its own vessel to install and maintain over 4,000km of HVDC cable from Morocco to the United Kingdom.[8] Both of these companies represent an innovative model for delivering exceptionally long interconnectors that require significant investment and a long-term commercial model. But, again, it is the commercial imperative driving development and procurement not national strategic interest.

The Future

The augment of Artificial Intelligence and the Internet of Things evidence society's new information reliant reality. Historically, Britain has played a leading role in the invention, development, and pro-liferation of submarine cables – both fibre-optic and HVDC. Through telecommunications and power cables, the nation's maritime sector has helped carry maritime Britain into the 21st century, connecting bus-inesses and people across the world and powering their operations. Yet, our ever-increasing dependence upon this integrated system is creating a metaphysical chokepoint where delays in production, commercial prioritisation of cost and efficacy and the lack of ships capable of carrying out timely repairs have put Britain at a strategic disadvantage. Moving forward, it is imperative that when discussing submarine cables, they are examined holistically as a strategically important system. One cable is equivalent to only one of hundreds of neural pathways that form the broader network of the digital realm. To adopt a segmented approach to securing the nation's critical submarine infrastructure is to undermine the very nature of a networked system. To over-rely on the capabilities and availabilities of commercial partners and international allies is to increase vulnerabilities whilst simultaneously weakening the submarine cable system's overall resilience from a British perspective. The multi-faceted nature of the system results in various points of exposure, making submarine cables a potentially prime target for actors – both state and non-state – seeking to divert, disrupt, observe, or influence the metadata and power that is constantly traveling between countries and continents. This in turn could affect, amongst other factors, understanding, decision making, societal behaviour, and coherent responses to scenarios or in-cidents. The British Public Sector, in concert with the submarine cable sector, our partners and our allies, needs to work to better engage, understand, support, resource, and regulate our components of the industry. This should be part of a wider enduring effort to ensure that critical submarine cables and their strategic resilience and dependencies are well understood and considered from a UK strategic perspective.

1. "America," *The Times*, August 23, 1858. *The Times Digital Archive*.

2. W. H. Russell's *The Atlantic Telegraph* (1866).

3. https://www.suncable.energy/manufacturing.

4. https://www.prysmiangroup.com/en/insight/projects/leonardo-da-vinci-sister-ship-celebrates-her-official-birth.

5. https://newsroom.orange.com/the-sophie-germain-oranges-new-cable-ship-a-technological-achievement-supporting-global-connectivity/.

6. https://www.nexans.com/en/newsroom/news/details/2023/07/nexans-to-build-third-generation-cable-laying-vessel-to-drive-global-energy-transition.html.

7. https://www.nkt.com/products-solutions/high-voltage-cable-solutions/nkt-victoria.

8. https://xlinks.co/faq/.

Human–Technology Partnerships: Implementing Advanced Automation in Naval and Commercial Maritime Operations

Gordon Meadow

Abstract

Technology should enhance, not replace, human potential. This analysis delves into the critical role of human-technology partnerships concerning successful implementation and adoption of advanced automation into naval defence and commercial maritime operations. Amidst the backdrop of rapidly evolving maritime technologies, particularly the integration of uncrewed surface and subsurface vehicles (USVs and UUVs), this assessment emphasises the synergy between human expertise and technological advancements. It explores how these partnerships enhance operational capabilities, improve strategic decision-making, and will reshape the future of maritime operations.

The analysis presents insights into the technical aspects of advanced automation, emphasizing the transformative impact of USVs and UUVs on maritime strategies. It further examines the evolving nature of human-machine interaction, highlighting the shift from direct control to supervisory and decision-making roles for human operators. This shift underscores the need for intuitive interface designs, ergonomic considerations, and specialised training programs. Strategic implications of advanced automation are explored, revealing how these technologies extend operational reach, improve response times, and necessitate interoperability in multi-national operations. Through a series of anecdotal case studies, the analysis demonstrates practical applications and successes of these technologies in both naval and commercial maritime contexts.

Central to this discourse is the recognition of the human aspect as an indispensable force. The analysis advocates for a human-centred app-roach in technology integration, where human intuition and decision-making capabilities are not overshadowed but rather enhanced by machine precision and data-processing abilities. It discusses the expand-ed role of behavioural assessments in understanding and optimiz-ing human-AI interactions, highlighting the importance of continuous learning and adaptation.

Concluding on a forward-looking note, the analysis envisions a future of collaborative intelligence in maritime operations, where human and AI capabilities are synergistically integrated. It stresses the import-ance of ethical considerations and safety standards in this evolving landscape, underscoring the need for a maritime workforce that is equip-ped to thrive in a technology-rich environment. The analysis provides a comprehensive understanding of why and how human-technology partnerships are pivotal for the maritime sector's advancement, paving the way for a secure, efficient, and sustainable future.

Introduction

In the ever-evolving realm of maritime operations, both in defence and commercial sectors, the interplay between human capabilities and advanced technology stands as a pivotal element for current and future successes. This crucial synergy is not merely a trend but an essential strategy in meeting the intricate challenges of today's and tomorrow's maritime environments. For the current maritime workforce, as well as for the next and subsequent generations, grasping this dynamic is vital. The integration of advanced automation, particularly within naval and commercial maritime contexts, signifies a transformative shift in the execution and management of maritime missions.

Human-technology partnerships in this field transcend the simple use of sophisticated tools; they represent a fundamental change in operational paradigms. In this context, technology is not seen as a substitute for human expertise but as an augmentative force, enhancing human skills and broadening operational capabilities. This perspective becomes critically important when considering advanced automation, where the complexity and sophistication of technology is overshadowing the human component.

At the heart of this partnership is the combination of human and machine strengths. Machines bring precision, speed, and the ability to process large data volumes, while humans contribute with critical thinking, contextual insights, and adaptability. This amalgamation is particularly relevant in high-stake environments like naval defence and commercial maritime operations, where decision-making carries significant consequences.

This analysis aims to unpack the multifaceted role of human-technology partnerships in the realm of advanced automation in this setting. The focus is both on the technical aspects of such automation, emphasising the integration of uncrewed surface and subsurface vehicles, and also on the strategic implications. Importantly, it highlights the role of the human operator as a significant and empowered player in this technological era.

Furthermore, the discussion explores the trajectory of artificial intelligence and its symbiosis with human competence, underlining the importance of behavioural assessments in evaluating aptitude within these advanced technological environments. By combining theoretical insights with practical anecdotal case studies, this analysis seeks to provide a comprehensive understanding of the criticality of human-technology partnerships for the effective implementation and adoption of advanced automation in the maritime sector, impacting the current workforce and shaping the future for upcoming generations.

Technical Aspects of Advanced Automation
The maritime domain, encompassing both defence and commercial components, has witnessed significant technological advancements in recent years. Advanced automation now plays a pivotal role, revolutionizing operations from routine surveillance to complex tactical maoeuvres. The integration of sophisticated technologies such as artificial intelligence (AI), machine learning, and advanced sensor sytems could be instrumental in enhancing operational efficiency, safety, and decision-making capabilities.

A notable development in maritime automation is the increasing use of uncrewed surface vehicles (USVs) and uncrewed underwater vehicles (UUVs). These remotely operated vehicles are transforming thinking on aspects of maritime operations, offering several advantages over traditional crewed systems.

- **USVs**: Uncrewed surface vehicles are becoming more ubiquitous in a myriad of applications, including oceanographic data collection, mine countermeasures, anti-submarine warfare, and surveillance. Equipped with advanced sensors, these vehicles can operate in hazardous environments, providing real-time data while reducing risks to human life.

- **UUVs**: Uncrewed underwater vehicles can serve critical roles in underwater surveillance, environmental monitoring, and seabed mapping. Their ability to operate in deep and challenging underwater terrains makes them invaluable for tasks that are either too risky or impossible or not practical for conventional resources.

The adoption of advanced automated systems have the potential to markedly improve operational capabilities in several ways. Firstly, USVs and UUVs equipped with sophisticated sensors can cover vast areas of the ocean, offering enhanced surveillance and reconnaissance. Such systems can provide detailed and accurate data that is crucial for wider situational awareness and monitoring and which would be impossible to attain through traditional methods; a ship has limited sensor and visual horizons). Secondly, by deploying USVs and UUVs, maritime forces can conduct operations in hazardous environments without putting human lives at risk, especially in mine countermeasures and anti-submarine warfare. Thirdly, automation enables continuous and long-duration missions with reduced human fatigue, leading to more efficient use of resources and personnel using distributed teams. Finally, automated systems can offer opportunities to operate at a lower cost compared to crewed missions, especially in terms of lifecycle and maintenance expenses.

Regardless of the benefit, successful and effective implementation of these technologies into operations requires a forward-thinking and adaptable mindset. Organisations must prioritise continuous learning and should be open to re-evaluating and updating their strategies in response to technological advancements. Successful organisations cultivate a culture of innovation, where creative problem-solving and risk-taking are encouraged, and failure is seen as a learning opportunity. They also emphasise collaboration and communication across departments, ensuring that technological solutions are aligned with the organisation's broader goals. In this context recent events taking place in the Black Sea have created an interesting step change in the deployment of these new systems. Here we see adoption and deployment fuelled by necessity coupled to a clear mission purpose and relatively simple mission outcome. For a cash and equipment strapped Ukraine, R&D is not an option, and they are forced to adopt an 80/20 approach – use technology that exists now, which is cost effective, for a clear purpose that is just about good enough to get the job done. If your naval capability is more akin to Samson, as opposed to Goliath, as in the case of the Ukraine, you can still gain competitive advantage, but you need to think differently. This is contrary to conventional defence, still seemingly driven by technological transformation, procuring technology to trial and discover the art of the possible, all fuelled by the pressure of a fast-shifting adversarial technology landscape.

The reality of course is that the wider maritime environment cannot operate in an unregulated operational sandbox using a haphazard "fail fast" approach. Trust must be assured in the use and adoption of new and complex systems. But perhaps there is still a lesson that can be learned from the mindset of the Ukrainians. Evolution through marginal gains, which involves making small, incremental improvements in a system or process, could also offer a more cost effective and sustainable approach to technology adoption compared to the aspiration to transform everything all at once. Marginal gains foster a culture of continuous improvement. By focusing on small changes, organisations can adapt more quickly to new information and changing circumstances. This adaptability is crucial in the fast-paced world of technology, where new developments are constantly emerging. It allows organisations to stay up-to-date with the latest technological advancements without the need for periodic, disruptive overhauls. Success measurement and momentum building is easier to track by taking smaller steps. Each successful implementation is a marginal gain and can act as a proof of concept at the same time as delivering results, building confidence in the technology and its benefits by being clear about the application. Smaller successes can help in garnering support for further technological adoption, creating a positive feedback loop.

Challenges in integration

While the benefits of incorporating advanced automation systems are relatively clear, integrating these technologies into existing maritime frameworks poses certain challenges, chiefly interoperability; training and adaptation; and cybersecurity. Each of these can be mitigated against, but require clear thinking and appreciation of the risks. In terms of interoperability, ensuring that new automated systems can seamlessly integrate and communicate with existing platforms and command structures is crucial for effective operations. Given that automation is an adjunct or development of tools rather than replacement of people, then the current and future maritime workforce must be adequately trained to operate and maintain these advanced systems, requiring a shift in training protocols and skill sets. Lastly, with increased reliance on automation and remote operations, safeguarding against cyber threats becomes paramount to protect these assets, and their human operators, from potential vulnerabilities.

Human–Machine Interaction

The advent of advanced automation in maritime operations will significantly alter the roles of the human operator. In earlier paradigms, humans by and large were directly in control of most operational aspects. However, with the integration of advanced automation, human operators are transitioning to more supervisory and decision-making roles. This shift emphasizes the importance of effective human-machine interaction to ensure operational success.

Integrating human decision–making with automated processes

One of the critical aspects of human-machine interaction is the integration of human decision-making capabilities with automated processes. This integration requires a balance where humans can rely on automated systems for routine tasks while retaining ultimate control over critical decision-making processes. Such a model ensures that the strengths of both humans (e.g., strategic thinking, adaptability) and machines (e.g., speed, precision) are optimally utilised. As such, the design of user interfaces plays a crucial role in effective human-machine interaction. Interfaces must be intuitive and provide relevant information that aids human operators in making informed decisions. The goal is to reduce cognitive load while enhancing the operator's ability to monitor and control automated systems effectively. Achieving this means creating robust feedback mechanisms; an essential element in maintaining situational awareness. Real-time feedback from automated systems enables human operators to stay informed about system statuses and environmental conditions, facilitating timely interventions when necessary.

Training and skill development

As the role of human operators evolves, so does the need for specialised training and skill development. Training programs must be designed to equip maritime personnel with the skills required to effectively interact with and manage automated systems. This includes vocational training, technical proficiency, analytical skills, and an understanding of AI and machine learning principles. Advanced training using simulation can prepare operators for various scenarios, including such areas as system malfunctions and emergency responses. Simulated environments allow for safe, controlled training that mirrors real-world conditions. However, trainees must also evidence practical hands-on experience, therefore training and assessment must also be carried out using real equipment in real world environments. This is not to suggest that technical system specific training alone should be underpinned by using real world equipment. Vocational training must also adopt this blended approach. The link between rapid advancements in technology, continuous learning and skill development is imperative. This ensures that the workforce remains adept at utilising the latest technological innovations.

Ethical and safety considerations

Human-machine interaction also brings ethical and safety considerations to the forefront. Ensuring that highly automated systems are designed and operated ethically, with a focus on safety and compliance, is crucial. As AI plays a more significant role in decision-making processes, establishing ethical guidelines for its use is essential. This includes ensuring trans-parency, accountability, and fairness in AI-driven decisions. Robust safety protocols are therefore necessary to prevent accidents and manage risks associated with automated systems. This includes emergency response procedures and fail-safes to ensure human control in critical situations.

Strategic Implications

The adoption of advanced automation technologies has profound strategic implications for naval operations. Automation not only enhances existing capabilities, but also opens up new strategic possibilities, such as extending operational reach. Highly automated systems can operate in environments that are challenging or risky for human crews, such as extreme depths or in proximity to hostile forces. This extends the operational reach of maritime forces, allowing for more comprehensive coverage and strategic flexibility. Moreover, automated platforms can maintain a presence in critical areas for extended periods, offering continuous surveillance and situational awareness. This persistent presence could prove invaluable for strategic monitoring and reconnaissance, especially when one considers the physical endurance of a machine compared to a human.

Decision–making and response times

The incorporation of advanced automation significantly impacts decision-making processes and response times in maritime operations. The speed and accuracy of automated systems can enable faster and more informed decisions, which is crucial in dynamic and potentially hostile environments. Automated systems equipped with advanced sensors and AI can process vast amounts of data in real-time, providing decision-makers with timely and relevant information. This positively feeds into the decision-action cycle. The ability to quickly analyse situations and execute decisions can be revolutionised by highly automated systems, allowing for rapid responses to emerging threats or changing operational conditions.

Interoperability and coalition operations

With the increasing complexity of maritime operations, interoperability between different systems and platforms, as well as among international partners, also becomes essential. Highly automated systems must be designed to operate seamlessly within a diverse array of existing technologies and within the framework of coalition operations. Developing common standards and ensuring compatibility across different systems and platforms is vital for effective joint operations. However, as shown through the influx of NATO standard equipment to Ukraine, it is not enough for systems to be standardised; compatibility should be sought as the norm. This will enhance interoperability, the cornerstone of multinational operations. The ability of automated systems to integrate with different countries' technologies and protocols is crucial, ensuring cohesive and efficient joint operations for naval defence and for their commercial counterparts.

Impact on force structure and resource allocation

The integration of highly automated systems in maritime operations also affects force structure and resource allocation. As systems take on more operational roles, the composition and deployment of human personnel will continue to evolve. Automation is leading to more efficient use of resources, including human personnel, allowing for strategic allocation of people and material assets. This in turn means that both military and commercial maritime sectors will need to adapt their operational structures to integrate highly automated capabilities effectively, balancing between human roles and automated systems. It is not simply enough to integrate automated systems into existing force or operational structures, but instead wholly new structures will need to be designed to exploit and maximize the effect of automation.

Case Studies

Case study 1: autonomous systems in naval reconnaissance

A notable focus of advanced automation in naval operations is the use of autonomous underwater vehicles (AUVs) for reconnaissance and surveillance in contested maritime zones. AUVs, equipped with state-of-the-art sensors and AI-driven navigation systems, are being increasingly deployed to gather critical intelligence in regions with complex geopolitical dynamics, with reduced risk to their human operators and increased discrete or covert capabilities. AUVs can provide data from high-resolution environmental data to enemy movement patterns, with potential to significantly enhance situational awareness and strategic planning. Successful exploitation of these operations could increasingly yield strategic value of autonomous systems in high-risk environments.

Case study 2: leveraging highly automated systems in commercial shipping

In the realm of commercial shipping, maritime operators and product developers are embarking on initiatives to integrate highly automated systems on board their cargo ships. Examples are in equipping vessels with advanced automation technologies for automated navigation, engine management, and cargo handling systems. As such ships can be designed to operate with minimal human intervention, with a central control system overseeing various operational aspects.

The objective at first sight looks to be centrally concerned with the enhancement of operational efficiency, safety, and the reduction of environmental impact. Regardless, the implementation must involve rigorous testing and gradual implementation, ensuring that systems are dependable and can seamlessly work in conjunction with the ship's crews. The introduction of these systems may result in a significant increase in operational efficiency and a reduction in system error-related incidents. Ships will be able to maintain optimal fuel consumption, adhere to strict schedules, and better ensure the safety of the cargo and crew. Successful adoption has the potential to transform commercial maritime operations, paving the way for a new era in the shipping industry. However, we are seeing increasingly greater personnel shortages across both naval and commercial maritime. Therefore, we should not solely be focused on factors concerning operational efficiency, safety, and the reduction of environmental impact. We must also concern ourselves that we are running out of seafarers to operate ships, never mind working in conjunction with highly automated systems.

Case study 3: collaborative operation between crewed and uncrewed systems

Use of joint naval exercises involving multiple countries focused on the integration of crewed and uncrewed systems in a simulated conflict scenario. Exercises can include the deployment of UUVs and USVs alongside traditional human-centred vessels, demonstrating coordinated operations involving surveillance, mine countermeasures, and anti-submarine warfare. As joint naval exercises will continue to highlight enhanced operational capabilities achieved through human-technology collaboration. It must also, however, provide valuable insights into training needs, interoperability challenges, and the tactical advantages of mixed crewed-uncrewed force structures.

Case study 4: emergency response using automated systems

Support to humanitarian and disaster relief operations are an often overlooked but fundamental mission of both naval and commercial shipping. Highly automated systems have the potential to be utilised for rapid response during a natural disaster at sea, or in providing support from the sea to coastal regions, showcasing the potential of automation in humanitarian operations. Unmanned aerial vehicles (UAVs) and USVs have great potential to be deployed for search and rescue oper-ations, delivering supplies, and assessing damage in areas inaccessible to human responders. The operation of both UAVs and USVs could not only save lives but also demonstrate the versatility of automated systems in diverse operational contexts, from military applications to human-itarian assistance and disaster relief. A prime example of where rapidly deployable automated systems could have been used to great effect would be the survey of the Port of Beirut after the explosion in 2020; it was only by fortuitous circumstance that HMS *Enterprise* was in the region.

The Human Element as a Powerful Force

In this era dominated by technological advancements, a common theme exists across all case studies: the role of humans in maritime operations remains more crucial than ever. While automation and AI will bring unparalleled capabilities, the nuanced understanding, decision-making, and adaptability of humans remains critical. This section explores how human capabilities complement and enhance technological advancements in maritime operations.

Synergy between human intuition and machine precision

The true power of advanced automation lies in its ability to augment human skills. For instance, while AI can process and analyse data at incredible speeds, human operators provide the critical thinking necessary to interpret and act on this information in complex, real-world scenarios. After-all, humans excel in adapting to unexpected situations and making decisions under uncertainty. In a maritime context, this adaptability is vital, especially in dynamic and potentially hazardous environments subject to rapid change.

Human–centred design in naval and maritime technologies

Designing technology with the human user in mind is key to successful implementation. This includes ergonomic controls and intuitive interfaces that facilitate seamless human-machine interaction. As highly automated systems become more prevalent, training programs must evolve to equip maritime personnel with the skills to effectively interact with and manage these technologies. This includes understanding automated system functionalities and developing the ability to intervene when necessary.

The importance of human oversight

Even in highly automated scenarios, the importance of human oversight cannot be overstated. Effective human system teaming can ensure that operations remain aligned with overarching strategic objectives as well as ethical considerations. Moreover, in critical situations, the ability of human operators to quickly assess and respond to emergencies is still vital. While highly automated systems can handle routine tasks, human intervention is still essential in situations that require nuanced judgment and rapid adaptation.

AI and Human Competency

The introduction of Artificial Intelligence (AI) in maritime operations heralds a new era where the fusion of technology and human expertise is more nuanced and critical than ever. This fusion is not just about coexistence but about creating a symbiotic relationship where each complement enhances the other's capabilities.

Advanced behavioural assessment in human–AI interaction

Advanced behavioural assessment in the context of maritime operations goes beyond mere observation of human interaction with AI. It involves in-depth analytics of decision-making patterns, response times, and adaptability to automated systems. By leveraging data analytics and cognitive science, organisations can gain deeper insights into the strengths and limitations of their personnel in managing AI-driven systems.

By utilising these insights, maritime organisations can develop customised training regimes. These regimes are tailored to individual learning curves and competencies, ensuring that each member of the maritime workforce can effectively harness AI capabilities. This approach leads to a more skilled and adaptable workforce, capable of navigating the complexities of modern maritime operations.

Charting AI capabilities alongside human skills

In the maritime domain, AI's role can be seen as a decision support system rather than a decision-maker. AI algorithms can process vast amounts of operational data to identify patterns and trends that might not be immediately obvious to human operators. However, the final strategic decisions, particularly in complex or ambiguous situations, are best left to human judgment. Integrating scenario-based training where human operators interact with AI in simulated environments, therefore, can be invaluable. These scenarios can range from routine operations to crisis situations, providing operators with a wide range of experiences in managing AI systems. This training not only enhances human skills but also contributes to the development of more intuitive and responsive AI systems.

Future prospects and ethical considerations

Looking forward, the focus is on enhancing collaborative intelligence where AI and human intelligence are not just aligned but inter-dependent. This collaboration aims to create a more resilient, efficient, and responsive maritime operational framework. However, as we move towards this collaboration and as AI systems become more autonomous, establishing robust ethical frameworks and governance models will and are becoming increasingly critical. These frameworks should ensure that AI systems are transparent, accountable, and aligned with human values and safety standards. It is essential to maintain a balance where technological advancements do not overshadow the ethical and humanitarian aspects.

Conclusion

This analysis has explored the multifaceted role of human-technology partnerships in the implementation and adoption of advanced automation in naval defence and commercial maritime operations. From the technical advancements in USVs and UUVs to the strategic implications of such technologies onboard ships, it is clear that the future of maritime operations is increasingly intertwined with advanced automation.

The case studies presented attempt to highlight practical examples of how these technologies are either already reshaping maritime operations thinking or have the potential to enhance capabilities, or open new strategic possibilities. They also underscore the importance of human skills and decision-making in maximizing the benefits of these technological advancements.

Central to this discussion is the acknowledgment of the human component as a powerful force in maritime operations. The synergy between human intuition and machine precision forms the backbone of effective maritime strategies. This partnership is not about replacing humans with machines but about augmenting human capabilities with technological advancements. The expanded role and need for behavioural assessments in understanding and enhancing human-AI interaction further emphasises the need for a workforce that is adept at working alongside AI and automated systems.

In the future the focus should be on fostering a collaborative intelligence framework, where human and AI capabilities are not just aligned but synergistically integrated. This approach will be crucial in navigating the complexities of future maritime challenges, from geopolitical tensions to environmental concerns. As we advance, it is imperative to ensure that ethical considerations and safety standards are at the forefront of technological developments in this domain.

The path forward involves continuous learning, adaptation, and collaboration. The current and future generations of maritime professionals must be equipped with the skills and mindset to thrive in this evolving landscape. The successful implementation and adoption of advanced automation in naval and maritime operations will hinge on our ability to harmonise the strengths of humans and machines, ensuring that this partnership leads to a more secure, efficient, and sustainable maritime future.

Security and Defence

America's Sentinels

Maritime Prefectures – The Future of UK Coastal Security?

America's Sentinels of the Sea

Admiral Linda L Fagan, USCG

Prologue

The choppy waters of the Pacific Ocean slap against the side of the small fishing boat as the three men inside pray for rescue. It has been more than three days since their outboard engine failed during a routine fishing trip from their home on the island of Tarawa to fishing grounds less than 80 kilometers away. Without the engine, they have been swept by currents out into the open Pacific. Drifting and alone, they are a small speck in a vast sea, far out of radio and mobile phone range and unable to call for help. Sitting low in the water, their tiny, five-meter fishing vessel is nearly invisible to passing ships or aircraft. With no cabin to shelter them from the elements, they try to make themselves as comfortable as possible on the boat's rough wooden benches and a few pieces of old plywood. Their scarce supplies are dwindling as the time slowly ticks by.

The men don't know it yet, but help is on the way.

Launched from Barbers Point, Hawaii, an HC-130J 'Super Hercules' long-range maritime patrol aircraft has flown over 3,800 kilometers to search for the missing men. When they failed to return home, their families contacted the local authorities. Their request for assistance made its way from Tarawa to the Rescue Coordination Center in Fiji and on to the Joint Rescue Coordination Center in Honolulu. Arriving on scene, the aircraft's search area is huge – more than 10,000 square kilometers – and looking for the tiny vessel is like trying to find a 50 pence coin in London's Victoria Park. Nonetheless, the aircrew begins methodically scanning the water for the fishermen.

To the men in the boat, the airplane first appears as a dot just above the horizon, its form slowly taking shape. The men stand. Balancing on their bare feet, they wave their arms and shirts over their heads, frantically signaling the aircraft. The plane banks towards them.

Long before the writing on its wings and fuselage is clear enough to read, its identity is revealed by a distinctive mark. Rising up both sides of the aircraft and inclined forward, a thick band of red is followed by thin bands of white and blue, comprising the 'racing stripe' of the United States Coast Guard.

Around the globe, this iconic symbol brings hope to hundreds of thousands of people in need on the water and in coastal communities, an unmistakable sign that the United States Coast Guard is there to help. It is such a powerful symbol that scores of coast guards, search and rescue organizations, and maritime law enforcement agencies have adopted their own versions of it.

Sighting the boat, the airplane circles the vessel. The aircrew lowers the plane's cargo ramp and prepares a watertight container with a radio, food, and water. On the next pass, the plane comes in low and slow, and the aircrew times the drop. Blossoming a bright orange parachute, the container falls gently to the sea in front of the fishermen. As they haul the survival kit aboard, the aircrew begins searching for the next link in the chain that will ensure the fishermen can return home.

Eventually, the aircrew find a large steel fishing trawler in the area and direct it to the location of the drifting fishermen, who are pulled to safety aboard the larger vessel. As the men recover on the trawler, the airplane returns to Hawaii to await its next mission, completing one of the many operations that the United States Coast Guard performs every day.

Another day and half a world away from the rescued fishermen, the United States Coast Guard Cutter (CGC) *Spencer* plots a course through the Atlantic Ocean en route to Africa. Sporting the same distinctive racing stripe as the HC-130J, the 82-meter ship is the perfect size to conduct maritime exercises with West African nations and help counter illegal fishing activity in the Gulf of Guinea. Today, however, the cutter and her crew have a different mission.

Bobbing in the water a few hundred meters in front of the *Spencer* sits a Brazilian sailing vessel. Suspicious that the boat might be involved in smuggling, *Spencer's* crew received permission from Brazil to board and search the vessel. It will be a fruitful boarding. Crammed inside the sailing vessel, Coast Guard officers will find nearly 100 packages filled with more than 3,000 kilograms of cocaine bound for Europe. While impressive, this seizure will form a small percentage of the 140 metric tons of drugs that the U.S. Coast Guard will interdict at sea in the coming year as part of the ongoing fight against transnational organized crime.

Just as the United States Coast Guard works with partners to counter illegal smuggling, it also helps them confront other threats to their sovereign rights and interests. More than 8,000 kilometers from where

Spencer found the sailboat, a U.S. Coast Guard law enforcement team is underway in the Indian Ocean aboard the Seychelles Coast Guard patrol ship *Zoroaster*. Capable of speeds of 34 knots and covering 1,500 nautical miles without resupply, the 50-meter *Zoroaster* is modern and well-crewed but faces daunting operational challenges.[1] Alongside the other patrol vessels of the Seychelles Coast Guard, it is charged with overseeing the nation's 1.4 million square kilometer Exclusive Economic Zone,[2] a massive task for any organization, but a crucially important one for an archipelagic state whose economy heavily relies on the ocean.

Operating under a recently signed bilateral agreement, U.S. Coast Guard personnel are working with their Seychellois counterparts to counter illegal fishing in the region. Efforts like these combine the U.S. Coast Guard's law enforcement expertise with local officers' authorities to protect their nation's waters. Together, the U.S. and Seychellois boarding team will discover a vessel targeting dolphin – a locally protected species – which will result in the vessel being escorted back to port and the catch confiscated.[3]

This boarding is the product of a long chain of cooperation based on a shared commitment to maritime security and ecological protection. The agreement between the Seychelles and the United States is one of more than 60 multi and bilateral agreements that the U.S. Coast Guard maintains with international partners to increase interoperability, exchange best practices, and support each other's operations.

Varied and multi-faceted, the cases above reflect only a few of the operations that the United States Coast Guard conducts around the world every day. Later in the chapter we will discuss the unique capabilities of the U.S. Coast Guard, and the maritime challenges facing nations across the globe, but first we must address our enduring connection to the sea.

* * *

Maritime Nations

'Oh, where are you going to, all you Big Steamers,
With England's own coal, up and down the salt seas'
'We are going to fetch you your bread and your butter,
Your beef, pork, and mutton, eggs, apples, and cheese.'
– Rudyard Kipling "Big Steamers"

In March 2021, the world's attention was captured by the plight of the *Ever Given*, a massive, 400-meter-long cargo ship aground in the Suez Canal. For six days, authorities worked to free the trapped vessel as the impact of the closed waterway rippled through the global economy. While many were captivated by the plight of the trapped ship, it is safe to say that on a normal day the typical citizen of the United States or United Kingdom does not spend much time thinking about maritime shipping. Unless booking a cruise, or catching a snippet of the Shipping Forecast, most people don't think about the sea, let alone where all the *stuff* around them comes from. But the truth is, whether strolling through a Walmart in Texas, filling a car with petrol in Manchester, or grabbing takeaway in London, the sea and shipping underpins every facet of our daily lives.

Like the United Kingdom, America is a maritime nation, with its security and prosperity inexorably linked to the ocean. With over 153,000 kilometers of coastline, more than 40,000 kilometers of coastal and inland rivers, and 3,500 marine terminals,[4] the U.S. Marine Transportation System forms the lifeblood of the American economy.[5] The United States has the largest Exclusive Economic Zone in the world and has sovereign rights and interests in a vast swath of undersea Continental Shelf and Extended Continental Shelf (ECS) spanning well over one million square kilometers.[6] These zones, and their accompanying seabed and subsoil areas, make up a diverse U.S. maritime ecosystem spanning halfway across the globe.

The ocean is responsible for more than £11 trillion in global trade each year,[7] 17% of the protein we eat,[8] and half of the oxygen we breathe.[9] It contains vast natural gas reserves, the greatest potential for renewable energy through offshore wind farms, and rare earth elements essential for technology and energy innovation. Undersea cables transmit 95% of international communications and roughly £8 trillion in financial transactions each day.[10] The ocean must be protected, and effective stewardship of its resources is necessary to ensure the prosperity and security of the generations that come after us.

The global prosperity that we enjoy today is due in large part to the rules based international order that was established in the aftermath of the Second World War. Fundamental to that system is the free flow of trade, a commitment to responsible maritime governance, adherence to international rules regarding territorial integrity, and respect for sovereign rights regarding offshore resources. The sea is the connective tissue of our globalized world and disruptions – whether accidental like *Ever*

Given or malicious through deliberate attacks on shipping and port facilities – have a cascading effect on industries and livelihoods worldwide in ways impossible to imagine even a generation ago. The ability of like-minded nations to support and defend the rules-based order is paramount, including the use of sea power to guarantee a safe and prosperous maritime domain.

American naval power is comprised of three sea services – the United States Navy, the United States Marine Corps, and the United States Coast Guard. Strategic sealift, overseen by the United States Maritime Administration and manned by the U.S. Merchant Marine, is also a crucial element of American sea power, as is the United States' broad network of alliances and international partners. In many ways, sea power today remains a modern reflection of the paradigm established by the Royal Navy – it is about the ability to maintain a forward presence, project power, deter adversaries, and secure maritime commerce.

While the United States Navy is the most powerful and visible expression of America's commitment to global maritime security, it is the United States Coast Guard that protects, defends, and promotes the full spectrum of American maritime governance activities, having done so in some form since the earliest days of our Republic over 230 years ago.

The United States Coast Guard

After the American revolutionary war, the fledgling United States needed a way to generate revenue. Writing from New York in November 1787, Alexander Hamilton penned Federalist Paper No. 12 to articulate the benefits of commerce, emphasizing that "a nation cannot long exist without revenue," and advocating for a way to enforce customs duties on maritime shipping. Hamilton argued that "a few armed vessels, judiciously stationed at the entrances of our ports, might at small expense be made useful sentinels of the laws."[11] After being appointed the first Secretary of the Treasury in 1789, Hamilton followed through on his idea, and in 1790 Congress passed a law authorizing the building and equipping of "boats or cutters, not exceeding ten, as may be necessary to be employed for the protection of the revenue."[12]

The revenue cutters – eventually called the Revenue Cutter Service – would prove invaluable to the new nation. In addition to collecting revenues, they hunted pirates along the American Gulf Coast, aided vessels in distress, and joined the U.S. Navy in fighting British warships in the War of 1812. In a particularly remarkable feat of bravery and resilience in the late 1890s, Revenue Cutter Service officers from the cutter *Bear*, in conjunction with Native Alaskan guides, drove a herd of reindeer over 2,400 kilometers, in the middle of winter, to Utqiagvik (formerly Barrow) on Alaska's northern coast, providing food for a group of starving whalers stranded in the ice.[13]

In 1915, Congress passed legislation creating the United States Coast Guard.[14] In doing so, they combined the ships of Hamilton's Revenue Cutter Service with the lifeboat stations of the U.S. Life-Saving Service. While the Revenue Cutter Service had fought under the U.S. Navy in previous conflicts, the act creating the Coast Guard codified the agency as an independent military service and branch of the armed forces. However, unlike the other military services, the Coast Guard – like the Revenue Cutter Service before it – was in the Department of the Treasury (in 1967 the Service moved to the Department of Transportation and, in 2003, transferred to the new Department of Homeland Security). Although the modern Coast Guard was created in 1915, the organization counts its founding from August 4, 1790, the day President George Washington signed the law establishing the first revenue cutters.

With traditions of courage and action inherited from the Revenue Cutter Service and Life-Saving Service, the newly formed Coast Guard would go on to distinguish itself immediately. It protected convoys in both world wars, hunted German U-boats, performed harrowing rescues in dangerous sea conditions, manned D-Day landing craft in the invasion of Normandy, and put U.S. Marines ashore in battles through-out the Pacific.

Over time, the maritime functions of other organizations were consolidated in the Coast Guard, including the Lighthouse Service, the Bureau of Marine Inspection and Navigation, the U.S. Maritime Service, and the U.S. Army Corps of Engineers Bridge Program. The Coast Guard was also distinguished by the fact that it was the only U.S. military service with authority to conduct domestic law enforcement activities, the other military services being specifically prohibited from exercising law enforcement authority.

As times changed, the Coast Guard accrued additional authorities and responsibilities as policy makers sought to address new threats. For instance, in the wake of the 9/11 terrorist attacks, the Coast Guard became a member of the U.S. Intelligence Community. In 2002, the passage of the U.S. Maritime Transportation Security Act and Inter-national Maritime Organization's International Ship and Port Facility Security Code, expanded the Coast Guard's role in ensuring vessel and port facility security, and led to the establishment of the Service's

International Port Security Program. Likewise, the National Infrastructure Protection Plan designated the Coast Guard as the U.S. Federal Government agency charged with leading and supporting programs and activities to secure Maritime Transportation, outlining the Coast Guard's obligations to protect the Marine Transportation System from physical and cyber threats.

The result is a dynamic, modern Coast Guard with a wide scope of responsibilities and robust authorities. As an armed force, law enforcement agency, humanitarian organization, member of the U.S. Intelligence Community, and Federal regulator, the Coast Guard simultaneously defends America's sovereign interests, enforces U.S. and international law, acts as a first responder for natural and manmade disasters, and facilitates the safe flow of maritime commerce.

Comprised of 55,000 active duty, reserve, and civilian personnel, the United States Coast Guard carries out its duties with an array of cutters (any ship over 20 meters), airplanes, helicopters, and small boats. With eleven statutory missions ranging from search and rescue, defense operations, and fisheries enforcement to drug and migrant interdiction, marine safety, icebreaking, maintaining aids to navigation, and responding to maritime pollution, the United States Coast Guard plays a vital and well-established role in protecting America's maritime interests at home and abroad, and facilitating responsible maritime governance around the world.

The United States Coast Guard's expertise, capabilities, and range of duties makes it the perfect partner for organizations who are charged with safeguarding trade, protecting natural resources, saving lives, recovering from natural disasters, and stopping criminal activity. Moreover, it is the sea service that reflects the aspirations and requirements of most partners. Incredibly expensive aircraft carriers, submarines, and cruisers are indispensable for their war fighting missions but are not the ideal assets to police fisheries, conduct search and rescue, respond to oil spills, or interdict smugglers.

The Coast Guard matches up well as a trusted partner for those looking to enhance their maritime security, safety, and governance. This alignment is clear from its global footprint. It is a "global coast guard." It is not, however, *the* global coast guard. It is in the interest of each nation, especially those with maritime traditions, to build capabilities and partnerships that benefit our uniquely interconnected maritime security environment and can respond to the challenges and complexities of our changing world.

Global Challenges

As we have seen, the sea underpins our modern lives, and the health and security of the ocean is vital for our continued prosperity. However, threats – such as climate change, cyber-attacks, war, and political instability – have the potential to change both the physical maritime environment *and* security environment, with the impacts reaching every corner of our globalized society.

Changes to the ocean, caused by climate change, threaten global food security and place coastal communities at risk worldwide. For the nearly 10 percent of the global population that lives in low-lying coastal areas rising sea levels and stronger storm surges represent potentially devastating social and economic changes to their way of life.[15] Disaster response, long a U.S. Coast Guard mission, will likely demand even more attention in the coming decades. Simultaneously, receding sea ice in high latitudes has opened the potential for new shipping routes and resource extraction in the Arctic, as nations race to access the estimated 90 billion barrels of oil and 1.6 trillion cubic feet of natural gas believed to be in the region.[16] Ecotourism is also increasing in the Arctic, with the region seeing a 35 percent increase in passenger vessel traffic between 2013 and 2019.[17] The risk of all these activities is heighted by the remote, inhospitable Arctic environment. Where the U.S. Coast Guard once rescued ships caught in the ice, it now works to manage newly viable shipping routes and maintain cooperation on safety of life at sea in the face of emerging venues for geopolitical competition.

The way the world feeds itself is also changing. Fish consumption is skyrocketing, with the world consuming five times as much fish as it did 60 years ago, even as the oceans become warmer and more acidic, disrupting delicate ecosystems and threatening fish stocks.[18] The soaring demand for fish, coupled with increased scarcity creates a growing incentive for illegal fishers to take advantage of regulatory or enforcement gaps. As a result, Illegal, Unreported, and Unregulated (IUU) fishing rose dramatically in recent years, now accounting for as much as 20% of the global catch and perhaps as much as 40% in some developing countries.[19] This activity destroys ecosystems, undermines legitimate fisheries, and threatens the long-term food security of billions of people.

As changes to the ocean challenge our collective security, so too does the increasing digitalization of the maritime community. Approximately 90% of world trade travels by sea[20] – a system that relies on ships, ports, shipyards, stevedores, and freight forwarders whose assets are all subject to cyberthreats. Technologies like the internet and automation enable efficient, global shipping networks and are at the forefront of the sea's role in the modern economy. However, modern technologies dramatically expand the scope and scale of potential threats. Cyber-attacks against the shipping industry are on the rise,[21] including attacks against the four largest shipping companies.[22] Position-spoofing attacks, causing ships to believe they are in a different position, are also increasing.[23] As the world moves toward autonomous shipping, the need to mitigate cyber risks will be even greater.

Similarly, those who seek to exploit the high seas for illegal trade also continue to expand their networks. Despite advances in maritime domain awareness, transnational criminal organizations take advantage of the vastness of the oceans to smuggle drugs, weapons, and people. These activities drive instability. As criminal organizations grow stronger through illicit trade and exploitation of the seas, they erode legitimate institutions and freely elected governments ashore. At its worst, this results in rampant crime, murder, rape, and kidnapping, driving law-abiding citizens to flee their homes, and often their country, fueling mass migration. In the eight years between 2014 and 2021, 2.3 million people crossed the Mediterranean to Europe, 24,400 died attempting the journey, and tens of thousands suffered abuse along the way.[24] Whether by land or sea, thousands of similarly perilous migration journeys take place across the world each year, straining government response organizations and putting lives at risk.

The examples above are just a few ways that a changing climate and evolving threats are reshaping the maritime domain. The interconnectedness and complexity of our modern society means that the threats cannot be addressed by one nation alone, and cooperation among the world's coast guards and navies is essential.

Global Partnerships

From her position on the ship's bridge wing the Commanding Officer of the CGC *Munro* watched HMS *Spey* draw closer. Painted in grey camouflage and trailing a white wake, the 90-meter river class patrol vessel raced past the starboard side of the U.S. ship. Passing close by *Munro* in a coordinated set of maneuvers, *Spey* adjusted course until it was leading the small formation. The maneuver in the South China Sea was part of training exercises between the 127-meter *Munro* and her UK counterpart, a critical opportunity to work together to increase interoperability and understand each other's capabilities.

In addition to naval exercises like those between the *Munro* and *Spey*, the United States and United Kingdom have had some form of maritime law enforcement agreement in place for over 40 years. The most recent iteration supports joint law enforcement efforts across the United Kingdom Overseas Territories. This agreement, and others like it, enable the Coast Guard and its partners to fight drivers of instability around the world, including seizing thousands of metric tons of narcotics and countless smugglers. Over the last few years, the United States Coast Guard and Royal Navy also worked together more closely in extreme environments. Officers from HMS *Protector* sailed aboard the Coast Guard icebreakers CGC *Healy* and CGC *Polar Star,* and a Coast Guard officer sailed aboard HMS *Protector* during its first Arctic patrol. These exchanges promote training and coordination between the two countries, which are vital to our shared efforts to explore, secure, and protect the high latitudes – some of world's most remote and important regions.

While the 'Special Relationship' between the United States and United Kingdom continues to thrive, and the U.S. Coast Guard's partnership with the UK is unique in its closeness, it does not stand alone. Rather, it is part of a constellation of more than 60 multi and bilateral agreements that allow the Coast Guard to partner with nations in key regions on issues ranging from fisheries enforcement, counter-narcotics, and counter-proliferation, to marine environmental pollution, search and rescue, and anti-terrorism.

Multi and bilateral agreements, like the one which enabled the U.S. Coast Guard law enforcement team to embark the Seychelles Coast Guard's vessel *Zoroaster* for a fisheries patrol, formalize operational cooperation with our partners. They make combined efforts possible and efficient while also yielding the opportunity for the two sides to learn from each other.

The U.S. Coast Guard is committed to helping partners build maritime capacity. Each year, Coast Guard training teams fan out around the world to share expertise with partners. The one-to-two-week training courses delivered by mobile training teams are often bilateral in nature. Several recent iterations, however, point to an emerging paradigm emphasizing multinational and multilateral cooperation. For instance, a partner in South Asia recently hosted a course partnering U.S. Coast Guard trainers with students from the host nation and neighboring nations to bolster skills and build familiarity between personnel who may soon encounter each other on the water. In other instances, U.S. Coast Guard training teams are increasingly working with trainers from like-minded nations to deliver integrated training, yielding events where multinational groups of instructors prepare students from multiple countries to face collective challenges.

The training delivered by the U.S. Coast Guard is part of an ongoing effort, supported by the U.S. Departments of State and Defense, to build capacity on subjects ranging from boarding operations and engineering logistics to countering IUU fishing. In an average year, these training teams deploy more than 80 times to deliver training to students in partner nations. This effort puts Coast Guard personnel on the ground working with partners in their home countries and complements the training of more than 300 international students at Coast Guard facilities in the United States during programs ranging from a few weeks to four-year attendance at the Coast Guard Academy.

In addition to these efforts, U.S. Coast Guard personnel also deploy around the world as part of the Service's International Port Security Program. Under this program, Coast Guard port security assessors and International Port Security Liaison Officers collaborate with host governments to review anti-terrorism measures and provide expertise in managing secure port facilities according to the International Ship and Port Facility Security Code. In 2023, International Port Security Program teams visited over 90 countries across six continents to work with port officials in support of a safe and secure global Marine Transportation System. This number is expected to rise as the program returns to pre-pandemic levels.

The Coast Guard also continues to collaborate with like-minded nations in many international fora, including more than 50 years of engagement at the International Maritime Organization in London where the Coast Guard serves as the United States Head of Delegation to develop policy for safe, secure, and environmentally responsible global shipping.

Sentinels

The fishermen drifting away from Tarawa likely did not devote much thought to geopolitics or strategy, they cared about avoiding a grim fate. The United States Coast Guard answered their call for help and ensured that they returned home safely. While best known for search and rescue, the highly versatile Coast Guard is a unique instrument of national security. Using its distinct identity, it works with other nations, including those that might not otherwise engage with the U.S. military, to help bolster responsible maritime governance and the rule of law around the world. It offers the United States a tool to maintain its own security, while forging new partnerships that promote a better collective future.

Across the world, bad actors take advantage of seams in the global order and endanger the systems at the core of global peace and prosperity. IUU fishing, encroachment on one nation's waters by another, piracy, human trafficking, illicit trade, and threats to commercial shipping all run counter to the rules-based international order that underpins the global economy. Protecting the legitimate use of the seas, upholding the rules-based order, and conserving fragile ecosystems are critical yet daunting tasks that require international focus and cooperation on an unprecedented scale.

Single or unconnected organizations will not meet the maritime challenges of the 21st century. In an increasingly complex and interconnected world, relationships built on shared values, like those between the U.S. Coast Guard, Royal Navy, and UK maritime agencies, are more important than ever. The United States Coast Guard looks forward to continued collaboration between our two nations and extending the best parts of our shared maritime tradition to new partners.

1. Patrick Joubert, 'New SCG patrol boat commissioned', Seychelles Nation, 30 June 2021, <https://www.nation.sc/articles/9573/new-scg-patrol-boat-commissioned> [accessed 19 January 2024].

2. 'Seychelles-US joint coast guard operation catches illegal fishing vessel with dolphin meat', Seychelles Broadcasting Corporation, 31 March 2023, <https://jrfseychelles.com/sbc2/2023/03/31/seychelles-us-joint-coast-guard-operation-catches-illegal-fishing-vessel-with-dolphin-meat/> [accessed 19 January 2024].

3. 'Seychelles-US joint coast guard operation catches illegal fishing vessel with dolphin meat', Seychelles Broadcasting Corporation, 31 March 2023, <https://jrfseychelles.com/sbc2/2023/03/31/seychelles-us-joint-coast-guard-operation-catches-illegal-fishing-vessel-with-dolphin-meat/> [accessed 19 January 2024].

4. 'Marine Transportation System', U.S. Department of Transportation Maritime Administration, (2023) <https://www.maritime.dot.gov/outreach/maritime-tportation-system-mts/maritime-transportation-system-mts> [accessed 23 December 2023].

5. 'Marine Transportation System', U.S. Department of Transportation Maritime Administration, (2023) <https://www.maritime.dot.gov/outreach/maritime-tportation-system-mts/maritime-transportation-system-mts> [accessed 23 December 2023].

6. 'Announcement of U.S. Extended Continental Shelf Outer Limits', U.S. Department of State, 19 December 2023, <https://www.state.gov/announcement-of-u-s-extended-continental-shelf-outer-limits/> [accessed 25 January 2024].

7. 'Shipping and world trade: driving prosperity', International Chamber of Shipping, <https://www.ics-shipping.org/shipping-fact/shipping-and-world-trade-driving-prosperity/> [accessed 23 December 2023].

8. 'The State of World Fisheries and Aquaculture 2022: Towards Blue Transformation', Food and Agricultural Organization of the United Nations, (2022) <https://doi.org/10.4060/cc0461en> [accessed 23 December 2023] (p. 86).

9. 'The ocean – the world's greatest ally against climate change', United Nations: Climate Action, <https://www.un.org/en/climatechange/science/climate-issues/ocean> [accessed 30 December 2023].

10. Collin Wall and Pierre Morcos, 'Invisible and Vital: Undersea Cable and Transatlantic Security', Center for Strategic and International Studies, (2021) <https://www.csis.org/analysis/invisible-and-vital-undersea-cables-and-transatlantic-security>.

11. Alexander Hamilton, 'The Utility of the Union In Respect to Revenue,' Federalist Papers, No. 12 (November 1787) <https://avalon.law.yale.edu/18th_century/fed12.asp>.

12. 'The Public Statutes at Large of the United States of America from the Organization of the Government to March 3, 1845', ed. by Richard Peters (Boston: Charles C. Little and James Brown, 1845), vol. I <https://tile.loc.gov/storage-services/service/ll/llsl//llsl-c1/llsl-c1.pdf>.

13. 'Report of The Cruise of the U.S. Revenue Cutter Bear and the Overland Expedition for the Relief of the Whalers in the Arctic Ocean, from November 27, 1897 to September 13, 1898', Treasury Department Division of Revenue-Cutter Service (Washington, DC: Government Printing Office, 1899), Doc. No. 2101 <https://archive.org/details/reportofcruiseof03unit/page/n3/mode/2up>.

14. 'An Act to create the Coast Guard by combining therin the existing Life-Saving Service and Revenue Cutter Service', 63rd Congress, Sess. III, Ch. 20 (1915), Chap. 38, Sec 800 <https://media.defense.gov/2020/Mar/04/2002258693/-1/-1/0/1915-ACT_CREATING_USCG_38_STAT_800.PDF>.

15. 'The ocean – the world's greatest ally against climate change', United Nations: Climate Action, <https://www.un.org/en/climatechange/science/climate-issues/ocean> [accessed 30 December 2023].

16. Kenneth J. Bird et al., 'Circum-Arctic Resource Appraisal: Estimates of Undiscovered Oil and Gas North of the Arctic Circle,' Department of the Interior: United States Geological Survey, ed. by Peter H. Stauffer, (2008) <https://pubs.usgs.gov/fs/2008/3049/fs2008-3049.pdf>.

17. 'As Arctic Marine Tourism Increases, How Can We Ensure It's Sustainable', Arctic Council, 10 May 2021 <https://arctic-council.org/news/as-arctic-marine-tourism-increases-how-can-we-ensure-its-sustainable/> [accessed 25 January 2024].

18. 'The State of World Fisheries and Aquaculture 2022: Towards Blue Transformation', Food and Agricultural Organization of the United Nations, (2022) <https://doi.org/10.4060/cc0461en> [accessed 23 December 2023] (p. 81).

19. Cristiano Minichiello. "Illegal, unreported, and unregulated fishing is one of the biggest threats to our oceans." Food and Agricultural Organization of the United Nations. 6 April 2021. <https://www.fao.org/fao-stories/article/en/c/1403336/>.

20. 'Shipping and world trade: world seaborne trade', International Chamber of Shipping, <https://www.ics-shipping.org/shipping-fact/shipping-and-world-trade-world-seaborne-trade/> [accessed 30 December 2023].

21. Linton Nightingale, 'Shipping is falling short in cyber preparedness', Lloyd's List, 01 March 2022 <https://lloydslist.com/LL1139994/Shipping-is-falling-short-in-cyber-preparedness> [accessed 19 January 2024].

22. 'Safety and Shipping Review 2023', Allianz Global Corporate & Specialty, (2023), <https://commercial.allianz.com/content/dam/onemarketing/commercial/commercial/reports/AGCS-Safety-Shipping-Review-2023.pdf> [accessed 19 January 2024] (p. 34).

23. 'Safety and Shipping Review 2023', Allianz Global Corporate & Specialty, (2023), <https://commercial.allianz.com/content/dam/onemarketing/commercial/commercial/reports/AGCS-Safety-Shipping-Review-2023.pdf> [accessed 19 January 2024] (p. 34).

24. 'No End in Sight', UN High Commissioner for Refugees – UN Refugee Agency, <https://storymaps.arcgis.com/stories/07502a24ce0646bb9703ce96630b15fa> [accessed 19 January 2024].

Maritime Prefectures – The Future of UK Coastal Security?

Cdr Alex Westley RN

The UK's maritime security is at a crossroads, challenged by emerging threats and the necessity for strategic reform. Drawing insights from the French Maritime Prefecture system, this chapter outlines a vision for the UK to transition towards a centralised maritime security model that promises enhanced cohesion, strategic clarity, and operational agility.

Introduction

Maritime security – integral to the United Kingdom's national safety and economic prosperity – faces contemporary challenges that test its historical prowess at sea. The UK's expansive coastlines are both commercial arteries and potential vulnerabilities where smuggling, terrorism, environmental degradation, and unchecked migration threaten sovereignty and security. This chapter critically examines the potential for adopting a Maritime Prefecture system akin to the French model, celebrated for its centralised command and comprehensive oversight of maritime affairs.

France has had a different approach to the sea in comparison to the UK, viewing it as an extension of its territory and treating it in a similar way as if it were land.[1] This resulted in maritime prefects with similar roles and responsibilities as the Prefectures on land, acting as the state's representative at sea, the government representative and the direct representative of the Prime Minister and each of the ministers.[2]

This chapter will discuss four main areas:

- Current UK Maritime Security Model: The current UK framework, identifying inefficiencies in coordination and response due to the fragmented structure of maritime governance. There will also be an examination of five case studies, including the 'Scallop Wars' and Operation ISOTROPE, to demonstrate the practical challenges and benefits of a more centralised approach.
- French Maritime Prefecture System: An overview of the centralised French system, noting its advantages in unified

command and comprehensive oversight of maritime affairs.

- Lessons identified from the French Model: Contrast the UK and French models and synthesise a comparative analysis to highlight the potential benefits a centralised system could offer the UK.
- Way forward for UK maritime security: Proposed options for change within the UK system to better prepare for future challenges.

The objective is to contribute to the maritime security reform dialogue, illuminating the UK's current challenges, and the French system's potential as a viable model. By doing so, this chapter seeks to inspire policy innovation and enhance the UK's maritime defence architecture. It will describe a potential centralised alternative to the current UK maritime security system; the creation of a Ministry for Maritime Affairs, how this ministry will be central to the assurance of maritime security through Maritime Prefects and, the changes necessary to the Royal Navy to support this new structure with the creation of Coastal Command. Whilst a significant change to the UK's maritime security, it has the potential to streamline operations, improve inter-agency cooperation, and enhance the ability to respond to the evolving maritime security landscape.

Current UK Maritime Security Model

The current fabric of the UK's maritime security is a complex web spun from the disparate efforts of numerous agencies to protect one of the nation's most vital assets – its 11,000-mile-long coastline. Within this intricate structure, the Maritime and Coastguard Agency (MCA), the Border Force, and the Royal Navy are key threads, each holding distinct and crucial responsibilities, from search and rescue missions to pollution control and border security. Despite the wealth of expertise these entities offer, their harmonisation is often less than seamless, leading to operational inefficiencies and communication gaps. Such fragmentation has been starkly revealed in incidents involving unchecked migrant arrivals or the clandestine transit of contraband across the North Sea.

In an endeavour to weave these strands more tightly, the UK government established the Joint Maritime Security Centre (JMSC) in 2019,[3] marking a significant stride towards an integrated 'Whole System Response.' The creation of the JMSC acknowledges the critical need for shared situational awareness and a collective strategic approach against the multifaceted threats to the maritime domain. It reflects an emerging

Fig 1: Organisations involved in UK Maritime Security.[4]

recognition that more than the sum of individual agency efforts is needed to meet maritime security's complex demands, and a more unified command structure is required.

Nevertheless, despite the JMSC's inception and strategic vision, the reality of UK maritime security reflects a system still in transition, characterised by an extensive, albeit fragmented, network of stakeholders. The JMSC's promise of synergy faces the enduring challenge of unifying these disparate forces under a comprehensive and cohesive framework that can dynamically counter maritime threats. This remains a pivotal issue as the UK navigates the turbulent waters of modern maritime security, balancing the need to honour its storied nautical legacy with the imperative to adapt to contemporary challenges.

JMSC represents the UK's recognition of the need for greater cohesion and a 'Whole System Response' to maritime threats, striving to emulate aspects of the centralised command structure seen in the French system. To best understand the issues of the current UK systems, it is worthwhile to critically examine some recent situations that demonstrate that implementing a more coherent 'whole system response' will best serve UK maritime security in the future.

The chosen case studies shed light on the multifaceted nature of maritime operations and the corresponding security challenges. Each case, whether addressing issues of fishing rights, migration crises, criminal activities, the protection of seabed infrastructure, or the integration of renewable energy sources, underscores the limitations of the UK's current decentralised maritime security system. These narratives advocate for a significant paradigm shift towards greater centralisation and adopting a unified command structure that can effectively address the complex issues that converge at the intersection of national security and maritime governance.

It is possible to discern the tangible benefits of a centralised approach by examining these case studies through a lens that considers the French and UK systems. This analysis aims to envision a future in which the UK's maritime security not only withstands the dynamic challenges presented by its territorial waters but also demonstrates resilience and adaptability in its responses. The case studies highlight the potential for streamlined decision-making, enhanced inter-agency cooperation, and a more strategic allocation of resources – key advantages that could stem from introducing a Maritime Prefecture-style system within the UK. The collective insights from these studies will be used to formulate strategic recommendations for UK maritime security reform, emphasising the need for a more integrated and forward-looking approach to maritime governance.

Case study 1: the scallop wars – conflict over fishing rights (a case for structural change in maritime security)

The English Channel, a historically fertile ground for scallops, has long been a source of contention. The so-called 'Scallop Wars' between British and French fishermen epitomise the complexities of maritime security where national interests, livelihoods, and international laws intersect. This case study analyses the contentious confrontations over scallop fishing rights in the English Channel, highlighting the intricacies of enforcing maritime regulations, managing resources sustainably, and resolving international disputes. The discord stems from diverging national regulations: French laws restrict scallop dredging to conserve stocks, whereas UK policy permits year-round fishing. This discrepancy set the stage for repeated confrontations as UK fishermen venture into waters near France during the French ban period.[5] The peak of tensions surfaced in 2018 when altercations at sea escalated, resulting in physical confrontations between vessels from both nations. The incidents were symptomatic of broader issues: the absence of a shared strategy for managing common fishing grounds and the economic pressures faced by fishermen in an increasingly competitive industry.[6]

The dispute brought to the fore the need for coherent policies aligned with international maritime law, particularly UNCLOS, which governs marine resource rights. It also highlighted the role of maritime security forces in de-escalating conflicts and enforcing regulations. The UK's Marine Management Organisation, the Royal Navy, and French maritime authorities were essential in managing the fallout. Diplomatic efforts resulted in a temporary detente, with a mutually agreed-upon restriction of larger British scallop dredgers in the disputed waters. However, this resolution was temporary and reactive, rather than proactive and sustainable.

What the 'Scallop Wars' underscore, are the importance of collaborative governance of shared marine resources, clear communication between stakeholders, and the enforcement role of maritime security in preventing conflicts. Nevertheless, it highlights the limitations of the current structure in being able to proactively prevent such conflicts and managing resources sustainably. This case suggests that a centralised maritime security strategy, such as the proposed UK Ministry for Maritime Affairs and Coastal Command, could address similar issues more effectively. By integrating environmental stewardship with security operations, the UK could proactively engage in bi-national or multi-national agreements to prevent such conflicts, safeguarding economic interests and international relations. The 'Scallop Wars' case illustrates a critical gap in the UK's maritime security apparatus – the need for a centralised body that can swiftly arbitrate and manage resource-related disputes. It points to the potential efficacy of a Ministry for Maritime Affairs, which could centralise command and control, enhance negotiation capacities, and ensure sustainable resource management in alignment with international law. It could provide a proactive and sustainable solutions to managing shared marine resources, thereby preventing future conflicts like the 'Scallop War'. Such a department could serve as a strategic and diplomatic tool, enabling the UK to effectively navigate and resolve similar disputes in its waters.

Case study 2: operation ISOTROPE – military coordination in maritime migration crisis

The sharp increase in attempts to cross the English Channel has prompted a robust response from the UK's maritime security apparatus, culminating in Operation ISOTROPE (March 2022 – January 2023). This military-led initiative aimed to strengthen the UK's maritime security posture and inter-agency collaboration against a "particularly challenging period for attempted crossings."[7] What Operation ISOTROPE underlines is the challenges posed by the absence of a unified maritime security structure in the UK, risking the reputation and efficacy of the Royal Navy. This case study scrutinises the operation's operational challenges and the imperative for a centralised maritime security framework.

Operation ISOTROPE served as a litmus test for the UK's maritime Command and Control (C2) structures. It revealed an apparent discrepancy between the strategic objectives of different government departments and the actual execution of the operation, with the Ministry of Defence and the Home Office holding divergent views on the operation's goals. The operation highlighted the friction between national security imperatives and international legal obligations, particularly regarding the safety of life at sea. Criticism emerged due to the need for explicit operational endpoints and realistic indicators of success, reflecting the need for a unified command to articulate and achieve strategic objectives.[8] The Royal Navy, Border Force, and other civil authorities played a pivotal role in Operation ISOTROPE. However, the operation's announcement was marked by premature policy disclosures and a lack of detailed planning, leading to concerns about the Navy's budget, asset allocation, and potential reputational risks.[9] It should be noted that, anecdotally, the French perspective during Operation ISOTROPE was that coordination was more straightforward as the military-to-military framework was more compatible. Operation ISOTROPE illustrated that without a centralised command, there is a significant risk of mismanagement and reputational damage to the Royal Navy. This stems from an ad-hoc approach to maritime crises and the absence of a single, clear strategic direction.

The operation's execution, while displaying the military's capability, also revealed profound shortcomings in the UK's current maritime security model. The inconsistencies and lack of clarity in operational objectives signify the necessity for a centralised maritime security system that could safeguard the Royal Navy's reputation by providing clear command, cohesive strategies, and well-defined operational roles. Operation ISOTROPE highlighted that enhanced cooperation is crucial for managing complex humanitarian and security situations. The UK should define clear operational objectives and realistic success indicators to ensure all participating agencies have a shared understanding of the mission's goals and parameters. Coordination of this through a national or regional operations centre would further ensure that objectives were met. Balancing security and humanitarian responsibilities is essential, especially concerning the safety of life at sea. Specialised training and readiness programs are necessary for personnel involved in maritime migration issues. International cooperation, especially with neighbouring countries, is crucial for managing maritime migration effectively and humanely. Clear public policy guidelines and effective communication strategies are also necessary to manage expectations and perceptions related to maritime migration crises. By addressing these implications, the UK can strengthen its maritime security model and ensure a more cohesive, effective, and humane approach to future maritime migration crises.

Case study 3: drug trafficking and UK maritime security

The sea has been identified as a critical entry route for narcotics destined for the UK market.[10] Drug trafficking through maritime routes into the UK has significant national security and law enforcement implications. Traffickers exploit commercial shipping routes and private vessels to smuggle contraband, presenting a persistent challenge to maritime security. This case study delves into the operational challenges UK agencies face in curbing drug trafficking activities, the strategies implemented, and the inter-agency collaboration required to address this transnational threat.[11] A notable incident occurred in 2019 when a sub-stantial narcotics shipment was intercepted off the coast of Cornwall: 1.4 tonnes of cocaine was seized onboard a private yacht.[12] The operation highlighted the value of intelligence-sharing and joint operations between the UK's National Crime Agency (NCA), Border Force, and other national and international partners. The collaborative effort resulted in the seizure of drugs worth £112M and the arrest of five individuals involved in the trafficking network.

Drug trafficking via maritime routes poses a threat to public health, safety, and security. It calls for robust maritime law enforcement measures and underscores the necessity of international cooperation under the 1988 United Nations Convention against Illicit Traffic in Narcotic Drugs and Psychotropic Substances. The NCA's lead role in intelligence-gathering and coordination with partners was instrumental in the operation's success. The incident prompted a review of maritime surveillance tactics and the implementation of advanced technologies for detection and interdiction. The case highlights the need for a comprehensive maritime security strategy that includes enhanced surveillance, dedicated resources, and international partnerships to combat drug trafficking. In France, the use of semaphore stations ensures that the majority of the French coast is under some form of surveillance and under the direct control of the appropriate Prefecture. This allows for coordinated operations to be conducted more efficiently and illustrates the importance of a centralised information hub, which could facilitate the timely exchange of intelligence across agencies and borders.

This case study reinforces the argument for a more cohesive UK maritime security strategy, emphasising the importance of an integrated system for information sharing and coordinated action. The proposed Ministry for Maritime Affairs could play a crucial role in unifying efforts to combat maritime drug trafficking, leveraging the collective capabilities of UK security agencies and international partners to protect national interests and promote regional stability. The establishment of an operations centre capable of efficiently coordinating operations against drug trafficking would significantly improve the effectiveness of counter-narcotic operations. Investing in advanced surveillance technologies can substantially boost the UK's capabilities in detecting and intercepting drug shipments. Inter-agency cooperation between agencies like the NCA, Border Force, and international partners is crucial for a more unified approach. Whilst JMSC is currently given the task of co-operation, its lack of ownership from a single ministry makes it reliant on joint funding and political will, which can be inconsistent or short term. A comprehensive maritime security strategy encompassing enhanced surveillance, dedicated resources, and international partnerships is needed to combat maritime drug trafficking effectively. Strengthening legal and policy frameworks, training personnel involved in anti-narcotics operations at sea, and ensuring international collaboration and legal compliance are also essential for the UK's effectiveness.

Case study 4: protecting the UK's seabed infrastructure

Undersea cables and pipelines are responsible for the transfer of a significant amount of global internet traffic and energy supply, and as such must be protected from accidental damage, natural hazards, and intentional hostile acts. The UK's seabed infrastructure is essential for communication and energy supply yet remains susceptible to various threats. This case study evaluates the challenges of safeguarding such infrastructure, concentrating on incidents of damage and subsequent security measures. It is prompted by an incident, in October 2022, involving the accidental severing of a vital undersea cable serving the Shetland Islands by a fishing trawler, causing substantial data transmission disruptions.[13] The event revealed the coordination needed between the Maritime and Coastguard Agency (MCA), telecommunications companies, and the Department for Digital, Culture, Media & Sport (DCMS) to restore services and evaluate the resilience of seabed infrastructure.[14]

The incident questioned the sufficiency of protective measures and emphasised the necessity for greater maritime domain awareness. It also highlighted the need for compliance with the United Nations Convention on the Law of the Sea (UNCLOS), which outlines the legal framework for submarine cable protection. The MCA's surveillance role and the DCMS's oversight of critical infrastructure proved crucial in addressing the incident's aftermath. These spurred initiatives to refine maritime activity regulations, especially regarding fishing activities near established cable routes.

The instance in question prompted a re-evaluation of the UK's security strategies, advocating for thorough mapping of seabed assets, real-time monitoring systems, and explicit guidelines for maritime operators. In total, this case emphasises the necessity for a strategic approach to protect the UK's seabed infrastructure, integrating security with environmental protection and commercial considerations. The proposed establishment of a Ministry for Maritime Affairs and a National Coordination Centre could significantly enhance the UK's protective capabilities, ensuring both economic stability and national security. Indeed, the vulnerabilities exposed by this case point to the need for a centralised maritime security strategy. In particular, whilst Operation ISOTROPE demonstrated the value of military command and control in coordinating a multifaceted response, the response to the cable's severing suggests that such a framework could be essential for safeguarding critical seabed infrastructure. Integrating military command and control capabilities could therefore ensure more effective protection and crisis management, strengthening the UK's overall maritime security posture.

Case study 5: exercise SANCHO and the implications for offshore renewable energy security [15]

With offshore renewables, especially wind energy, burgeoning in the UK, the necessity for comprehensive emergency response strategies has intensified. The marked absence of large-scale exercises since GUARDEX 2012 indicated a potential vulnerability in emergency preparedness – a gap Exercise SANCHO aimed to address. Exercise SANCHO represents a benchmark in UK maritime security's approach to offshore renewable energy frameworks, highlighting the crucial interplay between emergency preparedness and operational readiness. This case study delves into the 2022 Triennial Renewables Exercise (TRIREX) UK exercise, focusing on its objectives, execution, and the lessons learned for enhancing offshore emergency arrangements.

Conceived by the MCA and the Offshore Renewable Energy Emergency Forum (OREEF), Exercise SANCHO aimed to rigorously test emergency arrangements and response procedures within the offshore renewable sector. Spanning over a year of planning, the exercise's design encompassed multifaceted, live-action scenarios involving various emergency services and support organisations. In the face of pandemic-related uncertainties, Exercise SANCHO facilitated an extensive collaborative effort, integrating live resources to simulate a significant offshore renewables emergency. The exercise's complex nature provided a realistic platform for testing industry and emergency services' response capabilities, fostering a hands-on approach to crisis management. The success of Exercise SANCHO hoped to bolster emergency arrangement frameworks within the UK and internationally. By uniting disparate teams under a common objective, the exercise highlighted the importance of synchronised multi-agency exercises in improving industry-wide emergency responses.

Exercise SANCHO serves as a vital case study for future maritime security considerations, emphasising the need for regular, comprehensive training exercises. Its execution underscores the potential for a centralised maritime security strategy in the UK that could ensure a more cohesive and effective response to emergencies in the offshore renewable energy sector. The conclusions from Exercise SANCHO advocate for the establishment of a Ministry for Maritime Affairs within the UK, echoing TRIREX UK's intent for continuous improvement in emergency preparedness.[16] Such a department could centralise command and control, providing a strategic framework for operational excellence amid emergent maritime challenges related to renewable energy infra-structure.

Case study conclusions

These case studies provide a substantive insight into the current challenges and intricacies of the UK's maritime security landscape. From the resource management disputes highlighted by the 'Scallop Wars' to the complex humanitarian and legal issues posed by irregular migration and onto the strategic and operational demands of protecting the nation's burgeoning offshore renewable energy infrastructure, as underscored by Exercise SANCHO, each case study presents a scenario that tests the UK's maritime security response. Collectively, they underscore the limitations of the existing decentralised framework and illuminate the potential benefits of a more centralised, coordinated approach. Furthermore, they reveal a pattern where enhanced cross-agency cooperation, underpinned by clear command and control as evidenced during TRIREX UK, could lead to more effective outcomes.

As the challenges the UK Maritime Security model faces have been examined using these case studies, it appears clear that a more centralised and coordinated means of assuring the security of the UK's waters is required. The French system is centralised and coordinates multiple agencies to achieve its security ambitions. It is, therefore, a system worthy of study. Considering the lessons identified through these case studies, particularly the collaborative success of Exercise SANCHO, there is a compelling argument for the UK to contemplate adopting a centralised structure similar to the French. Such a model would foster continuous improvement in emergency preparedness, streamline maritime oper-ations, and ensure that the UK remains a frontrunner in domestic and international maritime security. The case studies collectively act as a clarion call for reform, guiding the way towards a more unified and robust maritime security framework for the UK.

The French Maritime Prefecture System

France's Maritime Prefecture system provides a striking counterpoint to the UK's maritime security strategy, showcasing the advantages of a centralised model steeped in a strong tradition of maritime governance. The French prefecture system is based around three maritime zones:

- Channel and North Sea – Based in Cherbourg
- Atlantic – Based in Brest
- Mediterranean – Based in Toulon

Each prefecture is headed by a Maritime Prefect (a 2-star French Admiral) who acts as the state's representative at sea. Tasked with a broad spectrum of responsibilities, the Maritime Prefect oversees the enforcement of national and international maritime law, the coordination of search and rescue missions, environmental protection efforts, and the economic exploitation of maritime resources. This expansive role is facilitated by the centralisation of maritime command, which allows for a unified response to maritime incidents and a strategic approach to steward maritime interests.[17]

Under the Maritime Prefect, France's approach consolidates the efforts of the *Marine Nationale* (French Navy), *Gendarmerie Maritime*, *Douanes* (Customs), and other pertinent agencies. These bodies collaborate under a unified strategy to address contemporary maritime challenges ranging from illegal fishing and pollution to safeguarding maritime borders and critical infrastructure. The French model's integrated framework is a product of its historical context and contemporary strategic vision. It allows for agile and coordinated responses to maritime incidents. It reflects a governance system where military and civil authorities work together, guided by comprehensive national strategies such as the National Strategy for Security of Maritime Areas (*Stratégie Nationale de Sûreté des Espaces Maritimes*).

Maritime prefecture system

Created in 1800 by the order of Napoleon Bonaparte, the French Maritime Prefecture system epitomises a centralised paradigm of maritime governance that has matured and adapted to the shifting tides of the maritime security landscape. With historical roots deeply anchored in France's maritime heritage, the system is a testament to the nation's proactive stance on maritime sovereignty and the comprehensive management of its vast maritime domain. The operational efficiency of the

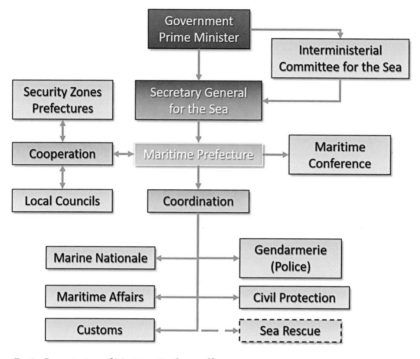

Fig 2: Organisation of Maritime Prefecture.[19]

French system is further reinforced by integrating various state agencies within the maritime security framework. The *Marine Nationale* plays a significant role in executing the Prefecture's directives and providing the military muscle necessary for enforcement actions at sea. However, the *Marine Nationale's* responsibilities extend beyond traditional naval duties, encompassing a wide range of operations reflecting maritime security's multifunctional nature such as, protection of critical national infrastructure, fisheries management, environmental safeguarding, and countering illegal activities at sea.[18]

This comprehensive approach indicates a system adaptable and responsive to contemporary challenges. The French model's emphasis on a centralised command structure and the integration of military and civilian capabilities contrasts the more segmented approach of the UK's maritime security strategy. Delving further into the French Maritime Prefecture system reveals its success in creating a harmonised maritime security environment. The system's strength lies in its integrated command structure, operational adaptability, and incorporation of a wide array of capabilities to address and manage maritime risks effectively.

This centralised approach contrasts starkly with the UK's structure which, despite benefiting from the specialised knowledge of various agencies, often experiences delays in inter-agency communication and decision-making processes. Such delays were notably apparent during the 2019 migrant crossings in the English Channel, where a more compartmentalised command structure led to slower responses to critical incidents.

The *Marine Nationale*, as part of the Maritime Prefecture, is crucial but not the only actor; it operates alongside the *Gendarmerie Maritime*, which provides law enforcement and public order at sea, and the *Douanes*, which handles fiscal and border enforcement duties. This multidimensional approach allows for a versatile and comprehensive response to maritime challenges, from environmental protection to the suppression of maritime criminal activities.[20]

The French system also demonstrates an acute awareness of the evolving nature of maritime security, with the Maritime Prefecture taking a proactive role in adapting to new threats such as cyber-attacks on port infrastructure, the increase in maritime piracy, and the illicit trafficking of goods and people. The integration of civil and military efforts under a unified command not only streamlines operations but also ensures that responses are swift, coordinated, and effective. Acting as both protector and promoter of marine resources, the Prefect navigates the complex interplay of economic, environmental, and security interests. This role is critical in fostering a safe, secure, and prosperous maritime domain that aligns with France's strategic maritime objectives. The effectiveness of the Prefect in these multi-farious roles is a testament to the centralised approach of the French system, which consolidates command and facilitates a unified execution of state policies at sea.[21]

The analysis herein underscores the advantages of a centralised command in the French maritime security system and poses the question of whether similar benefits could be realised in the UK. By exploring the functions and impact of the Maritime Prefect, this section lays the groundwork for considering how a unified command could enhance the UK's maritime security strategy, leading to a more agile and coherent response to maritime challenges.

Lessons Identified From The French Model

Before comparing the maritime security models between the UK and France, it is essential to recognise the distinct paths each has taken. The

UK's model, marked by a diverse coalition of agencies with specific maritime roles, faces challenges in coordination and rapid response due to its decentralised nature. On the other hand, the French Maritime Prefecture system operates under a centralised command that unifies various functions and agencies under the strategic direction of the Maritime Prefect. This centralised approach enables a cohesive strategy for managing the maritime environment, harmonising efforts in areas such as law enforcement, search and rescue, and environmental protection. By contrast, the UK's model has historically resulted in segmented operations, with agencies such as the National Crime Agency, Border Force, and the Royal Navy each addressing maritime security from their specialised perspectives, which can lead to inefficiencies and delays in action.

Strategic coordination: state's action at sea

The State's Action at Sea (Action de l'État en Mer), as directed by comprehensive strategies like the SNSEM, showcases the dynamic and responsive nature of the French maritime governance system. This approach demonstrates the strategic coordination essential in addressing the broad array of contemporary maritime challenges. The French model combines military capacity with civilian oversight, providing a holistic response to diverse issues, from illegal fishing and marine pollution to emergent threats impacting maritime traffic and critical infrastructure. This alignment of military and civilian maritime capabilities under a singular strategic vision allows for agility and coherence in decision-making and operational execution that is emblematic of France's maritime security policy.[22]

Broad agency collaboration in french maritime security

A broad constellation of state agencies sustains the French Maritime Prefecture's robust framework, each playing a pivotal role within the maritime domain. The *Marine Nationale* is a crucial component, but its role is complemented by the *Gendarmerie Maritime, Douanes,* and police, all unified under the Prefecture's direction. This multi-agency collaboration enhances France's maritime governance, ensuring a comprehensive approach to law enforcement, fiscal regulation, border control, and public order in coastal and port areas.

The effectiveness of the French model is rooted in this inter-agency cooperation, which allows for a more dynamic and nuanced response to maritime issues. The upcoming sections will contrast this approach with the UK's current maritime security framework, evaluating how the French model's emphasis on broad agency collaboration and centralised command might inform potential reforms within the UK maritime security strategy.

Civilian oversight and the french maritime prefecture

The French Maritime Prefecture's operational framework stands out for its civilian-led governance, operating under the auspices of the Prime Minister's office. This delineation from the military chain of command, which falls under the President and the Chief of the Defence Staff (CEMA), is a deliberate design that underscores the multifaceted nature of maritime governance. Such a structure ensures that the Maritime Prefecture's activities are not confined to military objectives but encompass a broader spectrum of national interests, including economic, legal, environmental, and public safety concerns. This civilian oversight is crucial for maintaining a balanced approach to maritime governance that integrates the full breadth of state capabilities while navigating the delicate balance between national security and civil liberties. It also facilitates greater inter-ministerial cooperation, enabling the Maritime Prefecture to draw upon diverse resources and expertise across the government spectrum.

Comparative analysis

Having reviewed the French Maritime Prefecture system, it becomes clear that the UK's maritime security framework reveals distinct structural and operational differences when compared to this centralised model. With the Maritime Prefectures, the French system's cohesive approach contrasts sharply with the UK's more segmented maritime governance, where responsibilities are scattered across various agencies. This comparative analysis highlights the need for the UK to adopt valuable lessons from the French experience, especially in addressing emerging maritime security challenges with a centralised strategy.

The adaptability of the French model is particularly notable in its proactive response to contemporary challenges, such as cyber threats, technological advancements in autonomous maritime systems, and the broader implications of climate change.[23] The French approach, character-ised by its agility and forward-thinking, contrasts with the traditionally reactive nature of the UK's maritime security efforts. However, recent strategic shifts in the UK indicate a growing recognition of the need for a more integrated and anticipatory strategy that encompasses the full spectrum of maritime security threats.[24]

The insights derived from the case studies advocate for the UK's adoption of a centralised model, potentially involving a specialised Ministry for Maritime Affairs and a specialised Coastal Command within the Royal Navy representing the Ministry of Defence, which could significantly enhance its maritime security capabilities. This approach would align with the French model's effectiveness in managing complex operations and adapting to a rapidly evolving maritime land-scape. The UK needs to consider how the principles of proactive evolution and centralised command, as demonstrated by the French Maritime Prefecture, could be integrated into its maritime security framework. This integration should respect the UK's unique maritime traditions and legal context, especially in the post-Brexit era. The goal is to create a tailored command system that preserves the strengths of existing British agencies while drawing on the centralised efficiency of the French model.

Looking to the future, the UK must strategically balance adopting a centralised command with maintaining its sovereign maritime traditions and operational practices. This balance will be crucial in shaping a robust and agile maritime security strategy for the UK to address current and future challenges in the maritime domain. The way ahead for UK maritime security lies in learning from the French experience, adapting it to the UK's unique context, and setting a course for a more integrated, responsive, and comprehensive maritime governance model.

Way Ahead For UK Maritime Security

A synthesis of the UK and French maritime security models suggests a progressive way forward for the UK – a path honouring its rich naval tradition while adapting to the demands of contemporary maritime security. Such a fusion would aim to create a more resilient and responsive security posture well-equipped to navigate the dynamic challenges of the modern era. The UK's adaptation could incorporate the centralised efficiency of the French Maritime Prefecture system, balancing it against the need to preserve the autonomy and specialised knowledge of British agencies. This could involve establishing a central coordinating body akin to the Joint Maritime Security Centre but with expanded authority and capabilities to ensure a unified command structure. In this context, the UK would benefit from a system that promotes seamless inter-agency collaboration, enhanced information sharing, and strategic coordination of national maritime security efforts.

By doing so, the UK could better leverage its diverse maritime capabilities to address complex issues such as territorial disputes, illegal fishing, human trafficking, and the protection of maritime trade routes.

Understanding the practical aspects of such a transition will be necessary, including the potential structures, resources, and legislative changes required to operationalise a more centralised command system within the UK's maritime security framework. It will also be necessary to consider the cultural shifts and stakeholder engagement required to implement this successfully and sustain these reforms.

Navigating legal and operational reforms

As the UK contemplates the adoption of a more centralised maritime security framework, navigating the requisite legal and operational reforms is essential. Drawing from the French model's adaptability, the UK must consider recalibrating its maritime governance to imbue it with greater coherence and efficiency. This recalibration involves scrutinising existing legislation that governs maritime operations and identifying areas where enhanced central authority could streamline responses to maritime threats and challenges.

Legal reforms include consolidating powers currently dispersed among various agencies and reducing bureaucratic layers that can slow decision-making processes. Operational reforms necessitate a cultural shift within organisations, fostering a climate that values integrated action and shared objectives over siloed operations. The UK's strategic shift towards a more centralised model would also have to consider the interplay of international maritime law, especially in the post-Brexit context, ensuring compliance with treaties like UNCLOS while asserting its national interests.

Implementing a centralised maritime security framework in the UK

The consideration of a centralised maritime security framework within the UK reflects a pivotal recognition of the need for strategic and operational enhancement. Drawing inspiration from the French Maritime Prefecture system, the UK faces the intricate task of tailoring a centralised approach that aligns with its unique maritime context and legal parameters. Implementing such a framework necessitates a comprehensive review of existing structures and a concerted effort to foster integration where fragmentation currently prevails. A potential UK adaptation is the evolution of a central coordinating body and an expansion of the remit and capabilities of the Joint Maritime Security Centre to serve as the nucleus of a more unified command system. This centralised body would streamline decision-making and harmonise the diverse array of maritime operations, from safety and enforcement to environmental stewardship. It would require a concerted push towards legislative reform, resource reallocation, and a cultural shift within and across the agencies involved.

Implications for UK maritime security reform

The proposal to transition UK maritime security to a model inspired by the French Maritime Prefecture carries profound implications for national security operations and policy. This paradigm shift aims to unify the UK's maritime security efforts, which are currently managed by disparate agencies, into a more centralised and coherent system. The reformed structure would establish a Ministry for Maritime Affairs to orchestrate the nation's maritime security through strategically (and geographically) defined Maritime Security Zones: North Sea, Channel, Irish Sea, Scotland.

- *Enhanced Operational Efficiency*: By centralising intelligence and operational control, the UK could streamline decision-making processes, ensuring quicker and more effective responses to maritime threats.
- *Improved Resource Allocation*: A central system would optimise resource utilisation, potentially leading to cost savings and better-equipped agencies.
- *Increased Interoperability*: Centralised management would enhance interoperability among different maritime agencies, improving joint operations and crisis management.
- *Strategic Alignment*: Defining clear roles and responsibilities within Maritime Security Zones ensures that all regional activities align with national security objectives.
- *International Law and Protocol Compliance*: The centralised model would facilitate adherence to international maritime laws and protocols, improving the UK's standing in the global maritime community.

The transition to this new model would require structural changes and a cultural shift within agencies towards embracing a unified operational ethos. It would necessitate significant investment in infrastructure, personnel training, and policy development, as well as a solid commitment to stakeholder engagement and continuous improvement.

Recommendations for UK Maritime Security Reform

A series of actionable recommendations are proposed to actualise the envisioned maritime security reform in the UK. These recommendations serve as a roadmap to guide the transition towards a more centralised, cohesive maritime security structure, reflective of the French Maritime Prefecture model but adapted to the UK's unique context.

- *Legislative Actions*: Draft and enact legislation to establish the Ministry for Maritime Affairs, solidifying its mandate and jurisdiction. Define the Maritime Security Zones' roles, responsibilities, and authority, ensuring they are empowered to act effectively within the UK's legal framework.
- *Infrastructure and Technology*: Construct a state-of-the art National Coordination Centre equipped with the latest communication and surveillance technology to ensure a unified operational picture across all zones.
- *Personnel Training and Development*: Develop comprehensive training programs for personnel within the Maritime Security Zones and the National Coordination Centre, focusing on areas critical to maritime security, such as threat analysis, inter-agency operations, and crisis management.
- *Policy and Protocol Development*: Formulate and implement robust policies that delineate operational conduct within the Maritime Security Zones, ensuring these policies adapt to national and international maritime challenges.
- *Engagement with Regional and International Stakeholders*: Foster a culture of collaboration by engaging regional maritime stakeholders to ensure the Maritime Security Zones operate with local expertise and are responsive to regional needs.
- Strengthen international partnerships to enhance the UK's maritime security network and ensure alignment with global maritime security efforts.
- *Pilot Programs and Evaluation*: Launch pilot programs within selected Maritime Security Zones to assess the efficacy of the new structure, using the findings to refine the approach before a broader rollout.

Each recommendation is designed to build upon the existing strengths of the UK's maritime security apparatus while addressing the known gaps and challenges. The successful implementation of these recommendations would mark a significant step towards achieving a maritime security posture that is robust, agile, and capable of meeting the demands of the 21st century maritime environment.

Implementation of a centralised UK maritime security framework

Within the envisioned framework of the UK's maritime security reform, the Secretary of State for Maritime Affairs emerges as a central figure, orchestrating a unified national maritime strategy and acting as a critical member of the National Security Council. Tasked with safeguarding the nation's maritime interests, the Secretary will spearhead policy development across commercial, security, and environmental domains within the maritime sector. This role requires adept navigation through the complexities of international maritime law and orchestrating the UK's response to emerging maritime security threats. The Secretary's responsibilities extend to diplomatic engagements, ensuring the UK's maritime policies are robustly represented globally and interwoven with national security imperatives. As an advocate for the UK's maritime interests, the Secretary will oversee a significant budget, driving strategic initiatives and fostering interdepartmental and international cooperation. In essence, the Secretary's role is pivotal in steering the UK's maritime security into a new era of centralised governance, aligning it with national security and resilience objectives.

The proposed reforms to UK maritime security call for the creation of a comprehensive departmental structure under the Secretary of State for Maritime Affairs. This structure would address the multifaceted nature of maritime governance, drawing parallels to the French Maritime Prefecture system's integration and breadth of authority.

Ministerial Roles and Responsibilities:

- *Minister for Maritime Infrastructure*: Overseeing development projects, maintenance of existing structures, and integrating new technologies to support maritime operations.
- *Minister for Maritime Security*: Focused on safeguarding the UK's maritime domain, coordinating security operations, and ensuring readiness to respond to threats.

- *Minister for Commercial Maritime Interests*: Ensuring the protection and promotion of the UK's commercial maritime sector, including shipping, trade, and fisheries.

Beneath the ministerial level, a series of directorates would each address specific elements of the National Strategy for Maritime Security:

- *Fisheries Protection Directorate*: Tasked with conserving marine life and enforcing fishing regulations.
- *Environmental and Ecology Directorate*: Dedicated to protecting the marine environment and ecological conservation.
- *Maritime Infrastructure Directorate*: Responsible for the upkeep and modernisation of maritime infrastructure.
- Other directorates would focus on areas such as pollution control, search and rescue, and maritime legal affairs.

Within this framework, Maritime Prefects would be appointed for each of the four Maritime Security Zones. They would possess executive authority within their respective zones, akin to the French Préfets, enabling them to oversee and coordinate all aspects of maritime security.

- *Executive Authority*: Empowering Maritime Prefects with decision-making capabilities to effectively respond to incidents and manage their zones.
- *Zone-Specific Structure*: Each Prefect would have a dedicated operational team, mirroring the French model's multidisciplinary approach, to cover the full spectrum of maritime security concerns.

The success of the Maritime Prefects would hinge on their ability to integrate operations across various maritime agencies and to collaborate effectively with international partners. This would ensure a holistic approach to maritime governance, from resource management to crisis response. The proposed system draws inspiration from the French Maritime Prefecture in its centralisation and the delegation of authority to regional leaders. However, it would be uniquely tailored to the UK context, respecting the nation's legal traditions and operational requirements.

Implementing this reformed maritime security framework represents a significant organisational transformation for the UK; by mirroring the

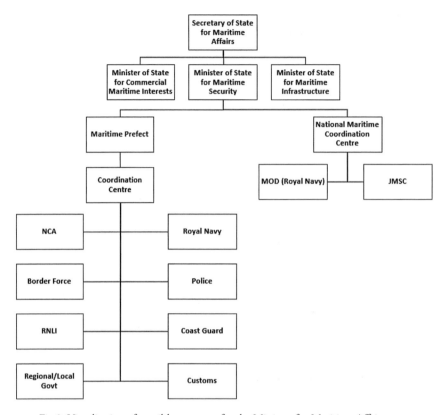

Fig 3: Visualisation of possible structure for the Ministry for Maritime Affairs

practical aspects of the French system, such as the integration of diverse maritime functions under a centralised command, the UK can enhance its maritime security capabilities. This new structure, with its ministerial and directorial levels culminating in the authority of the Maritime Prefects, would provide the UK with a robust, adaptable, and comprehensive approach to maritime governance for the 21st century.

Restructuring for a coherent UK maritime security enterprise

The transformation into a coherent maritime security enterprise requires strategic decoupling of maritime functions from existing government departments and their integration under the Secretary of State for Maritime Affairs. This process involves reassigning responsibilities and resources to create a centralised, focused department dedicated to maritime affairs. Functions currently spread across the Department for

Transport, the Home Office, and the Department of Environment, Food, and Rural Affairs, among others, would be realigned under the Ministry for Maritime Affairs. Assets and personnel pertinent to maritime security operations would be transitioned to the new department to consolidate expertise and capabilities.

In order to achieve this, it would also be necessary to create a command structure that unites all maritime security functions, ensuring swift decision-making and cohesive action. It would need to foster an operational environment where inter-agency collaboration is the norm, supported by shared objectives and strategies. This would be aided by formulating a singular budget for maritime security to streamline funding and eliminate financial inefficiencies across departments.

The Ministry for Maritime Affairs would operate with autonomy to ensure focused leadership and accountability. However, it would also coordinate with other departments on cross-cutting issues such as international trade, environmental policies, and national defence. Existing agencies with maritime responsibilities would adapt to support the new structure, potentially maintaining specific operational functions while aligning strategically under the Ministry for Maritime Affairs. Clear legislative guidance would delineate the new department's authority and ensure the smooth transfer of functions, whilst effective consultation with affected agencies, industry stakeholders, and international partners would be required to manage the transition effectively and maintain operational continuity.

The proposed restructuring under the Secretary of State for Maritime Affairs would be designed to create a unified maritime security enterprise that addresses the UK's modern maritime challenges. By consolidating disparate elements into a single department, the UK would enhance its maritime security posture, creating a more coherent, efficient, and responsive maritime enterprise. The process would by necessity be meticulous, requiring careful planning, change management, and a commitment to preserving the highest standards of maritime governance.

Adapting the royal navy's role within a centralised UK maritime framework

In a centralised maritime security framework, the Royal Navy would maintain its primary allegiance to the Ministry of Defence (MoD) while also playing a pivotal role in supporting the objectives set out by the Secretary of State for Maritime Affairs. This dual-support role necessitates careful consideration to ensure the alignment of defence and civilian maritime operations.

In order to best address these considerations, it would be necessary to establish a structure within the Royal Navy that interface with the Ministry for Maritime Affairs. This structure would be headed by a 3-star flag officer (Vice Admiral/Lieutenant General Royal Marines) who oversees explicitly Royal Navy operations in support of the Secretary of State for Maritime Affairs. This officer would coordinate Navy contributions to maritime security, including resource deployment and operational support. This structure would ensure that Navy operations align with broader maritime security goals while remaining under the MoD's command. It would be necessary to implement a dual command framework where the Royal Navy can be seconded to support civilian maritime operations under the guidance of the Ministry for Maritime Affairs without compromising its defence responsibilities. Creating a third 3-star flag officer, reporting directly to the First Sea Lord, would ensure that the forces allocated to protecting the UK's home waters would be under a separate command structure to the expeditionary elements under the Fleet Commander. The idea of a US-style Coast Guard, would likely be offered as an alternative solution, however, the creation of a whole force and the associated administration, human resource, and logistics burden would almost certainly rule this out on financial grounds. The ability, during a crisis, to exchange resource between two commanders within the same organisation would likely allow a flexible response where a unit under one commander could rapidly be re-tasked to support the other.

Whilst the name would likely be a subject of debate amongst experts and historians, the 3-star structure created within the Royal Navy would be its force. The creation of this command within the Royal Navy could indeed be instrumental in aligning military support with the objectives of the proposed Maritime Prefectures. This command would provide a dedicated military structure to oversee and integrate defence assets and capabilities into the maritime security framework, enhancing the UK's coastal defence and support for civilian maritime operations.

A dedicated Coastal Command would centralise the oversight of naval operations pertinent to the UK's territorial waters, providing a focused approach to maritime security challenges. A separate, distinct command from other naval operations would also facilitate the allocation of military assets to support the Maritime Prefectures, ensuring that surveillance, counterterrorism, and other defence-related maritime activities are effectively coordinated and tasked within each zone. Regarding Civil-Military Integration, the command would bridge civilian maritime governance and military defence operations, ensuring synchronised efforts and that military support is provided seamlessly and under civilian directives. It could also be the structure to which enhanced constabulary powers were allocated. This command would enhance interoperability amongst the armed forces, other government departments, and the Ministry for Maritime Affairs, optimising joint capabilities in maritime security.

The introduction of this Command for units in support of the Ministry of Maritime Affairs within the Royal Navy offers a strategic opportunity to fortify the UK's maritime security posture. By providing a military command dedicated to supporting the operational needs of the Maritime Prefectures, the UK can ensure that military and civilian maritime operations are closely aligned, responsive, and capable of addressing the spectrum of threats facing the nation's maritime interests. This approach would embody the synergy and comprehensive security strategy the proposed maritime security reform seeks to achieve, enhancing national defence and maritime domain protection.

Financial analysis of proposed UK maritime security reforms

The financial implications of transitioning the UK's maritime security to a centralised model necessitate a comprehensive analysis. This section examines the anticipated costs, benefits, and strategic financial considerations associated with implementing reforms inspired by the French Maritime Prefecture system. Cost Considerations:

- *Initial Investment*: Establishing a Ministry for Maritime Affairs, constructing a National Coordination Centre, and creating Maritime Security Zones will require substantial upfront investment. Costs will encompass infrastructure development, technological systems, legislative processes, and personnel training.
- *Operational Expenditure*: The new model will incur ongoing costs, including salaries for specialised personnel, maintenance of advanced communication systems, and operational expenses for regular maritime security activities.

- *Efficiency Savings*: Centralisation is expected to yield long-term savings through streamlined operations, reduced duplication, and optimised resource utilisation across maritime security agencies.

Benefit Analysis:

- *Security Dividend*: While qualitative, the enhanced protection of national maritime interests and improved response capabilities are expected to yield significant strategic value.
- *Economic and Legal Advantages*: Ensuring compliance with international maritime laws may prevent financial penalties while safeguarding critical infrastructure could avoid costly disruptions to commerce and communication.
- *Indirect Economic Benefits*: A robust maritime security framework can foster a stable environment conducive to maritime trade and investment, indirectly bolstering the national economy.

Financial Evaluation:

- *Return on Investment (ROI)*: A long-term ROI analysis will compare the financial benefits of the centralised model against the initial and ongoing costs, projecting the reform's value over time.
- *Break-Even Point*: Identifying when the accumulated benefits of the reform will offset the initial investment costs will be crucial to justify the transition.

Funding and Risk Management:

- *Budgetary Reallocation and Partnerships*: Exploring internal budget reallocations and potential public-private partnerships can support the reform financially.
- *Risk Mitigation*: Considering cost overruns and economic fluctuations, a robust risk assessment will be integral to the financial planning. Contingency funds and phased implementation strategies will be essential to mitigate these risks.

The shift to a centralised maritime security model represents a significant financial undertaking for the UK. However, the strategic benefits, potential cost savings, and long-term economic impacts justify the investment. Careful financial planning, including risk assessment and mitigation, will be paramount to these reforms' successful and sustainable implementation. Regular financial reviews will ensure transparency and accountability throughout the transition, safeguarding the financial integrity of the UK's maritime security reform.

Conclusion

The comparison of the UK's maritime security model, as informed by the case studies and the French Maritime Prefecture system, culminates in a set of strategic conclusions that are pivotal for the future of UK maritime governance. The case studies have demonstrated the importance of adaptability and resilience in maritime security operations. A centralised framework would allow the UK to be more responsive to emergent threats and challenges, ensuring a robust defence of national interests. Maritime security would also facilitate the UK's engagement on the international stage, ensuring compliance with international laws and contributing to global maritime security initiatives.

Reform is an ongoing process that requires a commitment to continuous improvement, regular evaluation, and adaptability to feedback and changing circumstances. The UK must remain committed to refining its maritime security strategy to stay ahead of the complex array of threats that characterise the modern maritime domain. The UK's maritime security reform should be forward-looking, anticipating future trends and challenges in the maritime domain. This includes embracing technological advancements, addressing the implications of climate change, and preparing for the geopolitical shifts that impact maritime security.

Adopting a centralised maritime security model marks a significant shift in the UK's approach to maritime governance, steering away from a dispersed system towards a more unified and integrated framework. This shift promises to streamline operations, improve inter-agency co-operation, and enhance the UK's capability to address and adapt to the evolving maritime security landscape. The role of the Secretary of State for Maritime Affairs, integral to this new architecture, has been outlined as a linchpin for integrating the UK's vast maritime interests across security, environmental, and commercial sectors. This position would bridge the national security directives as a member of the National Security Council with the operational execution of maritime strategy.

In conclusion, the UK stands at a critical juncture in the evolution of its maritime security strategy. The recommendations provided offer a path forward that builds on the strengths of the UK's current system while addressing its weaknesses. By considering the implications of these reforms and adopting a strategic, integrated approach to maritime security, the UK can protect its maritime interests for generations to come.

1. Lalanne de Saint-Quentin, Julien, 'France and Britain: Opposing Traditions of the Law of the Sea', Council on Geostrategy, 2023 https://www.geostrategy.org.uk/britains-world/france-and-britain-opposing-traditions-of-the-law-of-the-sea/ [accessed 18 November 2023].

2. 'Le préfet maritime – Préfecture maritime de l'Atlantique' https://www.premar-atlantique.gouv.fr/page/le-prefet-maritime-5630 [accessed 23 October 2023].

3. National Strategy for Maritime Security: Presented to Parliament by the Secretary of State for Transport by Command of Her Majesty (2022), p. 16.

4. National Strategy for Maritime Security, p. 47.

5. Sommerlad, Joe, 'Scallop Wars: A Brief History of British and French Fishermen Musselling in on Each Other's Catch', The Independent, 30 August 2018 https://www.independent.co.uk/news/uk/home-news/scallop-wars-britain-france-fishing-rights-english-channel-history-a8512871.html [accessed 14 November 2023].

6. Karasz, Palko, 'French and UK Fishing Boats Clash in "Scallop War"', The New York Times, 29 August 2018 https://www.nytimes.com/2018/08/29/world/europe/britain-france-scallop-war.html [accessed 14 November 2023].

7. Great Britain. Parliament. House of Commons. Defence Committee, Operation Isotrope: The Use of the Military to Counter Migrant Crossings: Government Response to the Committee's Fourth Report of Session 2021-22: Oral and Written Evidence (2022).

8. Great Britain. Parliament. House of Commons. Defence Committee, Operation Isotrope: The Use of the Military to Counter Migrant Crossings: Government Response to the Committee's Fourth Report of Session 2021-22: First Special Report of Session 2022-23 (2022).

9. Great Britain. Parliament. House of Commons. Defence Committee, Operation Isotrope: The Use of the Military to Counter Migrant Crossings: Fourth Report of Session 2021-22. Report (2022).

10. National Crime Agency [NCA], 'The Threat from Drug Trafficking' <https://www.nationalcrimeagency.gov.uk/what-we-do/crime-threats/drug-trafficking> [accessed 29 October 2023].

11. National Crime Agency [NCA], 'The Threat from Drug Trafficking.'

12. BBC News, 'Cocaine Smuggling: Five Guilty over £112m UK Trafficking Bid', BBC News, 21 March 2019 https://www.bbc.com/news/uk-england-cornwall-47626979 [accessed 29 October 2023].

13. Carrell, Severin, 'Shetland Loses Telephone and Internet Services after Subsea Cable Cut', The Guardian, 21 October 2022 https://www.theguardian.com/uk-news/2022/oct/20/shetland-loses-telephone-internet-services-subsea-cable-damaged [accessed 8 November 2023].

14. National Strategy for Maritime Security, p. 97.

15. Offshore Renewable Energy Emergency Forum: Exercise SANCHO Report – ORE, ORE, 2023 https://ore.catapult.org.uk/?industryreports=offshore-renewable-energy-emergency-forum-exercise-SANCHO-report [accessed 21 November 2023].

16. Offshore Renewable Energy Emergency Forum: Exercise SANCHO Report.

17. 'Organisation de l'action de l'Etat en mer - Préfecture maritime de l'Atlantique' https://www.premar-atlantique.gouv.fr/page/organisation-de-l-action-de-l-etat-en-mer [accessed 23 October 2023].

18. 'Action de l'État en mer', Gouvernement.fr https://www.gouvernement.fr/action-de-l-etat-en-mer-sgmer [accessed 23 October 2023].

19. 'Organisation de l'action de l'Etat en mer – Préfecture maritime de l'Atlantique.'

20. 'Sûreté, ordre public et lutte contre les trafics illicites en mer – Préfecture maritime de l'Atlantique' https://www.premar-atlantique.gouv.fr/page/surete-ordre-public-et-lutte-contre-les-trafics-illicites-en-mer [accessed 23 October 2023].

21. 'Missions opérationnelles – Dossiers – Préfecture maritime de l'Atlantique' https://www.premar-atlantique.gouv.fr/pages/missions-operationnelles [accessed 23 October 2023].

22. 'Action de l'État en mer', Gouvernement.fr.

23. 'Organisation de l'action de l'Etat en mer -Préfecture maritime de l'Atlantique' https://www.premar-atlantique.gouv.fr/page/organisation-de-l-action-de-l-etat-en-mer [accessed 23 October 2023].

24. Fondation Méditerranéenne d'Etudes Stratégiques [FMES], Territorialisation Des Espaces Maritimes (Pumbo, 2023).

Seascape Art

Nigel Waters

Biographies

Biographies

Editor Biographies

Kate Jamieson is a naval and maritime historian with over a decade of experience in the private maritime security industry, most recently as a project manager at Solace Global Maritime. Holding an MA in History from the University of Exeter, alongside council positions for The Society for Nautical Research, The Navy Records Society and The 1805 Club, Kate is regularly invited to deliver talks and lectures on naval history, exploration and maritime security by such organisations as the RN, RAF, British Army and United States Naval Academy. In addition to her academic work, Kate is also frequently invited to contribute her expertise in both broadcast and published media.

Dr Kevin Rowlands is Head of the Royal Navy Strategic Studies Centre. A captain in the Royal Navy, he left the regular service after a thirty-year career. He has been the Secretary to the Chiefs of Staff Committee and other senior MoD boards and was the Course Director for the UK's Advanced Command and Staff Course. Kevin holds a PhD in War Studies from King's College London and is the author of books on Admiral Gorshkov and on naval diplomacy, and has written various other book chapters, articles and commentaries.

Andrew (Andy) Young is the Fellowships Officer for the Royal Navy Strategic Studies Centre. A former Royal Navy Training Management officer specialising in professional military education, Andy previously worked at the Royal United Services Institute (RUSI) in Whitehall. He is a PhD candidate at the Laughton Naval History Unit, King's College London, focusing on the historic relationship of amphibious doctrine development with British maritime strategy.

Contributor Biographies

Matthew (Matt) Bowden is a Director at Red Penguin Marine having joined the company shortly after finishing a career in the Royal Navy. Providing market leading support and strategic guidance to the global submarine cable sector he advises on the submarine interconnectors, offshore grids, renewable energy (including US Offshore Wind sector) export cables and telecommunications. He regularly engages with key stakeholders on CNI and submarine cable resilience and is a member of the CH!RP Charity Global Maritime Advisory Board. Matt also sits on European Subsea Cables Association, and International Cable Protection Committee sub-groups, and a founding member of the Department for Science, Innovation & Technology's Subsea Cables Communications Industry Group.

Commander Matthew (Mat) Court RN is a Royal Navy officer with significant operational experience in the Atlantic, Barents, Mediterranean, Indian & Pacific Oceans, and the South China Sea. Currently the Commanding Officer of HMS PORTLAND he is completing a PhD in Organisational Psychology, and attributes his values and accomplishments to the patience and support of his wife and children.

Dr Tegan Evans is a geographer and works as a research associate with the University of Portsmouth Centre for Blue Governance and the Global Plastics Policy Centre. Her more recent research focuses on the many faces of transformative change towards the blue economy and sustainable ocean governance. Her findings notably illustrate the need for diverse understandings of transformation, and the need for multiple points of intervention across many scales to create change.

Admiral Linda L. Fagan is the 27th Commandant of the United States Coast Guard. As Commandant, she oversees all global Coast Guard operations and 55,000 active duty, reserve, and civilian personnel. Admiral Fagan has served on all seven continents, from the snows of Ross Island, Antarctica to the heart of Africa, from Tokyo to Geneva, and in many ports along the way. Possessing extensive interagency and intergovernmental experience, Admiral Fagan has worked with both the International Maritime Organization and International Labor Organization on flag state and port state issues. This work includes the development of the International Ship and Port Security Code and the Consolidated Maritime Labor Convention. Admiral Fagan is the longest serving active-duty Marine Safety Officer in the U.S. Coast Guard and holds the distinction of being the Service's first-ever Gold Ancient Trident.

Professor Pierre Failler is the Director of the Centre for Blue Governance at the University of Portsmouth. He holds the UNESCO Chair in Ocean Governance. He has coordinated complex research projects with multidisciplinary teams for more than 25 years in Europe, North America, Africa, Asia, the Caribbean, and Pacific coastal countries in collaboration with national research institutions and universities in close link with policy bodies. He has recently coordinated the Blue Economy Strategy for the African Union, the Regional Action Plan for the Blue Economy of the Indian Ocean Commission, the Blue Economy Strategy of IGAD, SADC, ASEAN as well as the Blue Economy Strategy and Action Plan for many coastal states of the Indian Ocean and Caribbean Sea regions. He has authored and co-authored numerous journal articles, book chapters, research reports, consultancy reports, etc. He is also a Scientific evaluator for several research councils in the UK, Europe, North America, Africa, and Asia.

Dr Joanne (Jo) Fallowfield is a former university Senior Lecturer in the Sport, Exercise and Nutrition Sciences. She has worked at the Institute of Naval Medicine since 2006, initially as Head of Applied Physiology, and more recently as the Royal Navy's Head of Musculoskeletal Injury (MSKI) Mitigation and Nutrition. Jo is the co-lead of the Royal Navy's MSKI Mitigation Programme, which is developing, implementing and evaluating a health and performance service for the Royal Navy and Royal Marines.

Dr Matthew Heaslip is a Senior Lecturer in Naval History at the University of Portsmouth. He is also a Visiting Fellow at the Royal Navy's Strategic Studies Centre. His research focuses on the application of naval power in littoral environments, both in peace and war, and how the twentieth century Royal Navy exploited its global dominance through gunboat diplomacy, amphibious operations, and imperial policing. His first book Gunboats, Empire and the China Station explores the Royal Navy's operations in East Asia during the 1920s. It examines the reasons behind some of the most violent clashes involving British service personnel during the interwar period.

Dr Melanie Holihead completed her DPhil at the University of Oxford. She was winner of the 2013 Sir Julian Corbett Prize for Modern Naval History, and the 2018-19 Doctoral Prize awarded by the British Commission for Maritime History. Her Naval Seamen's Women in Nineteenth-Century Britain is due for publication by Boydell and Brewer in 2024.

Dr Carl Stephen Patrick Hunter OBE is Chairman of Coltraco Ultrasonics, a high-exporting advanced manufacturer, Director-General of the Durham Institute of Research, Development & Invention (DIRDI) at Durham University, Director of the Centre of Underwater Acoustic Analysis (CUAA) for the Royal Navy, Professor-in-Practice at Durham University Business School, Chairman of the Council on Geostrategy Forum, Visiting Fellow of the Royal Navy Strategic Studies Centre, Fellow of the Royal Aeronautical Society and of the Institute of Marine Engineering, Science & Technology and is Chairman of the British Exporters Association. He supports several Government departments in various public service roles. A former Greenjacket Officer, his company has twice-won the Queen's Award for Enterprise. He holds an Honorary Doctorate in Science from Durham University and the University Senate's highest Dunelmensis Award, for his contribution to undergraduate development and scientific research. He speaks and writes on leadership, the UK Defence-UK Science-UK Industry relationship and of the United Kingdom as a Global Maritime & Underwater Power.

Devon A. Johnson is a graduate of King's College London with a BA in History & International Relations, an MA in War Studies and a PGDL. She has consulted for the Ministry of Defence on the UK's High North strategy and is a published author, frequently writing articles on subsea infrastructure security. Her graduate dissertation, "The Hidden Jugular? The Strategy and Security of Subsea Cables", produced a qualitative analysis of the threat landscape, an excerpt of which was published in the SubTel Forum industry magazine. As a Trustee for the Worshipful Company of Security Professionals' Charitable Trust and Deputy Chair of their Young Members' Committee, she is always eager to support initiatives that give back to the industry community and promote education and development amongst aspiring security professionals.

Dr Rob Johnson is the Director of the Secretary of State's Office of Net Assessment, Analysis, & Challenge, and Director of the new Oxford Strategy, Statecraft, Science, and Technology Centre (2024) also known as The Changing Character of War Centre at the University of Oxford. He is the author of a number of books on strategy and armed conflict, including Military Strategy for the 21st Century (Hurst and Oxford University Press, 2020) and NATO and Russia's War in Ukraine (Hurst and Oxford University Press, 2024).

Monica Kohli is a senior solicitor specializing in Maritime law. She is dual qualified in India and England & Wales and has been practising shipping and trade law for the past two decades; as a barrister in India, and as a solicitor in UK. For the last 15 years she has been a Senior Lawyer in Gard, the largest of the Protection and Indemnity Clubs, advising Ship Owners, Charterers and Traders on legal issues pertaining to shipping and trade worldwide. She has worked on internal projects looking into legal tech and innovation – including AI and NLP – making in house legal work efficient and lean. She read maritime law at the University of Southampton and studied for an MBA (Shipping and Logistics) at Copenhagen Business School. She speaks at events in the city and abroad on legal tech, diversity and inclusion in the maritime industry and on issue of interest in shipping law. She is currently President of "Women's International Shipping and Trade Association, UK" (WISTA UK) and the Chair of Indian Maritime Association UK (IMA, UK). She is also a Maritime Skills Commissioner; a trustee on the board for organizations focusing on maritime welfare, and on environmental law; and a Visiting Fellow at the Institute of International Shipping and trade Law, Swansea University.

Professor Andrew Lambert is Laughton Professor of Naval History in the Department of War Studies at King's College London. After completing research in the Department, he taught at Bristol Polytechnic (now the University of West of England), the Royal Naval Staff College Greenwich, and the Royal Military Academy Sandhurst. He is a Fellow of the Royal Historical Society and Director of the Laughton Naval Unit housed in the Department. In 2020 he was made a Fellow of Kings College London (FKC).

Glenn A Lipsham is the Senior Consultant at Red Penguin Marine. He is highly regarded in the international submarine telecommunications industry and has been a cable owner/operator, supplier and consultant to the industry for 27 years, with offshore and onshore experience throughout the entire life cycle of a submarine cable system. Particularly experienced in the Operations & Maintenance of submarine cable systems his technical expertise extends to crossing agreements, marine and terrestrial maintenance agreements, submerged plant fault location and repair, and management of third-party damage claims. Glenn has chaired the European Subsea Cables Association marine sub-group and regularly engages key stakeholders on CNI and submarine cable resilience.

Gordon Meadow is founder and CEO at SeaBot Maritime, a Chartered Marine Technologist and a Fellow of the Institute of Marine Engineering Science and Technology (IMarEST). He is an industry advisor on training development and speaks internationally on workforce assurance, skills and training development for the operation of uncrewed marine systems. He is committed to driving the maritime digital skills agenda and is at the forefront in the development of competencies, skills and training requirements for the operation of remote and autonomous marine systems. Gordon is a member of several maritime autonomy working groups and industry forums leading on next generation skills development. He co-created the International Maritime Competency Development Working Group, MASSPeople. Currently, with 8 nations as members, the group is capturing and defining new and emerging roles, and mapping competencies between humans and machines to co-exist alongside automation in maritime.

Dr Sophie Quintin is a senior research associate at the University of Portsmouth Centre for Blue Governance who specialises in international relations, law and security. Building on a career of 20 years managing large international aid projects and policy advice in complex conflict contexts in the Balkans and Africa, her research explores ocean governance with a focus on maritime security and the emergence of West African navies. As an amateur ocean racer and qualified skipper, she has sailed many maritime spaces leading her more recently to examine the intersection between offshore yacht racing and ocean sustainability.

Sub Lieutenant Joseph Reindler RN is a practising maritime artist and serving officer in the marine engineering branch of the Royal Navy. As an artist, his historical works have featured in publications namely from the United States Naval Institute, Navy Wings and the Royal Australian Navy. He is a Richmond Fellow of the Royal Navy Strategic Studies Centre.

Daisy Turnbull is a current split-site PhD student at the University of Portsmouth (UK) and Högskolan I Halmstad (SE). Her background is as a maritime archaeologist, coastal historian and museum specialist. Her current research looks at the wrecking of ships on the coast of Britain and Sweden between 1700-1850. She has previously published theoretic work on the materiality of urban coastal space in the UK.

Nigel Waters is a British landscape photographer based in Worcestershire, navigates the world through a lens, capturing nature's beauty through his artform. Waters discovered his passion for photography amidst the picturesque landscapes of his childhood in rural England, although formally embarking on his professional journey in the late 90s. Through his art, Waters captures the sublime beauty of diverse terrains, from misty mountain ranges to serene coastal vistas, exploring the interplay of light and shadow, showcasing a meticulous attention to detail that transforms ordinary scenes into visual masterpieces.

His evocative compositions tell stories of the land and sea, inviting viewers to immerse themselves in the raw, unspoiled beauty of the natural world. Indeed, Nigel Waters' legacy extends beyond his stunning visuals as Waters actively engages with his audience through workshops and exhibitions, imparting his knowledge and passion for the craft to aspiring photographers. As he continues his journey through untamed land-scapes, Waters remains dedicated to capturing the essence of Earth's wonders, leaving an indelible mark on the world of landscape photography.

Cdr Alex Westley RN is a Royal Naval Officer who, after a seagoing career on Swiftsure, Trafalgar, and Astute Class submarines, is currently serving in Paris within the STRATPOL Office of the Head of the French Navy. He has conducted staff assignments in the training and Intelligence domains. A recent graduate of École de Guerre in Paris, he is a First Sea Lords fellow.

Index